Ivanni Delgado

I0153223

Where This Civilization Is Going

A Dangerous Trend

Carmen & Son

Where This Civilization Is Going

Author: Ivanni Delgado

http://www.carmen-usa.com/haciadondevaestacivilizacion.html

Copyright © 2020 by Ivanni Delgado

Library of Congress Control Number: 2020909040

ISBN: 978-0-9910720-6-4

```
                              $21.00
ISBN 978-0-9910720-6-4
                              52100>

9 780991 072064
```

Published in USA by Carmen & Son, Houston, Texas

www.carmen-usa.com

Follow us on:

Second Edition

To The People

For his prominence in building our civilization

I want to dedicate this book to the people who have been the great protagonists of our civilization and who really have the power to keep it alive. The town is the group of people who live in the same place and who together are called people. We are all the people.

Thanks to their talent and thinking, the people have been heavily involved in all aspects crucial to humanity's progress. After discovering agriculture, they managed to get wealth to emerge. After they invented writing, they developed science. And in developing authority, they gave rise to power.

The people have developed revolutions, cultures, wars, cities, empires. They took civilization from Mesopotamia to Egypt, India, China, and the rest of the world. In the Western world, in Greece they invented philosophical thought based on reason and knowledge for the purpose of understanding their world and... they succeeded, thanks to philosophers such as Socrates, Plato and Aristotle. It was this thought that paved the way for science with the participation of Tales of Miletus, Pythagoras, and Archimedes. It was also in Greece, right in Athens, that power ceased to belong to a ruling elite to pass into the hands of the people with the rise of democracy. So, people must always stand by their democracy and defend it to preserve their power and enforce their rights.

With agriculture and wealth, the market economy would later emerge, as the economic system that provides the most benefits to the people by generating better incomes for a better life. The people now have their two great allies:

democracy and the market economy, which are perfectly compatible.

However, neither democracy nor the market economy is perfect and today both present many problems and threats. Perhaps the most critical problems are social problems and corruption, while the most serious threats could be left-wing politicians and the media.

To curb the problems and threats of democracy and the market economy, people must better prepare to defend them and to do so, people must be involved in politics, economy, and the history of their country and the rest of the world. People must participate in solving social problems and fight against corruption. One of the things they must first do is choose prepared democratic politicians, with clear plans to solve social problems and that those politicians are honest to curb corruption and to ensure the continuity of democracy and the market economy.

People must also be more involved in matters related to their society, such as investigating the management of public money, as the fight against corruption must be frontal to prevent it from continuing to undermine the foundations of democracy and the market economy, which could eventually lead to total collapse. In addition, people must raise their voices to reverse the negative effects of the media, and in this way helping on the fight against the problems and threat of democracy and the market economy.

All the problems of our civilization today show a clear dangerous trend. For this reason, I decided to write this book entitled "Where This Civilization Is Going" so that we the people can avoid its collapse.

TABLE OF CONTENTS

ACKNOWLEDGEMENT

Go my thanks to each and every person who has served in some way of inspiration to write this book. To all those authors who have written in relation to the theme of where this civilization is going. And to all institutions—such as the Discovery Science Channel™, the History Channel™, and the National Geographic Channel™—that have served as a means to bring a message of knowledge to all people everywhere. I also want to thank my whole family for their great support in the culmination of the book.

INTRODUCTION

Prehistory is the time of human evolution ranging from the emergence of the first beings in Africa to the invention of writing, and it is divided into the Stone Age and the Metal Age. The Stone Age is the time when our ancestors used stone in their natural state at the beginning of that time and later carved it to make their first utensils.

The stone age is divided into the Paleolithic period covering 99% of human history and ranges from about 2.6 million years ago to about 12 thousand years ago; and the Neolithic period that follows after finishing the Paleolithic until about 6 thousand years ago.

During the Paleolithic, our ancestors used stone in their natural state, knew and learned to control and use fire; they were in groups living off hunting, fishing, and fruit harvesting; and lived in caves. At the end of this period, they performed the first artistic manifestations through rock art mainly. During the Neolithic, our ancestors used carved and polished stone; discovered agriculture and livestock; they made the first pieces of ceramics; and built the first stable towns.

The Metal Age is the time when metal objects began to be made, ranging from about 6,000 to some 3,000 years ago. It is divided into three periods according to the use of metal: the age of copper, that of bronze and that of iron. In the age of metals, the earliest civilizations appear, with some more complex societies where writing begins to be used.

With the invention of writing ends Prehistory and the History of Humanity begins. And thanks to writing, I have wanted to write part of that history since the human being, imitating nature, managed to develop agriculture and then build the first civilizations and everything they would require to sustain themselves as wealth and power to reach our current world where thanks to the permanent contact between the citizens of the world , those early civilizations would combine into one: our civilization.

In our world, however, we now encounter a number of problems and threats that, if we did nothing, could jeopardize all that immense work and effort of our ancestors. For this reason, I wanted to write this book, which I have called *"Where This Civilization Is Going"* so that we could know its history and do something to prevent its collapse, because the trend it carries is dangerous.

The book consists of 5 chapters with 5 subchapters each. In the first chapter entitled *"Civilization: Origin and Evolution"* we began our account from the origin and evolution of humans who left Africa during prehistory in search of food and water, for which they would have to travel long paths, until they reached the Fertile Crescent, in today's Middle East, where their lives would change forever by finding abundant food and beginning to become sedentary. Thus, they began to build the first stable settlements and with them love, family and early towns, whose people made the Neolithic revolution, during which they managed to produce their own food: a true revolution, the Neolithic revolution. The chapter tells the details of the events that led to the construction of civilization: the Neolithic revolution, the first settlements and towns, the events towards the flourishing of civilization, and the first cities. During the Neolithic revolution, the Natufians were the main protagonists in discovering agriculture, domesticating animals, developing Neolithic culture and its advances for prosperity. Among the events towards civilization, we have: the development of pottery and ceramics, the discovery of metals, the development of urban culture that laid the foundations of the first cities and with them the flourishing of the first civilizations.

In the second chapter entitled "The First Civilizations" we will be presenting each of the first civilizations since their origin in Mesopotamia, and their propagation to Egypt, India, China, and the rest of the world reaching the western part. We will see how during civilization in Mesopotamia our ancestors managed to make a great development in the political, economic, and social aspects. As well as religion, science, and arts. They even developed the first empires. As for Egyptian civilization, this first thing he achieved was the unification of the High and Low Egypt into a single territory. However, this civilization stood out for the construction of monumental works such as the great Sphinx and the famous pyramids, which have become symbols of Egypt. It is also known for its mummification.

In the third chapter "Writing and Science" will talk about the origin of writing and science, the first type of writings, the first observations that led to the emergence of science, as well as the first observatories built by our ancestors to deepen their knowledge. We will see what it was during the Mesopotamia civilization that writing was invented, with which science later emerged. We will see the contributions that the Mesopotamian, Egyptians, Greeks, and Phoenicians have made to writing and science.

In the fourth chapter *"Wealth and Power"'"* we present the topics about wealth, capitalism, power, religion and power, and the struggle for power. As for wealth we will see how with the development of agriculture and breeding, trade, economics, finance, and capitalism; our ancestors were able to create wealth.

With the surplus of agriculture, they could feed other people who were engaged in other activities such as breeding and handicrafts. So, the farmer traded part of his surplus from his crop to the shepherd or craftsman for some of his animals, or crafts, respectively. This exchange in the form of barter gave rise to trade and with it emerged the first means of transport by land and rivers. With these activities of production, trade, transport, and consumption emerged the basics of the economy.

When trade began to be done with the payment of money by buying products, replacing the barter system, the market and commercial economy arose. Finance also emerged to study the circulation of money between individuals, companies, or states. The economy later became a science encompassing different economic systems such as capitalism, which is now based on private ownership of the means of production, as well as on the principle of free market, whose objective is the accumulation of capital. Capitalism is therefore based on ownership of the means of production and resources, from which trade profits are extracted.

As for power, we will see how this arose during Mesopotamian civilization, when one of the town's families, with a prosperous trade, managed to accumulate more wealth than the others. Eventually, the wealthy family took control of the town, which also acquired the economic power and authority of the town. Afterwards, the authority of the town created the first institutions such as the council of the elders and the first assembly with the important people of the town. Power was represented by the participation of the religious, political, military, and judicial sectors.

However, religious power was always closely linked to the other powers. Then with the rise of the cities, the first kingdoms appeared with kings considered gods with absolute power over all aspects of society. These kingdoms would develop wars to increase their power. After originating in early civilizations, power and its structures spread into the Western world. In Greece in the city of Athens arose the democracy with which power first passed from kings to the hands of the people to elect the government.

There has always been a constant struggle for power since its inception with the development of human beings in Prehistory, for which wars and governments have been invented, even the people have been in this struggle, establishing groups or factors of power.

In the fifth chapter *"The Current World: A Dangerous Trend"* we talk about the geopolitical situation including the threat of coronavirus; the decline of the political system, as well as that of institutions for world peace; the collapse of the economic system; social problems; and how to avoid the collapse of civilization, given the dangerous trend that it carries.

In our world today, attention is focused on the coronavirus pandemic, according to geopolitics. The main political systems in most countries of the world are democracy and dictatorship. The basic difference between these two systems is freedoms and respect for human rights, which exist in democracy, but not in dictatorship.

The main economic systems today are the market economy or capitalism typical of democracy, and the state planning system of socialist or communist countries. The basic difference between these two systems is private property, which exists in democracy, but not in socialism or communism, with the exception of some countries such as China and Russia that had to adopt market economies to prevent their collapse.

In our present world too, there are many institutions for world peace, such as the United Nations (UN),which show clear signs of decline by deflecting the goals for which they were created and instead embracing other interests on ideologies, with which they represent only countries with these trends.

However, there is still a solution if we can act in time to prevent the collapse of civilization. We see that the arrival of the coronavirus only accelerated the problems that democracy has already been presenting in large part by politicians with socialist or communist ideas supported by the media. Moreover, the attacks of institutions that were created to maintain the peace and well-being of the world such as the United Nations (UN) mainly, which by leaving aside their purposes have become a serious threat against democracy and the people. The other problems against our society must be addressed as soon as possible, as political decline can lead to economic collapse, which would make it more difficult to solve social problems. However, if the difficulties are addressed, we can avoid the collapse that threatens our civilization.

1

CIVILIZATION: ORIGIN AND EVOLUTION

In this chapter we will be talking about the Neolithic revolution, the first settlements and towns, the events towards civilization, the flowering of civilization, and the first cities. For this we will see first how everything would arise from the beginning.

All life, since the beginning of prehistory, our ancestors had lived off collecting wild fruits, hunting, and fishing. To get their livelihood they had to always move in search of food and water, naturally. This kind of wandering life is known as a nomad. This means, they always walked from place to place. They only stayed in one place for as long as they had water and food. However, they could stay longer in one place if the abundance of resources allowed. Then they went on their way to find another place with the resources that provided them with subsistence.

Their belief developed throughout their lives gave them the faith to move forward in search of their livelihood. They believed that all things that existed in their world, including it themselves, were made up of spirits with some power and that some of those things had supreme powers they called gods. To ask for favors to those gods they created rituals that accompanied with music that they made by imitating with their voice the sounds of nature and then accompanying their singing with musical instruments that they discovered and developed over time. As they sang and played, they also danced.

Thus, with this way of life based on their beliefs, their culture developed during the Paleolithic period, and with a climate still frozen as a product of the last glaciation of the Quaternary era, our ancestors about 20 thousand years ago wandered around the African continent in search of sustenance. However, when they found plenty of water, fruits, and animals, they remained in place for as long as necessary until resources ran out. Thus, they began to settle and built temporary settlements. In some cases, resources were reproduced before the resources of the previous harvest were depleted, allowing them to have a longer settlement and during it, they built more stable camps, thus raising the first villages dedicated to fruit harvesting and hunting. That is how sedentary lifestyle came.

Over time, a group of our ancestors, from Africa, had arrived in a region of the Middle East, known today as the Fertile Crescent, in which life would go through a series of changes in order to reach where we are today.

The Fertile Crescent was a crescent-shaped region with very fertile lands. This region went from Egypt, passing through Israel and then in route southward Syria to ancient Mesopotamia in what is now Iraq, to the Persian Gulf.

Thus, our ancestors entered the Neolithic period, which begins at the end of the last glaciation with a warm climate and with an abundance of water. In the Fertile Crescent, this new scenario caused nature to produce more plants with fruits and animals to eat and our ancestors became more sedentary.

However, then a short glacial period known as the "Younger Dryas" appeared and again the glaciers absorbed most of the liquid water and this, along with the wild fruits and animals that our ancestors ate also began to be scarce until they produced a cycle of famine.

To survive, our ancestors had to take the nomadic form again, to seek water and food. In their search, they found a region on Lake Galilee in the Fertile Crescent, in which, although it did have water, there were no edible plants, only pasture. Using their intellect, humans achieved one of their greatest discoveries: agriculture. After the end of Younger Dryas, the drought ended, and everything was better again as before.

During the Neolithic, megalithic art also emerged with its immense monuments formed by large carved stones such as the great temple of Gobekli Tepe in the Fertile Crescent, in what is now Turkey about 11 thousand years ago, one thousand years before the discovery of agriculture. Meanwhile, in Europe some 6,000 years later they built the Stonehenge monument in Britain with large rough stones erected.

Also during the Neolithic, very important events arose with great impacts on the way of life of our ancestors, which would have an immense influence on the way of living of modern humans today.

1.1   NEOLITHIC REVOLUCION

In this subchapter, we will be talking about the Natufians, agriculture, animal domestication, Neolithic Culture, and its advances towards prosperity, and the first settlements and towns. We will see how a group of our ancestors Homo Sapiens, called the Natufians were the protagonists of the Neolithic Revolution that began in the Fertile Crescent in the Middle East. A region with important stable rivers such as the Nile in Egypt, the Jordan in Israel, as well as the Tigris and Euphrates in Mesopotamia.

The Natufians led a nomadic life to the entrance of the Neolithic period, when they made a process of major changes in the life form of humans. From nomad they became sedentary and to live on the food provided to them by nature, they came to produce their own food with the discovery of agriculture, with initial crops of cereals such as wheat and barley.

Agriculture was possible with the efforts of many people, who built their houses near their crops, with which the villages would emerge and later the towns. With agriculture came the knowledge of plants, fruits, soils, irrigation, plowing and then trade. Later, this knowledge deepened by promoting more progress with better agricultural systems and tools. Agriculture began in the vicinity of what is now Israel, later arriving in Mesopotamia and Egypt where it made great progress. With time, agriculture spread throughout India, China, Europe, America, and the rest of the world.

For the domestication of other animals our ancestors, perhaps they would do it in the same way that they tamed the wolf, but this time with the help of the dog. During the huge drought of the "Younger Dryas" and given the huge shortages of food, our ancestors thought that it was possible and very convenient to retain, with the help of the dog, the live animals in a corral to eat their meat, only when necessary. Among the first domesticated animals, after the dog, were goat, sheep, cow, etc.

During the Neolithic period, humans would develop a number of things, ideas, and customs to survive and improve over time to achieve a better life. This is what is known as Neolithic culture with various advances towards prosperity such as wheel, better tools, and clothing. In addition to the development of basketry, pottery, and ceramics; with what they could make vessels to store, transport, eat or even drink their beer. With the surplus of agriculture, breeding and craft activities, trade arose, and the first settlements and towns emerged.

The Natufians

The last glaciation of the four quaternary-era glaciations, also called the ice age, lasted about 100 thousand years, and ended 12 thousand years ago marking the end of the Paleolithic period and the beginning of the Neolithic period. During this glaciation about 20 thousand years ago our ancestors, Homo Sapiens still led an errant or nomadic life in search of water and food in that cold climate. Their lives were based on wild fruit harvesting, hunting, and fishing. Where they found food, they stayed there until resources ran out. Then they went their way in search of their livelihood.

About 15 thousand years ago, when the climate was improving because the glaciers were melting, a group of those nomadic gatherers and hunters known today as the Natufians reached a region with a variety of plants that were mostly edible. It also had a lot of animals in that region. And of course, this region had plenty of water. Something our ancestors had never seen before. This was like a paradise for the Natufians who lived off what nature provided them with. They had everything to survive in one place. That region is what we know today as the Fertile Crescent, the region in the

Middle East that runs from Egypt in northeastern Africa to Mesopotamia in western Asia.

The name of the Natufians came in 1932 after the discovery made by the British archaeologist Dorothy Garrod when she excavated an areological site in the valley of Wadi an-Natuf. That is where the name came from and means: those who lived in Natuf. This place is in what is now Mount Carmel, a coastal mountain range over the Mediterranean Sea in Israel. There Dorothy Garrod discovered a body of a Natufians buried about 12 thousand years ago.

In this region the Natufians discover the herbs that produced dried grains, very nutritious and that could last for a long time without perishing, which allowed them to store it to guarantee their livelihood for a long time. This would change life forever and begin humanity's great progress.

These dry seeds that we today call cereals such as wheat and barley were very abundant in this region and could yield another harvest before the previous harvest. This resulted in our ancestors starting to store the surplus and eating it later when necessary. To store the grains, they dug holes in the ground and stored it there. They also used some containers such as leather bags or some pumpkin containers to take from one place to another.

Dry seeds could be stored for a long time. The abundance and consequent storage of food led the Natufians to stay much longer in these places, which made them start a more sedentary kind of life. Thus, they began to form the first settlements with huts of branches and straw where they also stored the grain. The progress of our ancestors was evident, for at first, they lived in caves, which they also used as storages of their belongings and food and even occasionally served burials.

The new settlements at first consisted of a small number of people. Over time, the Natufians learned to make flour by crushing the grains and by adding a little water to make their daily bread. Inside the huts they ground the grains to make the flour with which they made their bread, which was a kind of pita bread they cooked on some hot stones in a campfire.

However, not only on bread the Natufians lived. They also collected fresh sweet fruits and meat from animals they hunted with spears and waves. Among the animals they hunted were their favorite gazelles. In search of hunting animals, they moved according to the seasons and walked for weeks in their hunting activity.

Sedentary lifestyle brought many changes in our ancestors, perhaps one of the first was the sense of ownership. When nomads, they wandered around all the time and no one owned anything. The sedentary possesses everything they has achieved and would defend it even with his own life if necessary. This change would have serious implications in the future. However, sedentary lifestyle has a great advantage: it allows man to think to make his life easier and, in that sense, would try to ensure his livelihood, which would cause the nomadic population to follow this trend to enjoy its benefits as well.

In the time they were neither collecting fruits nor hunting, the Natufians were engaged in the manufacture of their weapons made with flint, stone, stick and bones. They came to develop an oz with the double blade horn handle for more efficiency in cutting plants to harvest cereals. They also made their blades, mortars, and even stone figurines with faces of people and animals. With shells, bones, and animal teeth they made their ornaments very aesthetic as necklaces and other garments.

During the storage of cereals, the Natufians observed that some of the grains in the storage hole and those that fell to the ground on the way when they carried them from the plants where they obtained them, germinated and formed new plants, in the same way as when these grains fell naturally from the plant to wet soil. This great observation would later lead to the discovery of agriculture.

The Natufians had led a rather prosperous life for about 2,500 years until the weather began to worsen again. After the last glaciation, a short period of glaciation called the "Younger Dryas" appeared about 13 thousand years ago, lasting just over a millennium. This new climate change adversely impacted the lives of our ancestors, as due to the formation of the glaciers, water in liquid form was diminishing with its corresponding impact on the scarcity of their food such as the fruits they collected and the animals they hunted to eat and survive.

Almost the entire Earth became cold and with a great drought, with its respective cycle of famine, forcing the Natufians to abandon their settlements around what is known as Jericho in today's Israel. Although some perished in the attempt, some others did achieve their goals. To survive, the Natufians had to spread as nomads, again, in search of water and food. They managed to find a new opportunity to survive on a lake in the Jordan Valley in a fertile region on the shores of Lake Galilee.

There the Natufians took refuge to try to start over. Although they found abundant water and a fertile soil, there were no plants with fruits, just a little pasture. So, they had to plant their own plants thanks to the great observation they had made before about how the new plants were born after the grains fell into the wet soil where they settled earlier when the wild fruits were abundant.

To sow their plants, they had to sacrifice the grains they carried in their leather bags to eat, and instead used them as seeds, which they put in hollows that opened with a stick, and with their bags they watered them with lake water, because they had already understood the importance of water. Then the plants were born, and they harvested their fruits and thus satisfy their hunger. Thus, the Natufians became the first farmers of the world. This simple act was the beginning of a new way of life that would transform the face of the Earth.

Meanwhile, the Natufians continued to adapt to their new conditions, which they did very impressively. Not only did they survive the "Younger Dryas" drought, but they also progressed during this period of calamity. After the end of "Younger Dryas," the drought ended, and everything was good again as before. The region where the Natufians had settled now had very favorable conditions for the development of agriculture.

They had begun to understand the importance of dry grains in their diet, as well as the great importance of choosing the soils to grow them from. And so, with this purpose in mind, the Natufians spread throughout the area that went from the Jordan to the Euphrates Valley in search of the best soils on which their crops would best thrive. It is likely that the Natufians had used irrigation channels for their agriculture. The truth is that this area allowed our ancestors large crops of their cereals, with a more productive grain.

Agriculture meant quite intense work. All his tasks from sowing to harvesting required teamwork, but well worth the effort. The abundance of the harvest caused the storage of dry grain to be now more organized and with specialized barns: the first silos emerged. Life had less free time. There was no longer time to make the original mortars, instead they used large stones with several holes where several people could grind large amounts of grain at the same time.

Besides producing their own food, they also hunted as much animal as they found. In addition to the abundance of crops in some places, the animals were also abundant mainly gazelles, as well as the wild goat and some birds. However, sometimes in some places, hunting was poached, leading our ancestors to develop the bow and arrow as a more effective weapon to compensate for the shortage of animals.

Our ancestors had settled more stably and for this they made their first circular huts of stone and mud with a door and thatched roof, which they burned from time to time to get rid of the little animals that could cause problems. Each hut served as housing for a family and had its own campfire. These were the first houses, the ones that came to form a community and then a town. With sedentary lifestyle, love and family emerge in a stable way.

Having at least, their secured sustenance, the Natufians came to manufacture a variety of tools that included snouts to cut the plants and then obtain the grains, made with stone blades embedded in a stick handle; stone mortars to grind the grains; fishing tools made of bone such as harpoons, hooks; as well as sewing tools such as needles and punches; they also made them woven baskets and mats; All this shows that the Natufians developed a very advanced lifestyle for their time.

The Natufians also invented the reciprocal exchange of ideas among villagers on how to best do planting, harvesting, tools, etc. Then came the simple exchanges of goods between the inhabitants of the villages. For example, villagers exchanged one type of fruit or tool for another or fruits for tools and vice versa.

The Natufians also excelled in their magical or religious art with the manufacture of statuettes and animal sculptures. They also stood out in their burials with their graves within their settlements and even, later, under their houses with funeral rituals. The deceased were buried with their most cherished belongings. Their tombs were considered sacred. The Natufians used to separate the deceased's head from the rest of the body already buried.

The Natufians always worked and socialized together, they were very creative, they learned to do things better to ensure their livelihood and shared everything among their people. Thus, they managed to develop a great culture that lasted between 15 and 11 thousand years, which would later give way to Neolithic culture. However, their great contribution was a simple act at the beginning of something that would change life on the face of the Earth: agriculture.

Agriculture

As we have already seen, agriculture was discovered by the Natufians about 11.5 thousand years ago in order to survive the huge drought of the "Younger Dryas". This discovery was made possible thanks to what our ancestors, the Natufians, had observed in times of the abundance of wild fruits about how the plants were born after their grains fell to the wet soil. What the Natufians really did was try to imitate nature. However, this agriculture was very incipient at first, but gradually began to progress.

The new activity of producing food, instead of collecting what nature provided, kicked off a new lifestyle because agriculture required a lot of work and several people working together. The work included tasks such as sowing, watering, cleaning crops, harvesting, storing, and grinding the grain to make the flour to make the daily bread.

To sow the seeds, they opened holes in the ground with a pointed stick or with a sharp stone tied to a stick, the same tool they used to remove roots from the earth. To irrigate the seeds, they were able to use containers, irrigation channels or wait for rainwater to fall.

To clean the crops had to remove the weeds constantly, a task that was normally done with the hands. To harvest, the stems of the plants below the spikes were cut with the oz. The spikes were then piled on the ground to be trite and separate the grains from the spikes. Then the grains were accumulated and stored.

To ensure the harvest, plants also had to be protected from wild animals and from the incursions of nomads that still prowled the region. All this work could only be accomplished by many people cooperating with each other. To take care of the crop, several farmers joined forces by building their homes in the fields of planting. It was important that the houses were close to each other, as this would make crop protection more successful. This is how the dwellings in the fields were increasingly piled up in the first villages. Given the intense work of agriculture, this activity had to be done out of necessity. However, it was worth the effort as it ensured survival.

Agriculture continued to progress slowly and by trial and error. Gradually the production of grains increased to the point that, to grind so much grain, our ancestors no longer used the small mortars of the Natufians, instead they used some made of large stones with several sections or hollows to grind with more people and faster to convert the grains into flour.

After the end of the "Younger Dryas" period, more than a thousand years later, the drought disappeared in the Fertile Crescent and better weather conditions arrived. The earth got wet again and everything became prosperous as before. As a result, the living conditions of our ancestors improved enormously: the abundant water of the melting of the glaciers caused more water sources such as rivers and lakes. In addition, the abundance of this water produced more fertile soils, which made agriculture prosper by transforming some areas rich in edible fruits, especially cereals such as wheat and barley. With agriculture, the population grew up and as it increased, more agriculture became more necessary to feed so many people.

The first plant species to be grown were wheat and barley about 10 thousand years ago. These two cereals were very nutritious, and their crops were very abundant. Then the crops of other cereals such as oats and rye emerged. And then they sowed lentils, peas and linen, the textile plant from which they extracted the fiber to make threads and fabrics with which they would make their clothes.

With agriculture knowledge of plants, fruits, soils, irrigation, plowing and then trade emerged. This knowledge was perfected over time to produce a real revolution. As for plants and fruits, our ancestors came to know the plants from which they could eat their fruits and those that did not. They differentiated edible plants from poisonous ones. Of the edible plants they managed to gain extensive knowledge of them. They understood that domesticated plants are genetically distinct from wild plants.

The first farmers had begun to manipulate natural selection and nature itself. By producing the first varieties of domesticated grain, it was larger and waited in its plant to be harvested, while the wild grain was smaller and fell itself from the plant. In addition, not all plants of the same species were the same. Some had a larger or better-tasting grain, so farmers started selecting the best grains to use as seeds in their next planting. Over time, they also came to discover medicinal plants.

As for the soils, farmers prepared the land where they would plant their crops. This included deforesting with stone axes to cut down trees and have more space exposed to sunlight and burn to clean it of weeds. Over time, they also used plow, fertilize for their crops with manure, and later used irrigation channels.

Irrigation channels were used in observation-inspired agriculture that our ancestors had noticed in the natural canals of rivers such as the Nile in Egypt and the Tigris and the Euphrates in Mesopotamia. Flooding during the time of river inundation was diverted to the fields, which once irrigated were ready for planting.

Agriculture began in the Fertile Crescent. Specifically, in the region that runs from Israel to Turkey and then spread throughout this region until reaching Mesopotamia and then Egypt. About 9,000 years ago agriculture had reached Mesopotamia, the region between the Tigris rivers to the east and the Euphrates to the west, which are born in the Taurus Mountains in Anatolia in present-day Turkey in the north and flow into the Persian Gulf to the south. These two rivers have different characteristics: The Tigris flows faster and is more turbulent, while the Euphrates is more stable and with better access.

Mesopotamia was a region divided into two parts according to its relief. The upper part to the north was formed by a high plateau with slope to the south, while on the contrary the lower part to the south was very flat and with little slope. Consequently, in that region agriculture was divided into two sections: high and low Mesopotamia.

Agriculture of upper Mesopotamia depended on rain for irrigation. But that of lower Mesopotamia, in the Sumer region, agriculture was irrigated, as this part did not have enough rain for agriculture to thrive.

In Sumer, agriculture became systematized and developed on a large scale with advances in agricultural and irrigation techniques. Some 7 thousand years ago, large irrigation systems had already been implemented. To irrigate the crops, water was taken from floods caused by the flooding of the Euphrates and Tigers rivers and then diverted through the canals to the crop fields. This irrigation system also served to drain the banks of rivers.

Later, the irrigation system also included a very simple piece of equipment known today as the "Shadoof", with which water was drawn from a river, canal or well to irrigate crops and for domestic consumption as well. The Shadoof consisted of a piece of stick that served as a lever by leaning on a stick run to raise the water from one fountain and throw it in another.

The crops of agriculture in Sumer, as in all of Mesopotamia were basically cereals like wheat to make bread and barley to make beer. Lentils, chickpeas, beans, onions, garlic, grapes, apples, figs, and dates were also produced; whose plants, the date palms require a lot of water. But that was no problem as the southern fields achieved great yields thanks to irrigation.

Also, in southern Mesopotamia emerged the plow about 6 thousand years ago as an evolution of the hoe to sow the seeds. With the plow grooves were made in the soil and inside them the seeds were laid and from there the plants were born in rows. At first the plow was operated or pulled by people and then by animals such as oxen and horses.

Initially the plow consisted of a single piece of stick or a tree branch in the shape of a hoe. Later with the arrival of the metals the plow became more sophisticated. It had the part of the hoe made of metal, which was connected to a stick handle. With the appearance of the wheel in Sumer, it was also adapted to the plow to improve its handling and efficiency. Plowing was an instrument of a breakthrough for agriculture. It made the fieldwork easier and in less time. In addition, it was one of the first sophisticated man-made instruments.

Around the same time that agriculture had arrived in Mesopotamia, about 9 thousand years ago it had also sprung up on the banks of the Nile River in Egypt. The rising rivers flooded the banks and deposited organic sediments or silt that carried the river current. This made these lands very fertile, which made them very suitable for agriculture.

The main crops were cereals such as oats and wheat with which our ancestors in this region made their bread and also made their beer. They also cultivated legumes such as lentils and chickpeas to eat, vines such as grapes to eat and make wine, fruits such as figs and dates to eat, the famous papyrus later used for writing, and linen to make their clothes.

Since agriculture depended on the floods of the river, the Egyptians invented 5.5 thousand years ago an instrument to measure the water level of the Nile River and thus plan their crops and food production. This meter was built of various types as a staircase corridor made of stones. This corridor began from the bank of the river and extended outwards. Each rung represented a mark indicating the level of the flood. Wells and other structures were also used to measure floods. However, the simplest type was a vertical column made of stones submerged in the river with depth marks at intervals to measure the level of floods.

The Egyptians used cow or ox plow in their agriculture. They also made irrigation channels and later built hydraulic irrigation systems. In addition, the river was its main means of communication to transport its agricultural products and other goods. To do this they used row boats at the beginning and then the sailing boats. They traded in the form of barter, i.e. they exchanged products for others.

After the Fertile Crescent, agriculture appeared elsewhere such as India, China, Europe, and the Americas. Then, a few thousand years later, agriculture had already been implemented in the rest of the world.

About 10,000 years ago agriculture from the Middle East had arrived in India entering for what is now Pakistan. In India agriculture began to develop around the Indo River, where wheat and barley were mainly cultivated. There they also used irrigation channels and plowing.

After India agriculture had arrived in China, in the Far East between the Huang Ho and Yangtze rivers. Rice cultivation developed in China and potato and soybeans were later also cultivated. In this region they also used irrigation channels and plowing in agricultural work.

Later, about 8,000 years ago agriculture also reached Europe by diffusion from the Fertile Crescent. The first crops were cereals such as wheat, barley, and oats. The people of the Fertile Crescent had begun to expand from Turkey to southern Europe bordering the Mediterranean. The first to leave were the merchants, who made their trips in small boats, in which they also carried seeds, some animals and the notion of agriculture. Arriving in Europe they found an immense continent with a new landscape and a different climate. And since the forests were impenetrable, they had to move through the rivers. The continent was of course inhabited by gatherers and hunters since glaciation. Agriculture and breeding had not yet developed.

Some 7,000 years ago the explorers of the Fertile Crescent had arrived in Slovakia where they met the Native Europeans to trade and negotiate. The natives offered antlers and skins in exchange for animals and seeds for Europeans to start developing their agriculture and breeding, as the people of the Fertile Crescent would teach them how to do it.

That is how that exchange of ideas began between these two different types of people. Explorers continued to search for good land for agriculture until this was possible, but on a small scale at first given to the constraints of forested land. Then they began to cut down the forest with a type of axe they had used in the Fertile Crescent to have more open spaces to grow. Eventually, both Middle Eastern merchants and European natives became farmers and together they built their own villages in Europe.

These farmers used the farming methods of the Fertile Crescent. But to avoid the adversity of the strong northern winter, they managed to determine the best time when to sow and harvest smoothly before winter. They also started using plow, which helped a lot to make their agriculture more productive. Another major change they made was the largest home manufacturing, where they lived with all their belongings including animals. In these houses the trees of the forest held the roof without cutting the trees.

Agriculture expanded from Europe east to Russia and west to France. The European continent now had abundant food. The Europeans also became shepherds, then improved the benefits of the dairy cow.

Then, some 6,000 years ago, agriculture had already spontaneously appeared, it is believed, in the Americas, where maize crops, potatoes, tomatoes and certain varieties of legumes such as beans in Mexico developed. In Mexico, the cultivation was developed by "Chinampas", which consisted of the construction of elevated fields within a network of dredged canals on the lakebed. In this way, nutrients carried by rains were recycled.

And so, agriculture spread all over the world. However, while our ancestors worked hard to develop this activity of great importance to humanity, by then our ancestors had also developed a close relationship with the wolf, which led them to the other great activity: the domestication of animals.

The Domestication of Animals

The domestication of animals begins with the dog when it was still a wolf about 15 thousand years ago in the region of the Fertile Crescent, too. It is likely that those who tamed the dog were also the Natufians, according to evidence found at a burial of a member of this culture with a puppy in Israel.

With the advent of the Younger Dryas period, the weather conditions became very unfavorable for our ancestors in finding their livelihood. Wild fruits as well as animals were very scarce. Then Homo Sapiens thought about domesticating other animals. The wise man realized that it was possible and very convenient to retain the animals to ensure their meat supply, as well as to dispose of their benefits afterwards when it was really necessary. Thus, began the domestication of the other animals using the experience they had with the domestication of the dog. Before domestication, humans and the wolf lived hunting in harmony for many years.

During the upper Paleolithic period at the time of the last glaciation, both followed the herds of the other animals they hunted. It is likely that by then they had already made a good relationship: at least they were not afraid of each other. Later it is likely that this relationship increased as the dog approached the places where humans camped, probably in search of the remains of food they left behind.

While they were nearby, humans may have noticed that wolves were trying to alert and defend them from other animals such as snakes or keep some scavenger and rodent animals away. So, there were its benefits in that relationship. Perhaps that's why both humans and wolves accepted each other and started getting along until they started hunting together and sharing their prey.

In the Neolithic when humans discovered agriculture, the dog was already with them and helped them to protect the crops. It also accompanied them when they went hunting and helped them take the prey. Sometimes wild animals were captured alive. These were then put in some kind of corral. In some other cases, these animals were cornered, i.e. directed, and tucked into a coral with the help of the dog, which had already established an alliance with Homo Sapiens.

Over time, especially during sedentary life, the relationship between man and dog became so close that they both became fond of each other to be part of the same family, a relationship that still remains today.

The dog also took care of the animals in the corral. These wild, cornered animals gradually became accustomed to living next to Homo Sapiens, who fed, cared for, protected, and even sometimes assisted them in giving birth. Domesticated animals changed their physical characteristics and behavior until they stopped looking like wild animals.

One of the first animals to domesticate about 5 thousand years later, after the domestication of the dog was the goat, then about 2 thousand years later the sheep was domesticated and then the cow about 3 thousand years after domesticated the goat. Then followed the domestication of the pig, lamb, cat, and camel, then the donkey and the horse.

During the process of domestication of animals, which lasted several thousand years, Homo Sapiens was discovering that the animals, in addition to their meat and skin, could bring other benefits. Thus, they discovered that some animals such as goat and cow could mainly also produce milk for their diet. Although the cow was also initially used as a cargo animal. The sheep could, besides producing meat, it also could produce wool to make yarns and fabrics to make clothes for Homo Sapiens. The horse was the engine of transport, as well as the donkey and the camel. The cat was very useful in removing or scaring rodents that ate cereal crops.

Breeding these animals would initially begin in the extensive steppes of Asia, making men shepherds. Over time and thanks to agriculture they could provide food for the animals as well.

At the end of the drought of the Younger Dryas period everything returned to prosperity and a very important event occurred: the shepherds joined the farmers. This gave both groups a constant supply of bread and meat, which made life much better. However, because these cultivating and breeding tasks were very different, the two groups had to adapt. But not all farmers and shepherds came together, as some of them remained independent in the management of their activities. However, both farmers and shepherds, together or separated, managed to make, through Neolithic culture, many advances towards prosperity.

Advances Towards Prosperity

The human being is a social being by nature, because he learned throughout his evolution that he needs from other humans to feel better and thus have a better development in doing the things he requires to survive. For this reason, we see it in a group, which gave rise to families, then to the first tribes, towns, and cities. Human beings have always needed other humans to achieve their livelihood. From the beginning of their lives, while some collected the wild fruits, others hunted animals and so on to obtain the food.

Since its appearance, the human has been in a constant struggle to survive, for that is what life is all about: fighting to survive. Now, in order to survive the man first needed to get the daily livelihood and second to successfully face the threats that could be presented to him in the pursuit of their livelihood.

During the Neolithic, to achieve their survival, humans used stick, stone, bone, and then metal tools when they were discovered. At first, life would not be so easy. However, as their thinking progressed to give birth to new ideas to develop better ways of doing things, achieving sustainment became easier and life also got better.

To achieve a better life, the human being used his intellect to constantly develop and improve throughout his life, a set of ideas, knowledge, beliefs, customs, and traditions. This is precisely what is known as culture and transmitted from generation to generation through language.

Thanks to their culture, the great capacity for learning and the adaptation of our ancestors for the early Neolithic, some 12 thousand years ago, a part of them had already been established and adapted in the Crescent Fertile developing the right attitude and aptitude to successfully exploit the resources available in that region.

Culture is the foundation of what human beings are and will have a significant impact on the future life of societies and all their social organization, spirituality, art, economy and all the activities that are required in the day-to-day life of being to achieve their livelihood. This set of disciplines forms the cultural identity of people and provides them with the necessary tools for their development. One of the ways in which people strengthen their culture and maintain their identity is through knowledge and practice of their own values.

Language is the fundamental pillar on which culture is based, this being the vehicle for the acquisition and transmission of the cultural knowledge and values of people. A key factor in having and maintaining a stable and strong culture is the organization of society.

Society is that set of human beings who share the same culture with their behaviors and objectives, and who interact with each other in full cooperation. At first, the society of prehistoric man was organized in a hierarchical way, where power was concentrated in a chief, perhaps the wisest or strongest of the group. During the Neolithic period, the form of organization of societies was undergoing some variations; Therefore, both culture and society are constantly evolving, because over time they are influenced by new forms of thought in human development.

With development and progress during the Neolithic, a larger art emerged. In the religious aspect, graves and burials in both the caves and the outdoors of the Paleolithic, were also made already in the Neolithic, but near or below houses with a variety of rites under the belief in life after death and that the dead could help the living. Another relevant aspect of the Neolithic was significant population growth. Outdoor settlements became camps and communities to form Neolithic society.

During the Neolithic Revolution, man perfected his stone tools by polishing the stone instead of carving it. Also, during this period and with the new economic model established thanks to agriculture and breeding, new tools were developed to carry out these two new activities.

For the harvest, the first snouts were created composed of two pieces of stick tied in the form of "L". On one piece of stick stone teeth were inserted to cut the stem of the plants and the other piece of stick served as a handle to be operated by hand. From the sickle were derived many of the other agricultural tools of prehistory such as the hoe or shed and even the plow itself. Those tools are still used today.

Progress also emerged during the Neolithic period in other activities such as trade and means of transport, including wagons and navigation; as well as the manufacture of better tools to perform, maintain and protect all the activities that allowed them to achieve sustenance, including, of course, agriculture and breeding.

To continue improving their lives, our ancestors also developed other activities such as basketry, pottery and ceramics, yarn, and weaving, as well as the construction of better homes. These other activities gave rise to craftsmanship: a true diversification of work. People became completely sedentary, and the towns grew significantly.

As for the manufacture of clothing, during the Neolithic period techniques were developed to obtain fibers of wool and linen. With the help of the loom invented more than 6 thousand years ago, they made the fabrics to make the clothes, which was no longer only to protect from the cold as was done more than 100 thousand years ago in the Paleolithic, but in the Neolithic, clothing was given an ornamental and decorative use, which also makes fashion emerge. This was an extraordinary advance, as the clothes used before in the Paleolithic were very rudimentary and was basically a kind of blanket made from the skins of the animals they hunted. To do this they scraped, cured, and softened the skin and then make their blanket. Over time they invented the sewing activity to make the blanket better adjusted to the body.

As for basketry, it began with the experience that our ancestors had had to make their ropes with which they built traps to hunt, rafts to sail and transport objects, as well as fishing nets. To make their baskets, they took their ropes, or some other materials such as guacos, twigs or fibers and weaved them to make baskets to transport objects such as grains. However, with these baskets, flour could not be transported, nor liquids such as water.

The baskets exceeded the limitations in terms of the shape and size of pumpkins or leather sacks. However, to overcome the limitations in terms of transporting liquids, the baskets began to waterproof with clay.

Upon discovering that the clay hardened by leaving it to the Sun and even more so if it was set on fire, our ancestors began to manufacture a wide variety of clay objects such as figurines, bricks, and containers. The statuettes were made for religious purposes, while the bricks were made of mud for the construction of houses. That is how pottery comes up.

To manufacture the clay vessels at first, they were made by molding them manually but later their manufacture changed with the invention of the wheel in Mesopotamia more than 5 thousand years ago. This wheel made of wood was used to build the potter's lathe to make the vessels. At first, the lathe consisted of a wooden wheel that the potter turned to mold with his wet hands the clay object and thus give the vessel its round and symmetrical shape. The great advantage of clay containers over baskets was that these containers could hold and transport liquids in addition to the other products they could handle with baskets.

Later the art of ceramics appears when cooking in a kind of high-temperature oven the object made of clay to achieve a sufficiently strong and resistant container for liquid leakage. They then developed techniques to decorate the ceramics with figures and colors. In addition to ceramic containers, utensils were also made to cook food and drink beer, which had already been invented, probably in Mesopotamia, more than 6 thousand years ago using cereals such as wheat or barley.

The wheel, in addition to being used to manufacture the potter's lathe, was also used to improve agricultural tools such as plow and some irrigation equipment such as noria. The other very important use of the wheel was in the manufacture of the first wagons pulled by animals to transport goods and people.

With all these advances, the internal organization of settlements became more complex. The cultivation of land and the rearing of animals could produce enough food and even with surpluses to solve the problem of food supply. As a result, the population increased considerably, forcing humans to expand farmland stock-land extensions, introduce irrigation and establish trade with surpluses. These new economic practices, unsurprisingly, further increased population growth.

With the surplus production of agriculture and breeding, other people engaged in handicrafts could be fed. In this sense, the craftsman changed his products to the farmer by part of his surplus. This gave rise to trade in the form of barter. It is with the surplus of agricultural production and that of breeding that prosperity begins.

Neolithic Culture

With the new economic activities, the concept of property became more accentuated. Humans considering their things, including the land they used to farm, as their property and that of their group, would be willing to protect and defend it. For this they formed villages and small towns with huts or houses very close to each other. Each tribe and town further developed the customs and traditions, religious beliefs, their art and the way of life that they had acquired throughout their entire evolution.

The Neolithic culture that had emerged in the Middle East spread from North Africa to northeast Asia and then spread through India and China to the rest of Asia. It later spread throughout Europe, America, and the rest of the world. The first thing to spread was farming and animal husbandry. With these two activities, the world would base its economy on food production, and with the surplus trade would emerge to further shape the world's economy.

In Europe, the Neolithic culture of the Fertile Crescent spread throughout the southeastern part about 6 thousand years ago. Over a millennium it had spread and consolidated throughout the Mediterranean coast. The European continent would also base its economy on food production and with the surplus trade would emerge to further develop its economy. However, this continent would develop its own customs and traditions, as well as its beliefs.

In Europe religion was also among the people and involved the Sun, the Moon and the stars that shone on their lives by providing them with the earth and water to produce their livelihood. People lived with some fear between life and death, as well as with some concern for the changes of the seasons. But by that time in Europe there were no elites organized like in the Middle East. Europeans rather lived in small communities. Their beliefs came from the influence of encounter with other farmers and from the local hunter-gatherers who joined them. These people also built great projects, thanks to all energy as a product of their economic development, with which they began to build their great stone monuments on meditation on life and death.

For 2 thousand years they raised large stones in the clear spaces of the forest. Later other farmers brought different beliefs and threw away the large, erected stones and built monuments of underground rooms for the burial of their dead. People could go to these places to see their dead through a long corridor, which was sometimes aligned with sunlight at a specific time of year. In those places people were going to visit their dead to communicate with them using some kind of hallucinogen. And in those altered states of consciousness they thought they really communicated with the spirits of their ancestors.

Over time, middle eastern traders who had come to Europe had forged a new culture: that of trade. So, people start marketing with their products and get others they did not produce. A type of people emerged with valuables such as horses, precious objects, even tall and large ceramic cups to drink alcoholic beverages. Which was reserved only for people of very high status.

Traders arriving in Europe from the Fertile Crescent also brought to the north of the continent the art of melting and the secrets of Middle Eastern trade. The technology to work metals was developed in the Middle East and then spread throughout Europe. Upon reaching this continent, copper technology developed more slowly. Its first manifestations appeared in the Cycladic Islands and Crete.

A thousand years later came bronze technology also and as in the Fertile Crescent, after tin was added to copper to obtain bronze, sharp weapons such as spears and swords appeared, which were symbols of power.

The wealthy people, of course, showed great interest in power, because they liked to have and accumulate any symbol of power such as bronze weapons, as well as the horse, which was a cargo animal until then, but could move at great distances and faster, although this animal was very expensive to have and maintain.

Iron technology would also be introduced to Europe some 700 years later. Metals technology made Europe a thriving continent. In addition, this change began to mark the end of the stone age in Europe.

The Europeans also learned to obtain from sheep's wool the yarn to make the wool clothes which was hotter for that kind of cold weather. Then the spinners began dyeing the fabrics and offering dresses for greater social status in colors such as red and blue taken from plants. They became well aware of plants until they got to know the medicinal ones in order to become healers, which marks the beginning of European medicine.

Wool dresses were favorites of Europe's elitist class. They were so dear that when the wealthy were buried with them and also with their other dear belongings as their weapons in coffins made of oak with the entire trunks of the trees they covered with earth in elaborate ceremonies. These tombs were surrounded by statues with figures of goddesses as guardians of tombs.

Trade continued its development and until later, it went from Europe to the Middle East, bringing amber to trade. Amber is the sap of fossilized pines. The exchange was then increased by including other products.

About 5,000 years ago there was a large increase in metals with the discovery of iron which resulted in the extensive production of cheaper and more effective agricultural and breeding tools giving rise to the iron age in Europe. The sword was produced and of course the soldier to create what Europe is today.

People who already had their weapons started trying to take over the farms, starting the violence. Farmers were losing their land to other people's friends and began building fences and fortresses around their settlements. The last farmers faced the warriors and their way of life disappeared forever. Four thousand years ago the last hunter-hunters living on the remote shores of Europe would disappear from the world of humans, for the warriors had taken up their lands.

Then, with the wagon, the horses and the weapons, everything would start to change. Foreigners from the Middle East would bring a series of changes to human life in Europe. But weapons are not the bad or lethal, but a new concept was introduced: mandate and obedience. People obeyed because they had a boss.

This created in Europe and then in the rest of the world a new society that would change the world with all its glory and horror. When command and obedience arose, the end of the stone age hunter-gatherer societies also appeared, which had begun about 3,000 years earlier in the Middle East.

However, Neolithic culture continued to spread around the world bringing prosperity to all regions. In Greece, sailing in the Aegean Sea developed until it reached the island of Crete. But each of the regions that Neolithic culture reached would develop its own customs and traditions, as well as its beliefs. With advances towards the prosperity of Neolithic culture our ancestors built the first settlements and towns.

1.2 FIRST SETTLEMENTS AND TOWNS

The contributions of the Natufians were essential to the way of life of the people who came after them. Consequently, Natufian culture was the basis for the culture that then continued throughout the Neolithic period to build the first settlements. This way of living then became the basis of new cultures including ours.

At first, thanks to the surplus of the wild fruits they collected and the animals they hunted in the region of the Fertile Crescent, our ancestors managed to guarantee their livelihoods and thus become increasingly sedentary and establish the first settlements with homes for their families. Over time the settlements grew and prospered to become towns.

With the advent of agriculture and animal husbandry, and then when the shepherds joined the farmers, the Neolithic Revolution took place, which radically and forever transformed human society. The discovery of agriculture and animal husbandry ended food shortages resulting from adverse climate changes during glaciations.

These two new activities: agriculture and breeding, began and then joined after the short glacial period Younger Dryas about 11.5 thousand years ago in the Middle East in the region between Israel and Syria. And then they spread out, following the trajectory of the Syrian corridor towards Mesopotamia.

With agriculture and breeding, our ancestors moved on to a totally sedentary life, when they devoted themselves entirely to sewing the land, raising animals, administering their products, and building their houses. However, by then, both people and animals lived together, which brought the first problems of public hygiene and with them new diseases.

To solve this chaotic situation, our ancestors began to build new settlements where people lived separately from animals.

The new communities have become bigger and more prosperous. Having their livelihoods safe, people began to plan their future. As the population grew, the first settlements began to spread from the Jericho area following the northern path to the Jordan Valley and Syria.

It should be noted that throughout the Fertile Crescent, the population grew, as there was enough food for all people thanks to agriculture and breeding. However, in some regions climatic conditions had also favored the abundance of wild fruits. And the more edible vegetation there was, the more abundant the animals were. This abundance of wild fruits and wild animals caused people in these regions to continue their practices as gatherers and hunters without having to resort to farming and breeding.

That abundance of food led people to settle and store the surplus of the crop to eat it when they needed it to survive and progress. This could explain why in some regions of the Fertile Crescent, people for that time became sedentary without the need for agriculture and still develop stable settlements until they formed villages and communities dedicated to fruit harvesting and animal hunting. As was the case of ancient gatherer-hunter villages in Egypt, as well as in Palestine south of the Canaan region.

However, as more was known about the advantages of agriculture, more peoples were joining it. Thus, in those areas where the Natufian settlements were from Jericho in Israel to Tell Abu Hureyra in Syria today, there has been evidence of the development of agriculture almost 11,000 years ago, albeit on a small scale. It is then seen that agriculture was an option that not only increased the chance of survival, but also increased the chance of progress. For, where it was practiced, agriculture caused an increase in the population, especially that of children, throughout this region. Children after a certain age also became part of the light-working team of agriculture.

Between 13 and 11 thousand years ago, early Natufian settlements emerged in Syria near the Euphrates River, which would be of great importance in the development of the towns of the region. These settlements lived at the beginning of wild fruit harvesting and animal hunting and fishing, but then adopted agriculture and breeding as their own way of producing their own food and thus guaranteeing their livelihood. These settlements included: Tell Abu Hureyra and Tell Mureybet, which stood out for their advances in house building.

Tell Abu Hureyra was a settlement located on a plateau in northern Syria near the Euphrates River. Its people grew rye, wheat, and barley. They also hunted their gazelles, donkeys, sheep, cows, rabbits, foxes, and birds, from which they later domesticated the sheep. At first this people lived in small circular huts with a roof of branches and reeds supported by wooden beams. The inhabitants of the settlement stored their grains under the hut.

Near Abu Hureyra was also the other Natufian settlement called *Tell Mureybet* with vegetation consisting of open steppes with pistachio trees and almonds with many wild cereals. Its people also lived at first in small circular huts. However, later they came to build larger rectangular houses with more than one room. The walls of these houses had stone columns buried on the floor.

Other settlements that emerged, around the same time by the northwest of Tell Abu Hureyra and Tell Mureybet, but in the southeast of the Anatolian peninsula in Turkey, were Nevali Cori and Cayonu, whose people were also at first gatherers and hunters, but who later adopted agriculture as their livelihood. These settlements stood out for their new designs of their houses and also for the construction of temples.

In *Nevali Cori* were built long rectangular houses that in addition to the residential part also included two or three parallel sections towards the bottom of the house. It is believed that these sections were used to store grains. These houses also had underground canals lined with stone slabs beneath the houses, perhaps to drain water from rains around the houses or to cool the houses, as the canals were open at both ends. In this settlement was also built a temple for worship with columns of stones. They also made clay figurines and sculpted some sculptures into limestone.

In *Cayonu,* also called Cayonu Tepesi, in southeastern Turkey near the Bogazkoy River, a tributary of the upper Tigris River. The people of Cayonu went on to grow the wheat and were the firsts to tame the pork. Its houses were made of rectangular stones and long as those of Nevali Cori. They also built buildings for their rituals such as the skull building with a chamber where they are believed to have practiced very mysterious rituals such as offering. They also made figurines of female deities as the double goddess to reinforce their religion.

As the settlements grew and developed, the first towns began to appear. One of those first settlements that later became a town and still stable to this day has been Jericho, built by the Natufians about 12 thousand years ago on a hill west of the Jordan River Valley near the Dead Sea in today's Israel.

Jericho had abundant water and fertile soils. At first the people of Jericho were gathers-hunters and lived in circular huts half-buried on the ground. Later, with the advent of agriculture, people were already producing their own food, mainly wheat and barley. The town was growing and by then had a population of about a thousand inhabitants, which was considered high for its time.

Later the famous walls around Jericho were built perhaps to protect the town from the floods of the Jordan

River or any invasion. These walls were more than 3 meters high and more than a meter wide. In front of the wall was a pit about 8 meters wide. The inhabitants of Jericho also built a conical stone tower within the wall, which was about 9 meters high and to reach the top of this tower they also built an internal staircase of 22 steps. It is believed that the purpose of this tower was to indicate the longest day of the year.

Another of the first towns was Catal Huyuk in what is today the Anatolian peninsula in Turkey about 10 thousand years ago. *Catal Huyuk* was a large settlement located near the Carsamba River about 87 miles from Hasan volcano. The people of Catal Huyuk, after some progress, lived in very remarkable houses for having their only entrance on the ceiling and with a very decorated interior. These houses were rectangular, made of adobe with ceilings made of wooden beams, on which they laid a kind of vegetable mats and then covered with mud.

The houses were built next to each other without streets, but with some common courtyards. This design provided the town with the protection of a wall. Access to these houses was made by the roof using two stairs: one outside to climb the roof and the other inside to go down to the house through the opening of the roof. If they wanted to walk around the town, they could walk through the roofs. These houses also did not have doors or windows. The ceiling opening in addition to allowing access to the house was also used as the only form of ventilation, as this allowed the entry of fresh air and the exit of the smoke from the kitchen and the odors of the house.

Inside the houses were divided into rooms whose walls were covered with a plaster finish with a very soft texture. These rooms were separate and were used for various purposes such as bedrooms, kitchen, and surplus storage of their agricultural production. In the bedroom there was a kind of beds to sleep in, as well as a kind of benches to sit on. In the kitchen there was a kind of oven to cook the bread. Some social activities could be done on the roof.

The people of Catal Huyuk buried their dead inside the town. It is believed that the bodies were exposed outdoors for some time before being buried. In some cases, when only the bones remained in the tombs, people separated the skeleton's head from their deceased to give him veneration. Sometimes the skulls were covered with plaster and painted with ochre to recreate the face of the deceased.

The villagers of Catal Huyuk also collected obsidian from the surroundings of the Hasan volcano, to make more resilient weapons and better tools. Obsidian is a volcanic rock, a hard, brittle material, which is also called volcanic glass. When broken or fractured, it produces slabs with sharper edges than those obtained with flint stone. This makes obsidian better material to make tools more efficient like knives, arrows, and spearheads.

Obsidian was also polished to make other utensils such as the first mirrors. In addition to these uses, the obsidian was also exchanged by the people of this place for other goods to the people of other settlements. The inhabitants of this region at first lived from fruit harvesting and hunting and fishing until they adopted agriculture and breeding to produce their own food. They grew wheat and barley mainly. Also, chickpeas, lentils, and linen. In addition, they ate deer meat, wild boar, donkey, and sheep as a product of hunting. Catal Huyuk came to cover an area of 13 hectares.

Very close to Catal Huyuk there was also another town called *Hacilar* about 9 thousand years ago. Its people lived off agriculture and animal husbandry. This was a walled town with houses, squares and perhaps also had a small temple. The houses had a stone floor, wooden and mud walls, and a flat roof. The interior of the houses was finished with plaster. These houses had rooms such as kitchen, living room, bedroom, and storage separately. The people of Hacilar made ceramic objects by hand, decorated with painted details. They also made clay statuettes, perhaps to represent some deity. Other towns emerged thanks to their advances in social organization, development and construction of their towns, and crafts. Among them are Jerf el Ahmar and Ain Ghazal.

Jerf el Ahmar excelled mostly for its architecture and social organization, which already included leaders. This town was located in Syria near the Euphrates River and near the Tell Mureybet settlement. Jerf el Ahmar was occupied about 11 thousand years ago. There the people at first were gatherer-hunters and then they lived off agriculture and they were very organized. To the point where they managed to build a special site for the common storage of harvested grain, which was then distributed among families, who were considered an integral part of the town and together practiced their religious ceremonies. It was an organized partnership with leaders.

At first, circular houses were built in this town, then oval-shaped houses with straight walls and later, about 10 thousand years ago, the first modern houses were built, albeit they were built next to each other. These houses were larger than the previous ones and were formed by rectangular walls made of stone with doors and windows, which were shaped by stone chisels.

They also built in the center of Jerf el Ahmar a very large public building made exclusively to pray, so that these people would fulfill their religious activities and thus fill the spiritual part of their lives. This building was a sanctuary where people would pray and left stone offerings with complex designs in the form of symbols and animals as if they wanted to tell a story. Obviously, it was matters of religion.

This shrine was something similar like the one that had been built in Gobekli Tepe a millennium before by our ancestors when they were still gatherers and hunters so that the people of the towns around them would continue to maintain their faith. This great sanctuary was built about 11 thousand years ago at the top of a mountain about 6 miles from the ancient settlement of Urfa, in the southeast of what is now Turkey, near Syria, around several neighboring towns before they began to practice agriculture and breeding.

The Gobekli Tepe shrine consisted of large "T"-shaped stone pillars decorated with a variety of animals and a kind of embossed religious symbols. The columns were carved with animals such as the bull, the lion, the snake, and the fox. It is believed that the columns were used as ritual platforms to put the dead so that the vultures would eat their flesh so that their spirit could be freed as they left the body.

For the first time religion had become commonplace and something very complex. With rituals carried out outdoors in a special shrine like this, which seems to have been attended by nearby communities on a kind of pilgrimage. It is believed that it was religion that prompted humans to colonize more lands so that there would be more participants in rituals in places like this.

After Jerf el Ahmar, the method of construction of the new rectangular houses was the same as that used in the other contemporary towns with Jerf el Ahmar and is the same one still used today. This new style of houses spread throughout the rest of the region to continue using it in housing construction, which was improved over time, to build other more sophisticated towns such as Ain Ghazal in Jordan more than 9,000 years ago.

Ain Ghazal also excelled at the development and construction of its town, its craftsmanship and its great prosperity. It had a kind of central street and on each side were the houses with their entrances where people accessed them from the street. It also had this town, a kind of square. The houses could be two-story, and some coated with a touch of plaster and painted red in some cases.

There people lived very well because they had abundant food thanks to agriculture and breeding. They lived in a lot of comfort. It was a very prosperous society. Those who were neither farmers, nor shepherds, nor house builders could use their talent to make more specialized tools such as special pink flint knives to make such tools.

Others were engaged in the manufacture of clay containers that dried in the sun and also to the manufacture of baskets used for trade. Some of these baskets were sealed with a clay or bitumen coating. Others were larger made or woven with herbs and reeds for larger tasks.

The first woven fabrics were also developed and designed with one of the first technological devices of the time: the first looms. To make the woven fabrics at first, they used a hairy, rough wool obtained from the sheep, but then the fabrics were improved. Later they made a linen cloth, which was softer. They also made the yarn to make the fabrics and to sew. With all these products, the exchange of goods between the people of the town and later with other towns was increased.

By then you could see the great progress that the Neolithic people made. Their quality of life improved and their houses had already become homes. These had grown to house larger families. These houses had separate bedroom kitchen to increase privacy. They also began to pay close attention to their household objects, just as we do today.

In Ain Ghazal, a large and very advanced town with hundreds of houses, our ancestors invented the first clean, soft, and water-resistant artificial material: the mortar. A material made of lime, sand, and water. The mortar was a kind of cement with which they glued the blocks of stones or bricks to make the walls of the houses. This material was very versatile with many applications. With the mortar, they even made the floors of the houses. The mortar became very popular and spread throughout the region. A whole new technology.

The people of Ain Ghazal also used mortar to recreate the face of their deceased from the dead man's skull. This skull was coated with mortar as a cult of veneration of their ancestors. These figures, related to the spiritual life of the first farmers, were very notable in Ain Ghazal.

But later the mortar would bring a very serious problem because lime does not exist as a natural substance. It was one of the first substances that man invented and to produce it had to take the limestone and burn it with large amounts of wood, which meant cutting many trees, which eventually began to be scarce.

When they found no wood to produce any fire, even for cooking or lighting, they began to use manure to make fire. The felling of the trees had led to deforestation. Another factor that contributed to deforestation was the effect caused by goats by eating the trees when they were still small, as they would never grow.

Communities had created an environmental problem for the first time. The population of Ain Ghazal began to decline and eventually abandoned the town after 2.5 thousand years of settlement. Many of the villagers had to become nomadic again to survive. However, the neighboring towns went ahead and even continued to use the mortar normally, but above all to reconstruct the faces of their ancestors to continue their faith.

To continue with the development and progress of the first towns we find *Teleilat el Ghassul,* a town very similar to ours that existed 6.5 thousand years ago, near Jericho and Ain Ghazal in the Jordan Valley of the Middle East, a few miles from the northern edge of the Dead Sea, in Israel. Its discovery came from excavations made since 1929 of our time. According to the findings, this town was made up of farming communities. Although the town was located in one of the driest places on the planet, fundamental ideas emerged on it that would lead to development and progress beyond the stone age.

Ghassul was located in a very strategic region that linked two other regions, which were two great emerging powers: the Sumerians in the Euphrates and the Egyptians on the Nile. At that time, there was a very complex economy in Ghassul for the time of prehistory. These people cultivated the olive tree on a large scale, whose crops spread through the hills of the whole town and then throughout the valley.

From the olives they took out their oil, which was given multiple uses mainly for cooking and to light the lamps for lighting at night. This olive oil was considered the gold liquid for that time in the Middle East. In addition to the olive tree they also cultivated the fig tree. The Ghassulian were the first fruit tree farmers in history: the first horticulturists.

Ghassul was a huge and very sophisticated town for its time, with very creative people filling its streets with a lot of energy, and a lot of life. They were people with many ideas. And they even gave themselves the luxury of importing things from Yemen in the south and from Afghanistan in the east, including very sophisticated items such as perfume and lapis lazuli, which was a semi-precious blue stone. It was a wealthy town, and everyone had the opportunity to thrive and get resources to lead a beautiful life. Ghassulian traded in very distant regions with large quantities of mass-produced products such as olives, oil, salt, and lentils. These products were packaged in ceramic containers, which were transported by donkeys to their respective destinations.

They made highly specialized ceramic containers with clay vats of all kinds heated by fire, large for transporting products and decorated for use in homes. They understood the importance of turning raw materials into more specialized products to give it better value such as milk and butter obtained from the cow. Then they also did the same thing when processing the wool of the sheep and with elaborate dyes raised their value. People paid high price for these luxury items to differentiate themselves from others. It was a very competitive society and aware of social and fashion status. They lived on the trade of the food they produced, which they preserved thanks to salt, which came to be considered as the white gold of prehistory. In Ghassul are the largest salt deposits in the region, right in the Dead Sea very close to Ghassul. The beaches of the Dead Sea were a large salt mine with which they preserved the olives and fish. These products were marketed with Egypt and Mesopotamia thousands of miles away on donkeys.

At first, they carried all this great economy of so many products that produced on a large scale and that they marketed massively without any accounting. However, they began to do something to identify the goods they sent using some symbols. To do this they made a clay ball and cut it in half and inside inserted small objects representing the products and then joined the two halves and sealed them and put a hallmark of the sender of the goods. When the products arrived at their destination, the seal would be opened. This method can be considered as the precursor to the written message that arose afterwards. These little balls started the basis of written language

Something really impressive yet, was to survive and progress so much in the middle of the desert in a place without water, so necessary to produce all the products they needed to survive. In addition, water was the center of their lives and faith. Very few rains fell there. To overcome this immense adversity, the Ghassulian built a whole network of irrigation canals and water descended from the hills by gravity. It was an achievement of the utmost importance and a lot of imagination. These canals were of many miles in length and required a lot of labor to make them, perhaps thousands of people working.

The Ghassulian were able to unite all the people in one project. This people made this great work of great wingspan about 2 thousand years before the construction of the pyramids of Egypt. This had to be the product of a very well-organized town. Also here came irrigation projects without having a river nearby as in Mesopotamia and Egypt, and they did so a thousand years before. This channel system should have been controlled by the local elite.

Ghassul was a peaceful society without armies or slaves. To encourage people to get involved in their big projects, they used religion, which had a social character. The priests were a kind of special elite, and they told people what the gods wanted them to do. Of course, the priests were connected with the large farming families and they, the priests, allowed society to conduct themselves in the way the mighty families wanted. That is like a transfer from the personal gods to the state gods. People moved to the sound of leaders because they believed their gods could punish them. Everyone was united by faith.

Perhaps related to that faith, there was the star of Ghassul, which represented the art of this people. This star is made of 8 points with a center formed by two concentric circles. Inside each of the circles is an 8-pointed star as well. The star of the first circle is white with a red background and the star of the second circle is also white with a black background. These stars were painted on some wall of some houses and for this they used substances composed of various minerals with which they made the colors black, red, white, gray and some colors of intermediate tone.

Meanwhile south of the Dead Sea, a long way from Ghassul, a great discovery had been made in *Wadi Feynan:* copper. Wadi Feynan was a small settlement in the valley in southern Jordan, contemporary with Jericho, which lived at the beginning of wild fruit harvesting and hunting, but then adopted agriculture and breeding to achieve their livelihoods. In this settlement appeared at that time after some flood, the green malachite at the bottom of the river. This stone is one of the sources of obtaining copper and there was much of this mineral in the mines around Wadi Feynan.

The green malachite was very easy to melt and then molded and melted several times at low temperatures. At first, color-inspired miners took the green malachite and ground it into smaller pebbles with stone hammers to make jewels without casting them. These jewels were marketed with their customers who had on the other side of the Dead Sea, in the Beersheba Valley 93 miles from the mines, where it was demanded it in large quantities. This *Beersheba,* rather called Tel Beersheba was a settlement in southern Israel that was located near what is now the city of Beersheba.

Tel Beersheba at the time had a monopoly on copper production from the Wadi Feynan mine. The people of Tel Beersheba sent Wadi Feynan, their miners, and traders to procure the ore, which was sent to them by donkeys.

But Tel Beersheba traders learned the exact way to heat the ore by blowing the fire with blowers and thus created in this region the first molten metal, which they kept as a secret. Copper was used to build everything from decorative objects to daggers. They could recast it several times in other ways and those processes were done in their settlements away from the mines.

These copper products then arrived in Ghassul several days or weeks away, the Ghassulian began to market them because their people liked to stand out among others and with copper could be made many fantastic and exotic ways to satisfy that market. Although those early products were used more as symbols of overcoming. With the advent of bronze some 5,000 years ago, rural society had become an urban society.

But life in Ghassul began to get in trouble. Its powerful customers in Egypt and Mesopotamia had also developed immense irrigation projects, grew their own olives and produced their own salt. This brought trade with Ghassul to an end, resulting in the disappearance of Ghassulian great culture in about a century. However, what it could survive from the town, was based on the agricultural and bronze economy. But the merchants of Ghassul spread to Egypt, Mesopotamia, Europe, and the rest of the world.

Meanwhile, from the southwestern part of the Fertile Crescent, the Neolithic towns continued to spread to Egypt around the Nile. The first settlements in Egypt date back about 11,000 years. However, the first peoples who adopted agriculture as their way of life date back about 8,000 years with migrants from the Middle East. Among the first agricultural towns we have Fayum and Merimde in lower Egypt and El-Badari in upper Egypt.

Fayum was a town on the western bank of the Nile River near the delta, about 62 miles southwest of old Memphis, modern Cairo. The town was initially very fertile with lots of fauna and flora, thanks to a canal with abundant water from the Nile River, which created a lake in which a lot of vegetation grew attracting many animals. This turned Fayum into an oasis, which in turn attracted the first settlers about 9,000 years ago.

Fayum lived off farming and breeding. Its main crops were wheat and barley and animal husbandry included sheep, goats, and pigs. They also made stone weapons and utensils with wooden handles, as well as ceramics, which they made simple. Everything indicates that people led a good life with lots of hunting, fishing and in the shade of large trees until about 3 thousand years later a drought appeared, and people had to migrate to the Nile Valley. People spread to form the great Egyptian towns of prehistory. However, the town of Fayum eventually evolved into the modern city of Medinet el Fayum, and which today is considered the oldest city in Egypt.

Merimde was a town that emerged about 7 thousand years ago on the western side of the Nile Delta, 27 miles from Cairo. The people of the town of Merimde lived from agriculture growing wheat and barley, and they also lived a little on hunting and fishing. They made their tools and utensils of stone, bones, and ivory, and also made primitive ceramics. People lived in small circular huts that they built with branches and straw.

The town of *El-Badari* also emerged about 7 thousand years ago on the banks of the Nile River in upper Egypt, whose culture flourished a millennium later. El-Badari lived from agriculture and animal husbandry, and fishing, during the era before the pharaohs. They grew wheat, barley, and lentils. They raised cattle, sheep, goats, and dogs; and hunted gazelles. They used stone tools such as scrapers, snouts, and arrowheads. In this region around El-Badari and other settlements, emerged a culture well known for its cemeteries in the desert where the dead were buried in graves with their heads lying to the south. The people of El-Badari made good pottery and anthropomorphic figures of terracotta and ivory. In addition, they made basalt vases. With the green malachite they made ornaments for personal use. The region had a highly developed trade with a social stratification.

Later, other towns emerged in upper Egypt, eventually becoming cities. Among them were Armant, El Kab, Naqada, Hieracómpolis and Abydos. *Armant* was a town on the banks of the Nile River, about 12 miles south of Thebes, present-day Luxor. In Armant arose the cult of the solar god of the war Montu, who was worshipped in human form with a hawk's head. This town was the original home of the first rulers of Thebes. *El Kab* or Nekhbet had a main temple dedicated to the goddess Nekhbet represented by a vulture figure. They also had another goddess, the famous Isis, the queen. In *Naqada* came the cult of the god Set or Seth, the god of chaos, the desert, storms, disorder, and violence. In addition, large tombs were built in this town. *Hierapolis* was the center of worship of the god Horus, who was the son of the goddess Isis, wife of Osiris. *Abydos* was a town that came to have many temples where many early pharaohs were buried including Pharaoh Narmer.

As the towns of Egypt continued to expand within their territory, the towns of the northern part of the Fertile Crescent had already spread through the so-called Syrian corridor, to the south following the course of the Euphrates and Tigris rivers to their mouths in the Persian Gulf. This land was ancient Mesopotamia.

At the foot of the Zagros Mountains northeast of Mesopotamia there was a settlement called Jarmo near the Shanidar cave, where a species of human being lived during the Paleolithic period, some 40 thousand years ago, as those who also lived in Germany, Europe called the Neanderthals.

Jarmo was one of the first agricultural settlements in Mesopotamia about 9 thousand years ago, with adobe houses with stone floors and roof of sun-dried muds. They grew wheat, barley, lentils and domesticated goats, sheep, and dogs. They used flint and obsidian to make tools. To work agriculture they made snouts, cutters, mortars, etc. They also made baskets waterproofed with tar to store and transport flours and liquids. They had a handcrafted ceramic with a simple design. Their clay figurines included pregnant women representing fertility goddesses.

In northern Mesopotamia there was enough rain to allow agriculture, which stimulated, about 8 thousand years ago, the development of Neolithic agricultural settlements, specialized in ceramics of very good quality. Among these settlements we have: Tell Halaf and Tell Arpachiyah.

Tell Halaf was a settlement in northern Syria today, near present-day Turkey. This settlement also produced a very good Neolithic ceramic with fine designs. In addition to ceramics, they also manufactured a wide variety of figurines and seals.

Tell Arpachiyah was a small settlement in what is now Iraq, with cobblestone streets and circular and rectangular buildings perhaps for some religious activities.

A little further south and near Tell Arpachiyah, another settlement came out called *Tell Hassuna* with adobe houses built around an open central space. These people worked pottery and ceramics, they also made tools such as hand axes, grinding stones, snouts and even ovens, all according to their own Hassuna culture.

Further to the center of Mesopotamia was a small town, from about 7 thousand years ago, called *Tell es-Sawwan,* located in present-day Iraq on the banks of the Tigris River and belonging to the Samarra culture with large houses built with sun-dried mud bricks. This was a town of farmers who came to use the irrigation of the Tigris River to obtain good crops, since in this region the rains were not very abundant. They are believed to have been the first to use irrigation practice. The downtown was surrounded by a pit about 3 meters wide and a strong adobe wall to defend the town from invaders. The way of life of this town, including its tools, its pottery, and its figurines, was very similar to Tell Hassuna to the north. Tell es-Sawwan was the ancestor town of today's city of Samarra. The Samarra culture was the forerunner of Mesopotamian culture.

Further south of Mesopotamia there was a town, about 7,000 years ago, called *Tell al-Ubaid* in southern Iraq, about 155 miles from the Persian Gulf. The people of Tell al-Ubaid lived in villages with adobe houses with open courtyards and paved streets. They got their livelihoods through irrigated agriculture and managed to make their own equipment to process their food. They also made many male and female figurines, especially those with lizard faces. Some of the Tell al-Ubaid villages achieved great development to become towns, which then continued their progress over time to lay the foundations of events towards civilization.

1.3   TOWARDS CIVILIZATION

What we mean today by civilization is a high level of a society on culture, customs, beliefs, ideas and knowledge that can be transmitted through the language to the members of society, to a town or group of towns at any given time of its evolution. A civilization is a society that has achieved a high degree of development in its forms of organization, its institutions, its social structure, and its economy. A society that is endowed with a political, administrative, and legal system, and which has developed scientific, technological, artistic, and cultural knowledge. The development of a civilization is transmitted among its members through mainly oral or written language.

The birth of our civilization took place about 5,300 years ago in the Sumer region, south of Mesopotamia. It was there that the world's first civilization emerged. And that would then expand for the rest of Mesopotamia and then to Egypt, in the Middle East. And later civilization spread throughout the rest of the world.

The towns that gave rise to these early civilizations had discovered agriculture and animal husbandry, trade, writing, and formed the first societies organized administratively by laws and standards for their proper functioning.

These early civilizations were characterized, among other things, by having developed around the basins of great rivers. The Mesopotamian between and around the Tigris and Euphrates Rivers, the Egyptian around the Nile River, the Indian around the Indo River, and the Chinese around the Yellow River. But of course, before reaching the level of civilization, the first towns that formed in these regions, with their constant development, managed to become the first cities.

It is important to note that, despite the distance among these early civilizations: Mesopotamia and Egypt, India and China; and the limited contact between them, these four civilizations shared several characteristics: they settled on the banks of large rivers and developed in extensive river valleys, so the basis of their economies was agriculture and livestock. All these civilizations had important urban centers, as in the case of Mesopotamia and Egypt they functioned as large political, commercial, and religious complexes. All these civilizations developed hierarchical and stratified societies in social classes according to their specialization.

These four civilizations are recognized for possessing huge architectural monuments, which are mainly associated with political power, and spiritual and religious manifestations, such as the construction of necropolises or cemeteries. All these civilizations made great strides in the scientific aspect, especially in the field of astronomy, mathematics, engineering, and medicine. These advances were applied to the construction of its great monuments and in works for public use.

In these civilizations usually the construction of their architectural and engineering works was carried out with labor of the people and some slaves, obtained as prisoners of war. These civilizations are also called hydraulic civilizations as they built irrigation systems to better harness river water to develop their agricultural activities and to ensure their livelihood.

Another characteristic of these early civilizations was the high level of development they had achieved in terms of agriculture, which was greatly favored by all the water provided by rivers and the fertility of the land of the valleys formed around the first agricultural settlements. This made it possible for agriculture to prosper widely to produce significant agricultural surpluses to meet the food needs of the population and still have a portion of the surplus to exchange for other products such as baskets, vessels, tools and utensils that other people made. This would lead to the birth of trade and the specialization of work, because in addition to farmers, artisans such as basket people and potters also emerged.

Given the importance of agriculture, it became necessary to the emergence of two other types of workers: those who protect the fields from attacks by some other people; and those who were responsible for making offerings to the gods, in which it was believed at the time, to enjoy good harvests.

The great effect of the agricultural surplus was the increase in the population, as there was enough food to feed more people. With agriculture and breeding in the Neolithic period, the towns of the Fertile Crescent experienced a great development. Religion emerged somewhat different from that of nomads, for in these early towns, religion was giving origin and form to intellectual life. From these kinds of people would later emerge priests, who would hold great positions in the growing society.

Agriculture and its consequent benefits of surplus, trade, and handicrafts; resulted in significant population growth and continued development of the region and the specialization of other types of work other than agriculture.

The need to record trade led to the birth of writing, which allowed peoples to become the first human societies organized administratively by laws and standards for their proper functioning.

With agriculture and breeding, and Neolithic culture, our ancestors would better develop pottery and ceramic, and work the metals after their discovery and then enter urban culture. Of these aspects, we will be talking in detail in this subchapter.

Pottery and ceramic are two events that have been closely linked to the development of the peoples. The pottery arose during the Upper Paleolithic period when our ancestors began to mold the clay to make the first objects made with this material and dried in the sun as vessels and figurines. The color of the objects could be reddish, ochre tones and even white, depending on the color of the clay being used. However, techniques for molding clay to make objects arose during the Neolithic some 12,000 years ago, when man had the need to collect and store his food.

With the emergence of agriculture in the Middle East, pottery continued its development by making objects for specific uses such as to store liquids, as well as solids. Later eventually they came to make pots for cooking, eating and drinking. Then, when our ancestors came up with the idea of using fire to dry their clay pieces, they realize that these pieces take on a higher level of hardening. This is how ceramic emerged about 9 thousand years ago.

Then human talent added decoration to these objects by printing stripes or symbols on the outer body of the object or by painting and transformed them into a real work of art.

At first, the shape of the vessels was not very symmetrical. However, with the invention of the wheel arose the potter's lathe about 5 thousand years ago in Mesopotamia. It is believed that this was the first use that was given to the wheel. This lathe basically consisted of a flat wooden wheel on which the clay paste to be molded, was placed. Turning the wheel conveyed a circular movement to the clay paste, giving it a cylindrical and symmetrical shape.

To achieve higher temperatures to produce better quality ceramics, the potter's oven emerged, some 500 years later also in Mesopotamia. This oven at first consisted of a hole in the floor and then walls were added to conserve heat and make cooking more efficient.

By using the potter's oven to achieve high temperatures to make pottery, our ancestors observed that some stones such as malachite and azurite subjected to intense fire could melt. This would give way to the discovery of the use of metals, which in turn would start the age of metals.

The Metal Age was the period of prehistory that began at the end of the Neolithic period when humans began using copper to manufacture some tools and utensils about 6,000 years ago. For this reason, this part of human evolution is called: age of metals, which is in turn divided into three stages that are named after the metals that man was progressively using in each of them. The oldest of these stages was the Copper Age, because this was the first metal worked, later came the Bronze Age and finally the Iron Age.

As in the case of agriculture and animal husbandry, metals were not discovered at the same time by all towns, so those towns who used copper were imposed on those who only used the stone. Afterwards, those who discovered the use of bronze and later iron were imposed on those who had fallen behind in terms of technology.

Humans first began to use metals that appeared in the wild such as gold, silver, and copper. Gold would be one of the first metals known to man, perhaps for its sun-like luster, to which they were always very attracted. Gold was found in the form of nuggets in the sands of rivers, or in veins containing gold, today called gold veins, where it also appears in the natural state.

Silver is also found in nodules, completely in the natural state, on the Earth's surface. But both gold and silver were very scarce and their distribution on Earth was very irregular. However, copper, like gold and silver, is also found in the natural state, but with greater abundance and regularity. So, copper would be the first metal used in greater quantity.

The Copper Age began with the use of this metal about 6,000 years ago when humans began working copper in a very simple way on the Anatolian Peninsula, northwest of the Fertile Crescent, in turkey today on the Asian continent. There is evidence of its use in Catal Huyuk. Copper then spread throughout the rest of the region and later through Mesopotamia, Israel, Jordan, and Egypt.

At first, they struck with a stone hammer the copper found in a natural or pure state at the ambient temperature. Subsequently, the hammering began to be done with hot copper, in order to avoid the fractures and partial losses of the metal, initiating this way the forging. Perhaps by accident by overheating the copper they discovered that it can pass from solid state to liquid and that this process was possible to manage by controlling the furnace fire, thus giving way to the casting, a very important process in the next stage in the elaboration of metal tools and utensils.

By melting the copper in the oven, they could give the desired shape by dumping it into molds. When they could no longer obtain copper in its purest form on the surface, then it had to be obtained from the mines. That is how mining was born. When the materials were extracted from the mines, melting, and alloying them with others, Steelmaking arose and then the metallurgy arose into finished metal objects. Copper metallurgy appears to be produced in various parts of the Middle East in Asia, the Balkans in Turkey and then expanded throughout the rest of Europe.

Copper is a malleable metal, soft and of little use for the manufacture of strong weapons and tools. So, with it were made rather ornamental objects such as necklaces, bracelets, rings, jewelry, and pins, which served as elements of luxury or social prestige for those who wore them. Some utensils such as campaniform vessels were also later manufactured. However, arrowheads, daggers and axes made of copper have also been found. But, given the low resistance of copper, stone tools were still used as they were more resistant. However, humans continued to seek a solution to the problem of low copper resistance until they discovered a more resistant metal that starts another period of the metal age: the Bronze Age.

The Bronze Age was the period that began with a great discovery. When the copper melted, humans saw that it was possible to mix liquid copper with other metals. That is how they discovered the alloys. In this way came bronze as an alloy of copper and tin. Bronze is a much harder metal than its two components and is easier to melt and work than copper. The use of bronze began about 5 thousand years ago, in the northern part of the Fertile Crescent, in what is now known as Armenia on the Asian continent and then in a short time spread throughout Europe and the rest of the world. The first bronze utensils mimicked the stone shapes, and thus the first metal axes had the same triangular shape and lacked a handle, like stone ones.

Progress in the use of bronze made it possible to make luxurious weapons and utensils. Among the weapons, the sword appeared, which would have an element that would determine the warrior character that developed at this stage. Other weapons made of bronze were daggers, knives, armor, helmets, spearheads, and shields to protect themselves in combat. With regard to luxurious objects, the pins, rings, jewelry, belt clips, necklaces and even mirrors, as well as statuettes of a magical-religious character, were highlighted. For most of the Bronze Age, agricultural utensils remained made of stone and wood. Only at the end of the period did bronze snouts begin to be used to harvest the cereals.

Bronze had been mainly used for the manufacture of ornaments and some weapons. However, the man at the time would continue his quest to make better tools, as he had done from his beginning to the present day. In that eagerness man discovered iron, which was most abundant. But there was one small detail: higher temperatures were required to melt it and our ancestors were not yet prepared to do so. Meteoric iron, which fell as a meteorite on the Earth's surface, has long been known in certain places such as Egypt and Mesopotamia about 4 thousand years ago to make small objects. However, the manufacture of iron objects required completely different knowledge and technology than bronze. But after a long process of trial and error our ancestors managed to master iron metallurgy as well.

The Iron Age began with the use of this metal. With iron they obtained much more resilient and powerful tools and weapons. New craftsmanship and new tools emerged: the tongs and the blacksmith's hammer. New iron technology demanded red-hot work, and it was a secret at first. The first to know this secret were the Hittites, inhabitants of the Anatolian Peninsula, in present-day Turkey, about 3.5 thousand years ago. They kept this secret very jealously for many years. After the fall of Hittite supremacy, the new iron technology began to spread elsewhere.

Iron had two advantages over bronze. The first was the abundance of this metal: almost all geographical areas have iron ore. On the other hand, bronze required the search, often in very distant places, for its two components: copper and tin. Secondly, iron weapons are more resistant, and although due to their flexibility they can be deformed, it is possible to repair them. In contrast, bronze weapons were brittle and often broke on impact. The iron would be used to manufacture all kinds of tools for the field and to improve the work and living conditions of the towns. However, during the Iron Age, certain bronze objects continued to be manufactured, such as bowls and cauldrons or all those of a religious or sumptuary nature.

The tools made of iron were very diverse: axes, knives, snouts, tweezers, hoes or weeds to dig and remove dirt, plows, chisels, hammers, limes, razors, wagon harnesses and horse bites, which is the part of the flange that is put to the horse in the mouth to control it. As we can see, these were tools for agricultural activity or daily life. In weaponry, swords, spearheads, daggers, combat shields, and helmets stand out. With the weapons of great resistance that were later manufactured during the metal age, mainly of iron, they were able to defend their lands. However, these weapons would also start wars.

With these new iron weapons came power with its respective military class to achieve whatever they wanted. A new kind of partnership with leaders and followers began. Leaders dominated community life with the help of followers, who were the workers who produced the basics to maintain society. The leaders began to accumulate fortune, with which they could pay for specialized craftsmanship so that they would work for the elite. Followers could also make wagons after the invention of the wheel in Sumer about 5.5 thousand years ago. The leaders offered food, social organization, and protection to followers. But this protection brought the danger of the warrior chief to the service of the leaders.

To combat the injustices of the wars created as a result of the invention of weapons of war during the metal age and to maintain social order, towns were forced to make their own laws. Definitely, life in society requires establishing rules so that men abide by them. In the beginning, before the invention of writing, the laws were based on usage and customs or traditional law that were transmitted orally. After writing, written law codes arose.

With an increasingly developed way of life, thanks to their intellect in developing agriculture and breeding, pottery and ceramic and metals, humans would route to the flourishing of civilization.

1.4 FLOURISHING OF CIVILIZATION

The changes that Homo Sapiens made in society were definitely significant. Among the most important changes were those of economic and social organization, which still have their impact on our modern life, such as the first forms of agriculture and domestication of animals and life in the first towns. With these changes appeared the modern humans and with them emerged a new social system based on new practices to achieve sustenance. The society of gatherers-hunters transformed its economy, now based on food production, with the introduction of agriculture and breeding. So Neolithic culture would give way to urban culture in order to lay the foundations of the first cities and with them the flourishing of civilizations.

During prehistory, several cultures emerged such as Natufians, Neolithic and urban culture. Culture changes as thought evolves. Thus, The Natufian culture, with agriculture and breeding, gave way to Neolithic and this in turn, with the advent of metals, evolved into urban culture, in which civilization would flourish in regions of the Middle East such as Mesopotamia and Egypt. Then with urban culture the stone age times of prehistory opened up to historical times and these in turn to our times.

It should be noted that urban culture was not an event that arose in one place, but that it occurred in different parts of the Middle East and then spread to the rest of the world. In addition, it took a long period of time for urban culture to fully develop, as its changes would take a long time to implement, perhaps several generations.

Urban culture included technological advances in metallurgy and their respective progress in agriculture and breeding. In addition, during the urban culture improvements in agricultural and livestock production intensified, as well as commercial exchanges, in addition to urban planning and the development of organized urban society.

During the Neolithic period, each family grew to have the food they needed to eat. But after this series of innovations and technological advances such as plowing and irrigation in urban culture, a higher crop yield was achieved, so each family would have a lot of food that it would not consume and that it could use to trade.

With the advent of metals there was a very important impact on the development of urban culture, as this would change the lifestyle that our ancestors had brought up to that time. With metals came metallurgy, with which other activities important for the development of towns such as mining and steelmaking emerged. High temperature furnaces were developed for iron smelting.

With metallurgy, many improvements were achieved in activities important to the towns' economy, mainly in agriculture. In this activity better harvests were achieved thanks to the manufacture of mainly iron metal tools such as plow, weeds, axes, snouts, and peaks. With the metal plow, the cultivation was achieved on a larger scale.

The technology to melt metals was a major advance of prehistoric societies. These deep advances were closely linked to urban culture. However, the new technology brought with it a new specialization of work and enhanced social hierarchy by giving rise to groups that would later hold power through the use of weapons developed with metals, thus accumulating great wealth. But, on the other hand, obtaining the raw material to make these weapons stimulated trade and cultural exchange between distant towns.

The metal tools improved the construction of irrigation channels, which made possible new crops such as the vineyard and the olive trees, with which the material was obtained to make luxury products such as wine and olive oil. These two products, in addition to being synonymous with economic well-being, were also the first secondary products of agriculture.

In livestock, secondary products arose according to the use of the animal. For the animals used as cargo transport, gadgets were developed to load the merchandise, such as the stretchers that were fixed to the animal and dragged carrying the load on them. Another gadget was the wheels to make the wagon. Derivative products such as butter, which was obtained from milk, arose from the animals used to obtain food. The wool was also used for the manufacture of textile products.

With urban culture came the flowering of civilization, which continued to expand as urban culture progressed to change the course of human history. Society had diversified to the point of including several more social strata, since now, in addition to gatherers, hunters, and fishermen, it also included farmers, shepherds, artisans, soldiers, and priests. All of them working together achieved great development for their society. Especially in agriculture, the most important activity since the economy of the first peoples was based on it.

With population growth, the work of stones and metals was perfected to make better tools and utensils. Farmers and shepherds were able to better study the behavior of plants and animals to improve practices for these activities. They also developed agricultural techniques to make agriculture easier and more efficient.

In lower Mesopotamia and then in Egypt emerged intensive cultivation, that is, the cultivation of the same species on a large scale, thanks to irrigation techniques, the use of better tools and specialized labor. This was how the towns became increasingly sophisticated and populated, until they finally became cities about 6,000 years ago.

Canals and dams were also built for excess water brought by rivers in spring to compensate with the little they brought during the rest of the year. As was the case with the Euphrates and Tigris rivers in Mesopotamia and the Nile in Egypt. Stored water was used to irrigate crops when the waters of these rivers were at a low level. This gave rise to irrigation agriculture, which made these regions the most prosperous of their time.

To build the dams, villages of people were built in lower Mesopotamia, as well as in Egypt. This resulted in constant production during the year with a larger surplus of production, which led to more diversification of work as more people could engage in producing or trading with other goods.

Trade and navigation had a very significant impact, due to the wheel and the construction of sailboats. But also, with the manufacture of more resilient and efficient weapons also emerged the soldier, armies, and wars.

During urban culture and thanks to the surplus production, people entered a more advanced way of life, and the first towns grew and developed to become complex urban societies in both political, as in economic and social aspects. In addition, with the increase of the growth and development of towns, wealth also increased.

Great works were built for the benefit of the towns, writing was invented, and trade was increased especially with distant towns. Art was also further developed, sciences specially emerged, and a highly organized society emerged.

Over time, some families would become richer than others thanks to trade among the inhabitants of the same town and with other towns further afar. At some point, one of these families took control of the town, becoming the highest authority and would rely on religion to justify their social standing and the accumulation of their wealth.

By increasing the growth and development of a town, it would become a kind of city or proto-city and become more important and powerful than the towns around it, producing a continuous flow of people from the towns towards the city, ensuring the growth of the population of the city or proto-city. This proto city was organized around authority and its headquarters, whether it was a palace or a main temple. Around that headquarters would be located the artisans and merchants. While on the outskirts and in the nearby towns would be farmers and ranchers.

To maintain and control the population, authority or monarch would have others working under their charge, thus leading to the emergence of public services. To keep the people who provided the public services, a tax system was established by which the inhabitants of the city or proto-city gave the authority a certain amount of their food or what they produced to be latter distributed it among its workers, also including the priests, as payment for the public services provided. Over time, proto cities developed so much that they became the first cities.

1.5   FIRST CITIES

The first cities were urban areas with a certain population density mainly dedicated to agriculture and breeding activities, with some urban planning, and some diversified economy and trade. In addition to having some centers of power and administration with political and religious participation.

These early cities originated in the Middle East south of Mesopotamia, in the Sumer region and then spread within the Middle East to the north of Mesopotamia to the Anatolian Peninsula and then south along the east side of the Mediterranean Sea by Syria, Phoenicia and Israel until reaching Egypt.

In its place of origin, in the Middle East, south of ancient Mesopotamia in the Sumer region, near the mouth of the Euphrates River in the Persian Gulf a short distance from today's Iraq, there were small villages more than 8,000 years ago formed by people who had arrived from neighboring regions, attracted by the region's great natural resources such as abundant water and food including, fishing and hunting. These people spoke the same language: the Sumerian. Of those small villages would later evolve, into something like about a millennium, the first cities such as Eridu, Ur and Uruk.

Being so close to the mouth of the Euphrates River in the Persian Gulf, Eridu and Ur had swampy or flooded areas, where canals were built to go from one side to the other. These floods made the land of this region very fertile and productive. At first wild fruits were very abundant, however, as the population of the city grew irrigation agriculture became necessary.

At first the people of *Eridu* lived in cane huts. But later, about 7.4 thousand years ago Eridu would become a city with several changes. The city had an area of about 25 acres with its architectural structures made of adobe bricks, which included in addition to adobe dwellings, a complex of sacred buildings such as the E-Abzu temple in honor of the god Enki, the god of water and wisdom. This temple was a truncated pyramid-shaped structure called ziggurat. Also, in the complex of sacred buildings was another building like the hall of offerings.

Eridu is believed to have been the city of the famous universal deluge of the Bible. But that big flood was just a local thing in South Sumer. It is also believed that it was over there, where the story of the construction of the famous ark to save life on Earth from the supposed universal flood arose. Given its close relationship with Sumerian mythology and magic, Eridu emerged as a center of religious power.

However, the city of Eridu declined some 4,000 years ago and was later rebuilt by the Babylonian empire, but only to use its temples given its religious history. However, as Eridu decayed, the city of Ur shone. *Ur* was another of those small villages, whose formation is contemporary with Eridu in the south of the Sumer region. Both were very close to only about 7 miles away.

Ur became a city about 6 thousand years ago and had achieved great development, because in addition to agriculture and breeding, other important activities such as handicrafts and trade emerged. Among the artisans were potters, carpenters, etc. The merchant community generated great commercial activity in and out of the city until it developed trade by sea to regions such as Iran and Afghanistan.

Ur was an important port in the Persian Gulf, where many of the raw materials that Ur lacked but needed for its continued development arrived from various parts of the world. From Iran they brought carnelian, a semi-precious stone to make ornaments, and from Afghanistan they brought lapis lazuli, and it is believed that they also brought tin to mix it with copper to form bronze. In addition, they brought wood from the Amanus Mountains in southern Turkey. This wood was transported along the Euphrates river to Ur.

In Ur also developed the cooked clay brick with which they built their houses of several rooms around a central courtyard. These houses were very close to each other with very narrow streets and alleys. The city was also walled.

Ur had three dynasties of rulers who extended their power to the Sumer region. The first king of Ur was Mesanepada about 4.7 thousand years ago. Then during the third dynasty came King Ur-Nammu, who started his rule about 4 thousand years ago and his dynasty lasted a long time. During his reign, Ur became very prosperous and the sacred area or the temenos of the city was built. This area was walled and included the Ziggurat, the temple of Giparu and the royal cemetery.

The Ziggurat was made of bricks and had three floors connected by exterior stairs and had a total height of 69 feet. At the top of the ziggurat was a sanctuary for sacred rituals, which resembled the ziggurat with a sacred mountain. The people of Ur worshipped Nannar, the god of the moon.

The Giparu was a temple made of mud bricks in honor of the goddess Ningal, the wife of the god Nannar and was located immediately southwest of the ziggurat. These two buildings were separated by a paved street.

The royal cemetery of Ur had about 2 thousand graves where they buried ordinary people, as well as royalty. The royals were buried with their precious objects of gold and silver, as well as other valuable things, of which some of great importance were found during the excavations made by archaeologists of our era, mainly the British archaeologist Leonard Woolley.

Among the important things found in tombs of royalty were the banner of Ur, the cylindrical seals of some kings, lire or harps and jewelry objects, figurines of deities and artistic vessels of pottery or stone in one piece. All these objects date back about 4,500 years.

The banner of Ur is a work of art in the form of a trapezoidal box made of wood with its front faces showing in horizontal stripes people, animals, and objects. On one of the front faces there were scenes of peace, so it is called the face of peace. While on the other front face there were scenes of war, and it is called the face of war. The cylindrical seals were instruments that had been invented in the city of Uruk and were brought to Ur. These cylindrical seals were carved in stone or other materials and were rolled to make prints on some clay tablets that could be used as a delivery note for commercial products. The harps would be the oldest string musical instruments. From these instruments it can be inferred that the people of Ur were already making music at the time. The so-called death pit in which human sacrifice was practiced was also found during excavations.

Later, after writing was invented in Uruk, King Ur-Nammu made his code of laws called the Code of Ur-Nammu, considered the oldest in the world, some 300 years before the code of King Hammurabi of Babylon. Ur-Nammu was succeeded by his son Shulgi, who turned out better than his father by consolidating the city and reforming his power in the region. Shulgi also ruled for a long time.

Ur had a stratified social system formed by the king; the highest political, military, religious and justice administrator authority; nobles and priests; senior officials with economic, social power and could even have land; traders and officials; a group of privileged people who could also have land and included the scribes; and finally the slaves who were usually the prisoners of war. Ur came to have about 65 thousand inhabitants in the Middle Bronze Age.

The city of Ur was later invaded by Elam, a region east of Sumer, which would later become the ancient Persian. During that invasion, the Elamites burned the city of Ur about 4 thousand years ago. However, it was resurrected because of the importance that Ur had as a religious center of the region, but later lost its importance. Although it lived a last great moment with the reconstruction of the city and its temples by the Chaldean kings of Babylon, until it disappeared some 400 years ago, perhaps by a change in the riverbed of the Euphrates river. Today only ruins remained of Ur, the city that became very important in Sumerian civilization. The Chaldeans were people from lower Mesopotamia, in the Summer region near the Persian Gulf.

Uruk was the other important city of Sumer about 50 miles north of Ur. Uruk emerged about 6.5 thousand years ago on the eastern bank of the Euphrates River in southern Mesopotamia. Uruk stood out for its great development to become the most important human society in the world by the time. It was the first city of great importance and well above the previous cities given its population, structure, and the great development of its urbanism.

With Uruk the concept of what we today call city was created, with all its characteristics: stable economy, culture, religion, writing, literature, social hierarchies, specialized occupations, political structures, and large architecture.

Uruk began its great economic development as a result of the great boom of its agriculture and breeding, and the great management of its surplus. At first, they produced only limited quantities of wheat, barley and peas, in addition to raising sheep and goats. To produce enough food steadily they spread to more fertile lands in the direction of the Tigris Valley. In addition to agricultural and breeding products, they also had many fish and birds from rivers and marshes. By this time, they had invented beer, which even had its own goddess named Ninkasi.

The origin of beer, like many other inventions, may have been by chance when some grains of barley to make the bread, were spontaneously fermenting, then when combined with water and with some natural yeasts resulted in an alcoholic beverage: the first craft beer. Everything seems to indicate that beer was invented more than 6 thousand years ago in Sumer and then spread throughout the rest of Mesopotamia until it reached Egypt where it developed even more and began to be marketed.

In Uruk, over time and to take advantage of river flood water, canal irrigation systems and dams were developed, which would increase agricultural production as the population grew. Animal husbandry had also thrived. And with the development of the city, its people began to change the way they dressed in clothes woven with wool or linen. With a larger surplus they could feed a larger population so that many others would engage in activities other than agriculture and breeding. As a result, the specialization of handicrafts such as pottery and ceramic, as well as trade, was substantially increased.

In Uruk the first architectural structures were built. The wheel was also invented about 5.5 thousand years ago, which was the driving engine of transport and was also the great impetus for the larger-scale development of the pottery with the invention of the potter's lathe. In addition, traders in this region invented a cylindrical seal, with which they marked clay containers with some hallmark of their owner or their contents. This invention of the cylindrical seal would later lead to the invention of writing about 5.3 thousand years ago. Thanks to writing today we can learn not only about Uruk, but of our entire history.

The writing emerged as a way to track trade transactions of growing commerce in the city. And to manage the growing economy came a kind of administration, which handled the already invented accounting. The details of how the writing arose will be seen later in subchapter 1.4 on "Evolution of Writing". The writing then expanded throughout Sumer, the rest of Mesopotamia and the rest of the Fertile Crescent for about two thousand years, with its variations of course.

According to the list of kings, an ancient stone tablet engraved in Sumer, Uruk was founded by King Enmerkar. It was also ruled by Eanna and then by the most famous of all: Gilgamesh, who was born about 4,700 years ago. The temples of Uruk played a social role in helping to keep people together.

The people of Uruk built temples with bricks and adorned them with colorful mosaics. One of these temples went to the god of heaven named Anu and the other for his daughter Inanna, who was later called Ishtar, the goddess of love and war. Who later became the patron saint of Uruk. The great city of Uruk was built around its sacred, political, and administrative sites such as temples and public buildings. These places represented the ruling class, around which the working class such as farmers, ranchers, craftsmen, and merchants rose.

In the rest of the city houses were built with courtyards for the inhabitants of Uruk. All over the city there were canals for agriculture and commerce that flowed throughout the city, which made Uruk look like today's Venice.

The city of Uruk developed a complex social structure with the ruling class led by a king and below the nobles and priests followed; then and below these were the scribes and public officials. In the stratum or class below appeared farmers, craftsmen and soldiers, and then there was the class of slaves, to which in addition to the people captured as prisoners of war, were joined by criminals or people who had large debts.

The ruling class exercised all authority and ruled Uruk and his resources by an authoritarian way, forcing work and tribute. This allowed the ruling king to complete large-scale projects such as large-scale irrigation agriculture. Uruk also came to have a very well-trained army.

About 5 thousand years ago Uruk came to have an area of about 600 hectares and a population of about 70,000 inhabitants. It was also surrounded by a brick wall about 15 meters high and about 9 kilometers long. This wall was built by King Gilgamesh. Uruk was the largest and most developed city not only of Mesopotamia but of the world for its time.

Uruk's development also included science, which in addition to agriculture and breeding, also encompassed mathematics, engineering, astronomy and literature, among others. Literature arose with the poem of Gilgamesh, one of humanity's earlier literary works. Gilgamesh was the great mythical hero born in Uruk.

Uruk was a city with a central and independent power, becoming one of the first city-States about 4.9 thousand years ago. It was a city with centralized institutions that controlled every aspect of social, economic, and political life. The impressive development of Uruk spread throughout Mesopotamia.

Uruk marked the beginning of the Sumerian civilization, the first in the world and had great influence throughout the Sumer region and the rest of Mesopotamia due to all its development in terms of its great city and progress. This also marked a reference, which is referred to as the culture or the Uruk period. However, some 4,000 years ago, Uruk began to struggle due to armed fights with the Elamites. But it continued to be inhabited until about 2,300 years ago.

After Uruk, Ur and *Eridu* also became city-States achieving more development and progress thanks to the rise of agriculture. Meanwhile the other towns that had sprung up also evolved in major cities such as Nippur, Lagash, Larsa and Umma to the west, and Kish and Isin north of Uruk.

The settlement of *Nippur* was established about 7,000 years ago on the east bank of the Euphrates River, about 93 miles southeast of Baghdad. Later as a city, Nippur was also among the oldest in Sumer, Mesopotamia. Nippur for thousands of years was the religious center of Mesopotamia with its various temples and public buildings. It was a highly literate city with a lot of work for the scribes, who managed to leave thousands of documents written in cuneiform on clay tablets including older versions of literary works such as the History of Creation and the Gilgamesh Epic, as well as administrative, legal, medical, commercial and school text documents.

Nippur had a very fine art made with metals and precious stones, woods, and exotic shells, as well as a highly developed trade with Egypt, Iran, and India. In addition, Nippur had several temples such as Ekur in honor of the god Enlil, the chief god of the Mesopotamian pantheon.

The city came to have an area of 135 hectares with a population of 40 thousand and was also walled. Nippur was considered a sacred city, which allowed it to survive several wars. The city received large donations from the region's rulers, who, according to Sumerian mythology, needed the support of the god Enlil of Nippur to achieve and maintain their reigns.

The city during its long period of existence became of much influence on the religious, intellectual, and political power of the region. It also became a center of convergence of other cultures of the region such as Sumerian, Akkadian and Babylonian. All this was because it had a very important geographical location among the other cities of Mesopotamia.

However, some 4,100 years ago, King Ur-Nammu of Ur rebuilt the shrine of Enlil of Nippur and then Hammurabi became king of Babylon about 3,700 years ago and Babylon became the new religious center of Mesopotamia and replaced the importance of Nippur, and it ended up being abandoned some 2,800 years ago.

Lagash was a city east of Uruk, near the mouth of the Euphrates and the Tigris in the Persian Gulf. At first Lagash was a town located southeast of another town called Girsu, but then these two towns became one under the name of Lagash, whose foundation dates back about 7,000 years. However, it achieved its great development between about 4,500 and 4,300 years ago during the Ur-Nanshe and Urukagina dynasties.

Among Lagash's most important works of art are the vultures' wake and the silver vase of King Entemena, successor to Eannatum. The vultures' wake was a carved limestone showing some vultures and various battles and religious scenes. This monument was erected to commemorate the victory of King Eannatum, grandson of King Ur-Nanshe, over the neighboring city of Umma in one of the world's first wars.

Lagash subsequently lost its independence to the Akkadians and eventually came under the control of Sargon I about 2,300 years ago. However, after more than a century, Lagash achieved another great moment with Gudea's government, about 2,200 years ago. This governor in turn subjected to the warrior town of Guti, who controlled part of Babylon from about 4,200 years ago. During Gudea's rule the temple was built in Eninnu dedicated to the god Ningirsu, son of the supreme god Enlil.

Larsa was a town in Sumer on the banks of the Euphrates River that existed about 5,000 years ago about 15 miles southeast of Uruk. At first, about 4,000 years ago, Larsa depended on Ur. However, it managed to become independent from Ur and form his own dynasty with the Amorite king Naplanum before the destruction of Ur at the hands of the Elamites. With King Naplanum, Larsa achieved its heyday making a lot of progress. Larsa was constituted as a city-State and was situated between two enemies: Isin and Elam.

A century later, Larsa gained great political ascent thanks to the dynasty of King Gungunum, which extended his control to the cities of Isin, Ur, Uruk, Eridu and Lagash, as well as extended his control to the capital of Elam. King Gungunum proclaimed himself king of Sumer and Akkad, the southern part of Mesopotamia and then conquered Nippur and Kish by converting a hegemonic kingdom into the area.

Some 3,800 years ago, a king believed to be an Amorite named Kudur-Mabuk took the power of Larsa and put his son Warad-sin on the throne. With him, Larsa managed to snatch Isin's control of Nippur until Nippur became independent in a short time. The Amorites were bellicose people who occupied Syria, Canaan, and the region west of the Euphrates River.

King Warad-sin was succeeded by Rim-Sin. During his reign, Larsa achieved its best moment. Rim-Sin was the last great king of Larsa, who managed to control Uruk and Isin and with it had control of the Sumer region. During this period, large temple construction projects and irrigation canals for agriculture were developed. Art and literature also flourished. Rim-Sin was the most powerful king until his fall at the hands of King Hammurabi some 3,700 years ago.

Kish was a city located between the Tigris and Euphrates rivers, at a very close point to these two rivers, 8 miles east of Babylon in present-day Iraq. Kish was founded about 5,200 years ago but was devastated by the great flood of about 4,900 years ago. However, it recovered and became a prominent city by having the advantage over the flow of the Tigris and Euphrates river irrigation systems, better than the other cities located downstream.

The list of kings of Kish covered a few, such as Jushur, who would be the first, followed by Kullassina-bel, then Etana, etc., but the only king who has been verified by archaeology was Enmebaragesi, the twenty-first king on the list. About 4,300 years ago, Sargon of Akkad proclaimed himself king of Kish.

Umma was another Sumerian city northeast of Uruk that emerged about 4,400 years ago. It was well known for its long border conflict with Lagash. However, as it faced off on this occasion, the triumph would be for Umma under the reign of King Lugalzagesi. With this King Umma reached its strongest time, about 4,300 years ago, after conquered the cities of Lagash and Kish and then took control of Ur and Uruk.

With his conquests Lugalzagesi unified the Sumer region and then extended his dominance to the shores of the Mediterranean. His 25-year reign ended when his fell to Sargon of Akkad some 4,300 years ago, and Umma became part of the Akkadian kingdom. Umma's patron was Shara, a minor god of war, who is believed to be Inanna's son.

Isin was a small town that grew into a city about 4,500 years ago. It was located 20 miles from Nippur. Its first ruler was Ishbi-Erra about 4 thousand years ago. Isin managed to repel the Elamites and thus gained control of Ur and Uruk, as well as the spiritual center of Nippur.

Isin flourished for more than a century. It became a city-State with its temples, public buildings and its code of law published by the fifth king of Isin Lipit-Ishtar during his reign from 3,900 to 2,000 years ago; a century before the Hammurabi code in Babylon. Isin managed to make large incomes due to lucrative trade routes to the Persian Gulf.

The city of Isin was very powerful, like Larsa, which competed with many other city-States by that time. However, about 3,700 thousand years ago, Isin ended up in Larsa's hands first and then in the hands of Babylon. With the fall of Isin, Sumer's power ended, which passed on to his Successors the Amorites. These who had been settling in the region for centuries assimilated Sumerian culture and then founded their own cities like Babylon, Ebla and Hamath.

The cities of Nippur, Lagash, Larsa, Umma, Kish and Isin also became city-States to form the Sumerian civilization, the first Mesopotamia civilization and that of the whole world. However, all Sumer city-States tried to compete for the power of the region. Meanwhile, other cities further north of Mesopotamia would emerge and also become very important. Among these cities we have Babylon, Sippar, and Akkad.

Babylon was a city in the north-central Mesopotamia that was founded some 4,300 years ago by people who spoke a language other than the Sumerian: the Akkadian. Babylon was located on the banks of the Euphrates River in today's Iraq, about 59 miles from Baghdad. Shortly after its founding, the reign of Sargon of Akkad, also known as Sargon the Great, began. However, Babylon became a military power under the dynasty of the Amorite king Hammurabi some 3,700 years ago. Babylon at the end of the Bronze Age had a population of about 55,000 people.

Hammurabi then conquered the city-States of Sumer including Isin, Larsa, Ur, Uruk, Nippur, Lagash, Eridu, Kish, among others, and formed a unified regime with the south and center of Mesopotamia, calling this entire region: Babylon. That is how he created the Babylonian empire. He also conquered Elam to the east and Mari and Elba to the northeast. Hammurabi gave Babylon its great power and influence. He built the city walls and created one of the most complete written law codes in the world known as the famous Hammurabi Code.

This code is considered to be one of the first attempts at legislation of humanity that was written on a stone or basalt wake about 7.38 feet high, some 3,700 thousand years ago. At the top of the wake appears King Hammurabi receiving the laws from the god Marduk and below this scene appear the laws. The code consisted of 282 laws on punishment of citizens according to their social status for crimes committed. The code is considered to be based on the Talion Law, as the punishment imposed is proportional to the crime committed as a principle of justice, which the Bible states as "eye for eye, tooth for tooth".

Hammurabi turned Babylon into the new religious center, replacing Nippur and Eridu. But, after the death of its great king, Babylon collapsed and became a small kingdom until it was looted some 3,500 years ago by the Hittites from the Anatolian region of Turkey today.

After the Hittites, the Casitas followed, people that it is believed to have come from southwestern Iran. Later, the Assyrians followed to the Casitas and dominated the region with the Assyrian king Sennacherib about 2,700 thousand years ago. However, Babylon revealed, and Sennacherib had the city plundered and dragged into the ruins. Shortly after this, Sennacherib was killed by his sons. However, Sennacherib's successor, the ruler Esarhaddon some 2,600 years ago, began the reconstruction of Babylon, bringing it to its glorious level before. But a few years later, Assurbanipal of Nineveh took the city, although it rose against it without success.

After the fall of the Assyrian empire, Babylon was ruled by a Chaldean named Nabopolassar, who created the Neo-Babylon empire. With the son of Nabopolassar, King Nebuchadnezzar II, Babylon began a period of flourishing becoming a very powerful state after defeating the Assyrians in Nineveh about 2,100 years ago. During the Neo-Babylon

Empire many luxurious buildings were built and works of art from the ancient empire were restored.

The most famous work of art of this period was the Ishtar Gate, which was the main entrance to the city center. The portal was decorated with bright blue enameled bricks and adorned with images of bulls, dragons, and lions. The gate of Ishtar gave way to the city's great processional thorough range, a half-mile decorated corridor used in rituals to celebrate the Babylonian New Year. The new year began with the spring equinox and marked the beginning of agricultural activity.

Also, in this period, the city walls were further fortified with three rings of additional walls of 40 feet high. Nebuchadnezzar II also built a series of shrines being the largest being the Esagila, a ziggurat dedicated to the god Marduk. It is believed that this ziggurat may have been the so-called Tower of Babel of the Bible.

It would also be this famous king who built the famous Hanging Gardens of Babylon as a gift to his wife Amytis to compensate for her nostalgia about the large vegetation and mountains with waterfalls of her native region, although no evidence of its existence in Babylon has yet been found. These gardens reportedly had lush vegetation with waterfalls on the terraces of the 75-foot-tall garden. They had exotic plants, herbs, and flowers with stunning fragrances. This wonder of the hanging gardens must have counted with a great work of irrigation engineering to bring the water from the river to the upper terraces.

It may also have been during the reign of Nebuchadnezzar II that the thousands of Jews were taken from the kingdom of Judah in the city of Jerusalem, according to the Bible, and that they had been held captive for almost a century in Babylon, until much later they returned to their homeland.

After the death of Nebuchadnezzar II, Babylon continued with its normal pace of important city. However, in less than a century, about 2,500 years ago, the Neo-Babylon Empire fell into the hands of the Persian king Cyrus the Great. Babylon passed to the control of the Persians. Under the rule of the Persian, Babylon flourished as a center of art and education. Mathematics, cosmology, and astronomy achieved great developments.

However, a couple of centuries later, the Persian empire fell to Alexander the Great, some 2,300 years ago and after his death, Babylon was decaying into ruins and all its glory was buried by time under the sands of the region.

The other cities that also existed in northern Babylon were Akkad, Sippar, and Mari. Akkad was a city located on the bank of the Euphrates River. The Akkadians were a nomadic village of Semitic origin of the Arabian Peninsula, from the region closest to the Mediterranean Sea that reached the Fertile Crescent attracted by its prosperity. They settled in northern Mesopotamia by the city of Kish. Over time they came to form an important city with Kish included.

According to legend *Akkad* was founded by King Sargon the Great, who ruled for more than half a century, about 4.3 thousand years ago. The city of Akkad was the seat of the Akkadian Empire, the first in the world, which ruled the entire region of ancient Mesopotamia. However, before Sargon, King Lugalzagesi of Uruk had managed to unify the Sumer region under his rule. But he was defeated by Sargon, who imposed his dominance on a larger scale and improved Uruk's model. Sargon conquered the entire south of Mesopotamia, part of Syria, Anatolia and Elam, which would later become western Iran. He also established the first dynasty or succession of Semitic kings. Sargon was considered the founder of the military tradition of Mesopotamia.

The city of *Sippar* was located southwest of Baghdad today. Sippar was part of the first Babylonian dynasty, but then about 3,200 years ago it was looted by Elamite King Kutir-Nahhunte. It was then recovered but was later taken by King Tiglath-Pileser I of Assyria. However, about 2,800 years ago King Nabu-apla-iddina of the eighth Babylonian dynasty rebuilt the great temple of Shamash.

Mari was a city located near the banks of the Euphrates River north of Mesopotamia near today's Syria. It emerged during the Bronze Age. where copper and bronze were worked until it became a large commercial center between Babylon south of Mesopotamia and the resource-rich Taurus Mountains of today's Turkey. Mari remained the important center of northern Mesopotamia for about 1,200 years until King Hammurabi arrived from Babylon and destroyed the city about 3,700 years ago.

Other cities that developed in northern Mesopotamia in the Assyria region were Ashur, Nineveh and Dur-Sharrukin. The city of *Ashur* was located on the bank of the Tigris River. At first it was part of Babylon and then it was the first capital of Assyria until about 2,900 years ago. But later Assyria with its capital Assur was taken and destroyed by the Medes, who were from present-day Iran about 2,600 years ago.

The Medes also took *Nineveh,* which was the oldest and most populous city in the Assyrian empire. Nineveh reached about 100,000 inhabitants in the Iron Age, about 2,700 years ago. It was located on the banks of the Tigris River where important trade routes of the north-south and east-west of the region were intercepted.

Dur-Sharrukin was a city located northeast of Nineveh. Built by King Sargon II of Assyria, about 2.7 thousand years ago. It was a walled city with 7 fortified gates. It also had the temple of the god Nabu, the royal palace and very good houses for important officers. Dur-Sharrukin came to an end with the battle of Sargon II.

The first cities originated in southern Mesopotamia, in the Sumer region and then spread north of Mesopotamia. Cities also appeared in Egypt, at the other end of the Fertile Crescent.

In Egypt we found that its first inhabitants came from the Sahara desert and settled on the banks of the Nile River. These first inhabitants were organized into a type of province called nomos, which came to form two kingdoms each ruled by a pharaoh. These two kingdoms were: Upper Egypt in the south and Lower Egypt in the north. Upper Egypt consisted of 22 provinces, with the important Hieracómpolis, Abydos and El Kab. His pharaoh wore a white crown; while Lower Egypt consisted of 20 provinces, of which the most important were Buto, Sais, Memphis, Merimde. His pharaoh wore a red crown.

However, some 5,100 years ago, Pharaoh Menes of upper Egypt invaded lower Egypt and unified the two kingdoms and since then the Pharaoh wore a white and red crown, Menes became the first pharaoh of the first dynasty of the thirty to rule Egypt until the Persians conquered Egypt.

Later the first cities continued to spread until leaving the Middle East and reached India and China. While in the north of the Mediterranean the first cities went out to the Aegean and the Balkans until they reached Europe. And then for the rest of the world to form the first civilizations.

2

FIRST CIVILIZATIONS

In this chapter we will be talking about the first civilizations including that of Mesopotamia, Egypt, India, China. As well as those of the western cultures and civilizations such as the Phoenician culture, the Greek civilization, the Hebrew culture, the Roman empire, and the American cultures such as Mayan, Aztec, and Inca.

The first civilizations were those of Mesopotamia and Egypt in the Fertile Crescent of the Middle East. Mesopotamian civilization included the Sumerian civilization, Acadian, Babylonian, and Assyrian. Then emerged the civilizations of India, China and later, the other cultures and civilizations around and beyond the Mediterranean Sea.

Civilization originated in Summer, Mesopotamia, a region with abundant water, but had no wood or stone to build buildings, nor metals to make tools and weapons. However, the Sumerians to achieve their great development used the only thing they had available: water and mud. With their only raw material they made clay, with which they made their bricks to begin the construction of their great architecture. Later, they obtained other raw materials such as wood and metals when they developed the ability to bring them from other places. From Sumer, the civilization spread throughout to the rest of Mesopotamia and the world.

2.1 MESOPOTAMIAN CIVILIZATION

Mesopotamia, the southwestern region of the Asian continent, in the Fertile Crescent, between the Tigris and Euphrates rivers; it was made up of two large regions: to the north, in the mountainous part, was Assyria and Accad; while, to the south, in the marshy part, at the mouth of the Tigris and Euphrates rivers, was Sumer.

Mesopotamia came to have the climate and resources to host the beginnings of our civilization through its people, which had been established in this region for about 16 thousand years, living from the harvesting of wild fruits, hunting and fishing, and forming small settlements with circular huts. Some 6 thousand years later, these people formed agricultural communities and lived on agriculture and animal husbandry. These agrarian communities began scattering in northern Mesopotamia and extending south to the Sumer region where they achieved great development into the first cities.

Summer was a region with abundant water and wild fruits and animals, but lacked wood and stone to build buildings, or metals to make tools and weapons. However, the Sumerians managed very well to have a great development using clay as their great raw material, with which they manufactured their adobe bricks to begin the construction of their great architecture. On other raw materials such as wood, metals, and precious stones; developed the ability to bring them from other places. Mesopotamia was the first civilization to develop, according to archaeological finds found so far. The origin of this civilization dates back almost 6 thousand years. Starting in southern Mesopotamia, specifically in the Sumer region, where an urban system was developed, that gave rise to several technical advances. This great development initiated the Sumerian civilization, the first in the world, which spread throughout the rest of Mesopotamia: Babylon, Accad and Assyria.

On Mesopotamian civilization we will be covering in detail, its society and development, its religion, the sciences, its art, and its empires.

Society and its Development

In Mesopotamia came the first inventions that would change our lives forever. Among these inventions we have: the adobe brick and the architectural arch to build the first houses in the first cities. In addition, the wheel, sailboats, maps, writing, written laws, sciences, the sexagesimal system and even the concept of time were invented. Mesopotamia began the development of civilization in the Middle East, which then spread to the rest of the world.

The first Sumerian cities, such as Eridu, Ur, Uruk and Nippur date back about 7,000 years. Later the cities of Lagash and Kish emerged. All of them became city-States and spoke the Sumerian language.

Uruk was the most important city due to its great development. This city was already about 5.2 thousand years ago, an important urban center. Its growth was the result of the merger of settlements to create the city. About 5,000 years ago, Uruk was a mega-city, with an area of about 225 hectares and about 50 thousand inhabitants. Uruk had great walls to protect the city. In addition, it had its ziggurats, structures in the form of a truncated pyramid at the top of which were platforms where temples and centers of worship operated. The city had several rulers, but the most famous was Gilgamesh. The development of Uruk was then spread throughout the rest of the cities that made up the territory of Mesopotamia.

Mesopotamian civilization made great progress in economic, political, and social. Economically, they made great strides in agriculture, the basis of their economy. Cereals such as wheat and barley were grown, as well as grapes and palm trees. Ox-pulled ploughing and sickle were used to mow. The Sumerians managed to have a good control of the water of the rivers, to the point of being able to build levees to contain floods and irrigation channels for irrigated agriculture to obtain large crops. The other part of its economy was the rearing of animals, mainly sheep for the food and clothing of the population, oxen for the work of agriculture and donkeys for the transport of agricultural products mainly.

Politically and socially, they were the first to create organized, independent cities called city-States governed by a governor called *Patesi*. He was regarded as a representative of God, who was responsible for regulating the activities necessary for the proper functioning of the city such as the distribution of water, the maintenance of the canals, the defense of the city, and the administration of justice.

Eventually, the Patesi took the title of king and formed the upper part of the social classes. He was then followed by the priests, who controlled the economic power of temples and great landowners. Then there was the part of the town, made up of small landowners and tenants, who were free men that with their taxes had to maintain the administration and the temple. Finally, on the social scale were slaves, whose condition they had gone through debts or being prisoners of war.

The city-States had their own laws. The rules by which they were governed were engraved in stones or steles that were placed at the entrance of the city. Some of them have come to our days, such as the stele of the Hammurabi Code about 3.7 thousand years ago. In this stele appears the god Shamash handing over the laws to King Hammurabi.

Religion

As for the religion of Mesopotamian civilization, this was polytheistic as its people believed and worshipped several gods representing the forces of nature such as the Sun, Moon, and stars. To worship their gods at first, they built the ziggurats in the south specifically in Sumer, important brick architectural structures. The ziggurats were temples built in honor of the gods and their top was used as an altar for worship and offering to the gods. Due to their height and open ceilings, these temples also served as the first astronomical observatories. The temples housed religious power and around them, the institutions of political and administrative power were grouped.

Among the most important gods were: Anu god of heaven; Enlil, god of storms and winds; Enki god of rivers; Sin the moon god; Ishtar goddess of war and love; Shamash god of sun and justice. In addition, there were the protective gods and almost every city had one. Marduk was the protector of Babylon, just as the god Assur was the protector of the capital of Assyria. The Mesopotamian gods were conceived in the image and likeness of human beings.

Science

In Mesopotamia science and art were developed. Science included mathematics, astronomy, medicine, engineering, etc. On mathematics, the Babylonians exceled in geometry and algebra. About 4.5 thousand years ago the sexagesimal system had already developed in Babylon, which is based on the number 60 and was used to measure time. Later, about 4.0 thousand years ago the decimal system came about based on 10, which was used in commerce and accounting. They also developed numbering systems with which they could add and subtract, but not multiply or divide. In order to perform these last two operations, they developed multiplication and division tables. Later, they also developed tables for taking square and cubic roots. They also knew how to work with fractions.

Babylonians also developed a system of measures of length, area, weight, and volume. The standard unit of smaller length was the *Digit*, equivalent to 1.65 centimeters. The area unit was the *Sar*, equivalent to 36 square meters. The weight measurement was *Gin*, equivalent to 8 grams. The volume measurement was the *Sila* equivalent 0.82 liters. They also had an agricultural measure called *Gur*, which was about 250 kilos of grains. This system of measures was key to the development achieved by Mesopotamians in trade with other regions. Although the currency did not yet exist as we know it today, but if they used metal bars with a mark indicating their weight, which was used as currency in trade. The concept of currency arose in Babylon.

As for astronomy, it emerged with a long series of observations of the skies from the top of the ziggurats. By then a simple form of the sundial had developed. The early astronomers were priests linked to political power. They studied the moon's trajectory in the sky and detailed its cyclical movement in order to predict *eclipses,* as they were intrigued by the disappearance of the moon during these events, as they feared that, in one of these eclipses, their civilization might also disappear along with the moon. Mesopotamians established that lunar eclipses were periodically approximately 18 years.

Also, in their observations, they detailed the trajectory that the Sun, the Moon and that of the planets, seen from Earth, were going through the firmament. In this way they invented the *Zodiac,* as an area of the firmament through which passes the ecliptic or the elliptical trajectory of the Sun around the Earth. The Zodiac is divided into 12 equal parts representing each one to a constellation identified with their respective signs: Aries, Taurus, Geminis, Cancer, Leo, Virgo, Libra, Scorpio, Sagittarius, Capricorn, Aquarius, and Pisces.

In addition, the Mesopotamians made important observations based on the movements of the Moon and the planets. From these observations they managed to relate the phases and cycles of the lunar calendar with the seasons of the year regulated by the course of the Sun. Thus, they managed to determine the *solar year* with a difference of only four minutes.

As for medicine, the Mesopotamians believed much in their gods to heal some of their diseases. However, they also used to consult a doctor for certain other conditions. This physician was able to observe the symptoms of these diseases, formulate a diagnosis and administer a therapeutic solution based on dissolved or crushed mineral substances. Mesopotamia was the cradle of early civilizations in developing the first surgical instruments.

In engineering, Mesopotamia also made great scopes in irrigation and agriculture, in the construction of canal systems, levees, gates and water storages. The preparation of the ground for the construction of these works required leveling instruments, measuring rods, drawing, and mapping.

Art

As for Mesopotamian art, it is represented by works such as cylindrical seals, steles, embossed sculptures, artistically decorated tombs, etc.; carried out in the different towns or regions of Mesopotamia. The art was made based on the natural resources available such as stones, shells, marble, alabaster, limestone, etc. The art of the Sumer region is very well represented by the *Banner of Ur,* which is a trapezoidal box with two panels: front and rear, three bands each. One of the panels represents war and the other represents peace. This work was made with shells, lapis lazuli and limestone for the purpose of representing the conquest of a civilization and the serenity of victory.

The most important work of Akkadian art is represented by the *Victory Stela of Naram-Sin* in Sippar, which was the first artistic work that represented a man as a synonym for a god. In this work made of sandstone, Naram-Sin is shown physically above all the figures on the stela, establishing himself as the most important person. He also wears a horn crown and stands under the stars that are close enough to the ruler to show how close he was to heaven. The work tries to show the divinity of Naram-Sin.

As for the most representative work of Babylonian art we have the Gate of *Ishtar.* This is without a doubt one of the most impressive and well-known works of Mesopotamian art. It is made of blue bricks and alternately decorated with images of dragons and wild cattle. It was commanded to be done by King Nebuchadnezzar II and was considered in its time to be one of the 7 Wonders of the World. This gate was dedicated to the Babylonian goddess Ishtar and played an important role in the religious festivities of Ancient Babylon.

The most important work of Hittite art is the *Stele of Hammurabi,* which represents the set of laws that the Hittite king Hammurabi of Babylon imposed and promulgated among the citizens of his kingdom. It is the first written code of law in history and a magnificent example of how society relied on art for organization, structure, and education. Hammurabi believed that he had been chosen by God to enforce his divine laws, to show this relationship with divinity, the Hittite king ordered the making of a sculpture that represented him by dialogue with the divine just above the list or code of laws he imposed.

Assyrian art is represented by the *Statue of Lamassu,* which is a combination of a bull's body with the wings of an eagle and a man's crowned head, representing the ultimate protection against evil. This statue was widely used as a permanent protector of many towns of the Fertile Crescent.

The Empires

At first, as some of our ancestors became more sedentary and settled somewhere by taking a batch of land to work it to produce their own food, some others who were still walking around as nomads, and when they reached that lot of land taken by other humans, the nomads tended to take the food and a few other things that they saw in that land. But those who had taken that land before felt it as their property and everything in it, for what they would defend it even with their lives. This originates ones of the first disputes and fights between humans.

As the towns developed and prospered, they were of great appeal to others who somehow tried to meet their basic needs for food and protection with as little effort as possible. This resulted in the towns preparing to defend themselves, thus the first soldiers emerging. Over time these towns prospered into cities and that, with the discovery of metals, especially iron, they managed to form the first civilizations. This resulted in the formation of the first armies armed with spears, axes, daggers, daggers, and swords, and also, protected with helmets and shields, starting wars to defend themselves.

Over time wars would become more frequent by bringing the culture of war to emerge, which would be used by some cities or territories to extend their territorial dominance to obtain irrigated or strategic spaces, or to obtain more food to sustain the growth of their population. Also, wars would be used to deal with the permanent coercion of some dominant groups, or to repel other towns prowling the boundaries of their river valleys with the intention of seizing their resources. All of this stimulated a major military culture, which brought forth the mandate and obedience to form leaders and followers.

The first major war originated in Mesopotamia between the Sumerian cities of Lagash and Umma 4.5 thousand years ago and lasted more than a century. This war has been depicted in the Stele of the Vultures of Lagash as a memorial to King Eannatum of Lagash.

Wars by a large military culture gave way to the beginning of empires as a form of political organization constituted by the power of a state that dominates other conquered states or territories. The power of the empire is exercised by a king, monarch, or emperor, who exercises all kinds of authority. The world's first empires emerged in Mesopotamia, including the Akkadian, Babylonian, and the Assyrian.

The first empire was the Akkadian between 4.3 and 4.2 thousand years ago. The Akkadians were nomads originating from the Arabian Peninsula and moved to Mesopotamia during the prosperity of this region. Its first monarch and the first in history was Sargon, who managed to conquer and unify southern Mesopotamia under his command. Sargon is believed to have arisen after being a servant of King Ur-Zababa of Kish and then revealed himself against him and took the throne. After seating over, he adopted the name Sargon. The succession of power by its descendants or Sargon dynasty of Accad had several rulers and was the first dynasty in history that dominated towns of different cultures. The fall of the Akkadian empire was precipitated about 4.2 thousand years ago with the invasions of a town called the Guti of the East Tigris River with people living in the Zagros Mountains.

The Babylonian empire dates from 3.8 to 2.5 thousand years ago. This empire was one of the most important in the world as Babylon, its capital, was a very sophisticated city with great developments in architectural works and sciences. The empire extended from Summer in the south to Assyria in the north. The influence of the towns of the empire led Babylon to become the most powerful cultural center of its time. However, despite this influence, Babylon retained its native language, the Akkadian, and wrote in cuneiform, the writing system of the Sumerians. Babylon also had a very advanced political organization. It was a monarchy controlled by a king, who was in charge of managing and leading the people. In addition, there were other groups of some power such as priests, the military, merchants, and owners of buildings, and finally there were slaves.

The Babylonian empire was divided into two parts: the first ancient or Paleo-Babylonian empire and the second or new empire also called Neo-Babylonian. The first empire was made up of the Amorites, who were from a Semitic town formed in turn by very aggressive nomadic tribes living in Syria and Canaan. The most famous king of the ancient empire was Hammurabi, who ruled for 42 years until 3.7 thousand years ago.

Hammurabi is well known for its famous code of laws. He also implemented highly efficient defense systems, justice administration, tax collection, trade control and agriculture. During the ancient empire, the arts and sciences flourished in Babylon. After Hammurabi's death, Babylon suffered several attacks until the city was finally looted 3.6

thousand years ago, when the Hittites, from Anatolia, invaded Babylon and looted it.

However, it was not the Hittites, but the Casitas coming from the east who took power. For the next 440 years the Casitas kings ruled Babylon until they were expelled about 3.1 thousand years ago.

Babylon was plunged into a time of turbulence and chaos until about 3,000 years ago. The Assyrians from the north ransacked Babylon and then took power, but the Assyrian empire was in full decline and then about 2.6 thousand years ago came a general named Nabopolassar, native of Chaldea, a region south of Babylon and reconquered and restored Babylon, thus beginning the greatest period in Babylon's history: the new empire.

The new or Neo-Babylon empire began about 3.9 thousand years ago and ended about 2.5 thousand years ago. During this period Babylon managed to conquer neighboring towns to establish their dominance and make important progress in the economy and architecture. Nabopolassar, who ruled some 20 years until 3.6 thousand years ago, turned Babylon into a powerful new empire. This great king defeated the Assyrians and took their lands. Later, his son Nebuchadnezzar, 2.6 thousand years ago, had defeated the Egyptian army at the Battle of Carquemish and was crowned king a little later. His reign lasted up to 2.5 thousand years ago. This was the king who brought the new Babylonian empire to the most outstanding point. Nebuchadnezzar continued his father's work and rebuilt Babylon with stronger walls, new palaces, and temples, as well as the beautiful hanging gardens of Babylon for his wife. Nebuchadnezzar widened the empire's borders by defeating Syria and Phoenicia on the shores of the Mediterranean. And then he went south to conquer the kingdoms of Israel and Judah, conquering Jerusalem in less than 2.5 thousand years ago. After this conquest, the king of Judah and thousands of

Jewish citizens were brought in chains to Babylon. Some 10 thousand years later, Jerusalem rebelled, the city was looted and again many of its citizens were deported to Babylon. After Nebuchadnezzar, the glorious history of Babylon was declining. His last king was Nabonido, an elderly and mysterious character who ruled for about 17 years to 2.5 years ago. This empire came to an end when they fell to the Persians.

Another major empire that emerged in Mesopotamia was the Assyrian Empire about 4.0 thousand years ago. The Assyrians were rather violent and bellicose Semitic nomads, who had settled in several towns on the banks of the Tigris River in Mesopotamia where they founded the city of Assur in honor of their god and made it their capital. Assur was the name of the god of life and represented the creation of everything. Over time the Assyrians expanded through Mesopotamia to become an empire and later compete with the Babylonian empire. The Assyrian empire was the most violent in human history for its brutal and devastating campaigns. Its form of government was autonomous dominant and theocratic. All power was exercised by a king, who influenced the whole religion. The empire was divided into provinces ruled by prefects. The Assyrians lived off the collection of tributes of all the provinces, as well as the agricultural and commercial activity, the latter had a chamber of commerce that granted loans, regulated interest, and solved financial problems.

This empire was characterized by a culture of violent and cruel wars and became a powerhouse in the region. However, during the reign of Sennacherib, the son of Sargon II, moved the capital to Nineveh making it a great city. Later Esarhaddon the son of Sennacherib managed to advance with his armies to Memphis the capital of Egypt by then and conquer it.

Then the descendant of Esarhaddon, Ashurbanipal continued to advance to Thebes, Egypt and towards the other end to Susa, Elam. With this outpost the Assyrian empire managed to spread further. Ashurbanipal is credited with building the large library in his Nineveh palace. After Assurbanipal's death began the fall of the empire, which came to an end 2.6 thousand years ago after having dominated for more than a millennium.

Mesopotamian civilization began the development of civilization in the Middle East and then spread through Egypt and the rest of the world.

2. 2 EGYPTIAN CIVILIZATION

Egypt, the country located in northeast Africa and surrounded by Libya, Sudan, the Red Sea and the Mediterranean Sea; it was the cradle of another of the first civilizations that developed around the Nile River, which is the longest river in the world with more than 6,500 kilometers of travel from its birth on Lake Victoria in the heart of Africa to the north of the continent where it takes its waters to end up pouring them into the Mediterranean Sea.

The Nile has floods of water in the summer months because of the rainy rhythm typical of a tropical climate. With the rains, its shores were flooded, and a silt was deposited that made the lands around the river very fertile. Precisely, it was the fertility of the river that made it possible for the people who inhabited these lands to survive from the harvesting of wild fruits, in addition to hunting and fishing. Egypt has always been fertile thanks to its river, even during the glacial period it still had a very rich flora and fauna. Much of Egypt's first settlers arrived from the Sahara desert as desertification increased.

Egypt was divided into two distinct regions, albeit linked by the river. These two regions were: Upper Egypt and Lower Egypt. Upper Egypt was located in the south, in the desert-dominated valley, whose only cultivable strip was the lands that were exposed when the waters of the river retreated. Upper Egypt consisted of 22 provinces, the important ones being Hieracómpolis, Abydos and El Kab. Its pharaoh wore a white crown. While Lower Egypt was in the north in the Nile Delta. Lower Egypt consisted of 20 provinces, of which the most important were Buto, Sais, Memphis, Merimde. Its pharaoh wore a red crown.

Egyptian civilization began some 5.2 thousand years ago, as the peoples settled on the banks of the Nile in both Upper and Lower Egypt. The unification of Upper and Lower Egypt by its first king, the legendary King Menes of Upper Egypt, laid the foundations for a powerful empire: Ancient Egypt, whose capital was established in the city of Memphis. After unification, the pharaohs of unified territory carried the two crowns combined into one: the white of Upper Egypt and the red of Lower Egypt as a symbol of the two regions of the empire.

The history of the political organization of Ancient Egypt began with the unification of the country about 5 thousand years ago. Menes started an empire ruled from the city of Memphis. The unified territory was divided into 42 departments or provinces called nomos: 22 in upper Egypt and 20 in lower Egypt. These nomos were ruled by representatives of the pharaoh called nomarcas. The nomarca was the head of the administration of the nomos and was responsible for the irrigation, agricultural yield, and storage of agricultural production, as well as for the collection of taxes and for setting property limits after the annual flood of the Nile.

This stage was also characterized by the construction of the great pyramids as architectural works symbols of Egypt, which were made of limestone to serve as home to the pharaohs after their death. Among the most important pyramids are that of Pharaoh Djoser in Saqqara, and those of Khufu, Khafre, and Menkaure in Giza. The construction of the pyramids of Egypt shows the great technical and organizational capacity of its people at that time. The pyramids were works of great magnitude. The pyramid of Djoser was the first to build and the most famous. It was a stepped pyramid whose architect was the famous Imhotep. The pyramids of Khufu, Khafre and Menkaure raised on the Giza Plateau near Cairo are the kind of classic construction with smooth faces. The pyramids of Egypt are now considered one of the 7 wonders of the world.

It should be noted, however, that before the pyramids as we know them today, during ancient times, the Egyptians built their tombs made of adobe or stone, which were like a truncated pyramid called mastabas. After the ancient empire, the pharaohs began to be buried in the pyramids, which consisted of mastabas on one another.

Egypt's great development has always been associated with the particularity of its river, which by providing good crops favored the increase of the population. The first towns achieved great development to become the first cities, which continued to evolve into large cities. Among these early cities were Memphis, Thebes, Giza, and Saqqara.

Memphis was built by the kings of the first Egyptian dynasty in Lower Egypt and was one of the important religious centers of that time. Memphis was Egypt's first capital and was located approximately 15 miles south of modern Cairo. The most adored gods in Memphis were those of the trio of gods or triad consisting of the god Ptah, his wife Sekhmet and Nefertum, his son. Of the then famous city of Memphis, today only ruins remain.

Thebes was located in Upper Egypt and was one of the most notable cities in ancient Egypt. It was also the capital city of the dominant dynasties of the Middle and New Kingdom. Its most adored gods were represented by the triad formed by Ammon, Mut and their son, Khonsu or Jonsu. In Thebes are located the important temples of Karnak and Luxor. It is also located in front of the city, on the western bank of the Nile River, the desert necropolis known as the Valley of the Kings and Queens. This necropolis is home to a number of monuments, tombs, and temples. This is where Tutankhamun's famous tomb is located.

Giza, also located in Lower Egypt, was a necropolis city for the royalty of the Ancient Kingdom. Giza is famous for the Great Sphinx and the pyramids built there. The Great Sphinx of Giza is a monumental sculpture with a lion's body and human head, which is oriented to the east and is about 20 meters high and 70 meters long. The Great Sphinx was sculpted on a mound of limestone some 4.5 thousand years ago. At first the Sphinx was painted bright red, and the ornament of its head was painted with yellow and blue stripes.

The Great Pyramid of Khufu, also built in Giza, is one of the last seven ancient wonders of the world, which rises to some 137 meters. The other known pyramids of Giza include the Pyramid of Khafre and Menkaure.

Saqqara was located in Lower Egypt. This city was used as an ancient cemetery. Among the most famous structures is the stepped pyramid of Djoser, also known as the stepped tomb. About 20 ancient Egyptian kings built their pyramids, which served as a necropolis for the kings who lived and died in Memphis. The continuous progress of the development of these cities made them larger cities and thus laid the foundations of civilization.

Egyptian civilization is well known in the contemporary world, in addition to its Great Sphinx and pyramids, for its mummification, which was used to preserve people's bodies when they died. At first, the first inhabitants of Egypt buried their dead in small wells or pits in the desert where the heat and dryness of the sand absorbed bodily fluids and rapidly dehydrated the bodies preventing their decomposition. This gave the bodies of the deceased a still living appearance of people for many days. These dead became natural mummies.

Later, the Egyptians began burying their dead in chests to protect them from the wild desert animals. However, they soon observed that the bodies inside the chests were more easily decomposed because they were not in direct contact with the heat and dryness of the desert sand. This observation caused the Egyptians to seek for centuries to perfect the techniques to preserve the bodies of the dead. These techniques were developed to such an extent that a living aspect of the dead could be maintained for years.

The mummification process includes embalming and cleaning the body, once performed the deceased is wrapped with fabrics and linen bands. This process took place in the houses of death and the people who did it became true artists. The process had 5 steps: it wrapped the body for 70 days to dehydrate it with a mantle impregnated with a natron resin, a saline mineral of hydrated sodium carbonate; the viscera and brain were removed, except for the heart and kidneys; the body was washed and purified with ointments, resins and perfumes; the body was wrapped in bandages and placed in a sarcophagus, which was buried in the tomb and with it its valuables, as well as food, drink, clothing and even money so that he could use them in the other life, according to their belief.

Mummification was done because the ancient Egyptians believed in life after death. When someone died, his soul left his body and then returned to him once the deceased was buried. However, the soul had to be able to find and recognize his body to enter it and thus live eternally. That is why the dead body has its mouth opened before being buried so that he could eat, drink and for the soul to enter the body again.

The viscera that were extracted from the body of the dead during the mummification process were initially stored in some vessels called *canopic jars,* but then over time the viscera were returned to the body once extracted and dissected. Given the laborious and costly mummification, this would eventually only be accessible to the upper classes.

The Egyptian civilization that lasted almost 3.5 thousand years reached its greatest splendor with the ancient empire between 4.8 and 4.2 thousand years ago. In which all the power of the state was represented in pharaoh. This stage was characterized by strict control of agricultural production. With their great advances in agriculture and breeding, the Egyptians managed to develop a great culture with a wide range of economic activities such as food production, irrigation techniques, mining, and trade.

In addition, they had made great strides in their political structure, religion, writing, literature, and sciences such as mathematics, astronomy, and medicine. Egypt also stood out for its art, especially architecture in relation to the world of the gods, temples, and tombs of the dead.

The organization of Egyptian society can be represented by a pyramid on whose peak the pharaoh was, regarded as a god, son of the Sun to be obeyed and worshipped. From him came every authority of the system of government, which was monarchical when led by the pharaoh, absolutist since the pharaoh had all the powers and theocratic because the pharaoh was seen as a god. The pharaoh was a supreme judge, head of the army, and owner of the entire territory. So, the economy depended on him, too. His powers were to be renewed every 30 years.

The priests occupied the immediately lower place, who as guardians of the temples had their riches, which comprised numerous lands with their consequent peasants to cultivate them. Then there were the administration officials, including the scribes, military chiefs and the nomarcas, that is, all those groups that were very close to the pharaoh. The lower steps were occupied by the rest of the people formed by artisans and peasants. These were free people forced to pay tribute to the pharaoh, either in kind as handing over a part of the harvest or in work by participating in the construction of public works. Most of the peasants were the so-called *Fellah* who cultivated the lands owned by the pharaoh or the temple, in theory they were free people, but in practice they were subjected to the will of the landowners. Finally, the slaves, who had come to this condition by being prisoners of war.

The main source of Egyptian wealth was agriculture, mainly dedicated to the cultivation of wheat, barley, grapes, and flax. They were also engaged in livestock and fishing. Because most of the land belonged to pharaoh or temples, the crops were deposited in silos or warehouses that were controlled by the pharaoh's priests, scribes, or officials. Trade with abroad was a monopoly of the pharaoh and was carried out through caravans that reached as far as present-day Lebanon through the desert.

Egyptian culture stood out for several unique aspects mainly for its writing and religion. They also had an important artistic development from which there have been traces in architecture, sculpture, and painting. Egypt developed its own writing, which at first was figurative, for each figure represented an idea. It was then improved with signs and symbols to become hieroglyphic with more than

500 signs and with it was engraved on stones and walls of temples and pyramids to bear witness to the history of Egypt.

The Egyptian religion was polytheistic because they believed in several gods. They worshipped *Ra* the god of the sun and life with a hawk's head and the solar disc on top, He was also the chief god of empire; *Osiris* god of agriculture and resurrection; *Isis* the goddess of fertility and love; *Horus* god of heaven with a hawk's head, son of Isis and Osiris; *Amon* god of the wind, who merged with Ra and became the god Amon-Ra, Egypt's most important. The Egyptians held several rituals to ask their gods for the floods of the Nile for agriculture.

The twilight of ancient Egypt ended in a transition marked by the weakening of the monarchy in the face of the growing power of local or nomarca rulers. This new situation ended with the transfer of the capital to the city of Thebes during the time of the Middle Empire. At this stage, the conquering spirit of the Pharaohs and the creation of a stable army produced a remarkable extension of the king's territories to the Nubian region of southern Egypt.

However, the invasion of the Hycsos later occurred when the capital of Egypt was Avaris, located in the Nile Delta of Lower Egypt. Avaris was a very active trading center during the rule of the Hycsos, including trade with Aegean Sea regions between Greece and Turkey. The Hyksos were a group of foreign nomads from various parts of the eastern Fertile Crescent, who arrived and settled in the Nile Delta and then took over. After a while they plunged Egypt into a period of political weakness. However, under their rule, they provided some technology such as the composite bow, the armor of scales made mainly of metal, daggers and curved swords made of bronze, the use of the horse and the war carts.

Eventually, the Egyptians ended up expelling the invaders to open themselves to the brightest stage of their civilization: the new empire. The capital of the new empire was in Thebes where the priests of the god Amon exerted considerable influence. To whom, the Egyptian dedicated two of the most important works of the time: the imposing temples of Karnak and Luxor.

Amon was a deity of the ancient empire elevated to the position of patron saint of Thebes. After the invasion of the Hyksos the god Amon acquired great importance to the point of merging with the sun god, Ra and thus forming Ammon-Ra, the chief god in the Egyptian pantheon. However, the supremacy of Thebes was interrupted by the accession to the throne of Pharaoh Akhenaten considered by some to be a heretic and by others to be a great revolutionary.

The original name of Akhenaten was Amenhotep IV, but because he disagreed so much power that the priests of Amon had, he changed the cult to Aton, a deity based on the solar disc. And he also changed his name to Akhenaten. This pharaoh introduced the first monotheistic religion: Atonism with his god Aton. And as if that were not enough, he also moved the capital of the empire to his city of Amarna, away from Thebes. Of course, these changes did not please the priests of Ammon, who felt threatened with losing their power.

Amarna was a city ordered to be built by Akhenaten to be the new capital of Egypt. The new city had large, sculpted steeds and large buildings such as the great temple of Aton, roofless for sunlight to enter; the city also had the royal and administrative palaces. After Akhenaten's death, Amarna was destroyed.

Akhenaten also stood out for his Great Royal Wife Nefertiti, who has been well known for her beauty and her great leadership skills. He also excelled at his successor Tutankhamen, who restored the traditional order. This young king was very famous for his burial mask. In this way the new empire went on to Ramesses II whose reign was the final flash of that stage of ancient Egypt.

The late era of Ancient Egypt stretched from the fall of the new empire to its incorporation into the Roman Empire, between about 3.1 and 2.3 thousand years ago. At first this new stage was characterized by a succession of foreign dominations that weakened Egypt, thus foreshadowing its decline. One such domination was that of the Assyrians who invaded Egypt some 3.1 thousand years ago, taking control of Memphis, the capital at the time and then taking Thebes. However, after this dark period and after succeeding in casting out the Assyrian conquerors Egypt achieved a kind of renaissance known as the Saita era, as the governor of the city of Sais in the Nile Delta came to the country's rescue.

But Egypt's prosperity was again interrupted some 2.5 thousand years ago as the Persians invaded, with its king Cyrus II the Great, Egyptian territory, which became part of the Achaemenid empire, the greatest of the Persian empires. Egypt lasted 35 years under Persian rule with some stability until the Egyptian people revealed against Darius I, the Persian king at the time, but this rebellion was suppressed by Xerxes the son of Darius I. Afterwards, Xerxes invaded Greece, but the Persians were repelled by an alliance between the Greek cities of Sparta and Athens. The latter became a naval and enemy power of the Persians. Finally, the Persians were defeated by Egypt thanks to an alliance with the Greek city-State of Sparta and then with Athens.

Egypt was later conquered by Alexander the Great of Macedonia, a region of Greece some 2.3 thousand years ago. With Alexander's victory over the Persians in Egypt, Alexander the Great was appointed pharaoh in Memphis and Egypt entered the so-called Ptolemaic era by establishing its capital in Alexandria, a small town that later became a great commercial and intellectual center. The Ptolemaic dynasty ruled Egypt from the death of Alexander the Great until a little over 2,000 years ago.

Greek dominators promoted large temples such as those on the island of File on the Nile of Egypt, while fostering the penetration of classical culture. Eventually, Egypt was annexed to the Roman Empire during the reign of Cleopatra, its last Queen. However, the world would continue to make way for other civilizations.

The Neolithic culture that had emerged in the Middle East spread throughout India, China, and the rest of the world. The first thing to spread was farming and animal husbandry. With these two activities, the world would base its economy on food production, and with the surplus trade would emerge to further shape the world's economy. However, each of these regions would develop their own customs and traditions, as well as their beliefs.

2. 3 INDIAN CIVILIZATION

India is a country south of the Asian continent with two rivers of great importance, the Indo, from which the name of India came from, and the Ganges. Both rivers were essential, as they overflowed every year, depositing fertile sediments, transforming the basins of these rivers into great agricultural potential and the basis for the development of the first towns on the banks of the Indo River among which were Harappa and Mohenjo-Daro. From them, the rest of the towns and the first cities from which civilization would emerge were derived, including the towns and cities that formed around the Ganges River. Indian civilization began to emerge less than 5,000 years ago and evolved within the model of Mesopotamia and Egypt's Fertile Crescent civilizations in the Middle East.

Indian civilization had a social organization with some class distinction unlike Middle Eastern civilizations. Society was divided into four castes: the Brahmins, the Chakras, the Vaishyas and the Shudras.

The Brahmins were a kind of priests in charge of teaching spiritually to the people and carrying out the various religious ceremonies and rites. The Chakras represented the warriors and also took care of the administrative side to ensure that the monarch's decrees and mandates were fulfilled. Vaishyas were mainly engaged in agriculture and breeding, trade, and handicrafts. The Shudras represented the lowest caste, composed of peasants, indigenous people and even slaves.

As for the political organization of Indian civilization, we see that, at first, the Indians did not form a single and united nation, but rather were a group of independent towns with at least three main political entities: kings, priests, and feudal aristocrats.

It was the kings who ruled the towns as absolute and monarchical authority and had divine origin. Sometimes these kings even fought to preserve and extend their territory. After the kings, there were the priests, who helped the king of the towns in the administration, including justice. Below were the feudal aristocrats, who held positions of officials with lower rank, but who could own enormous fiefdoms.

The economy of Indian civilization was mainly based on agriculture, breeding and trade. Its main agricultural products were barley, wheat, cotton, and sesame. As for the rearing of animals, they raised goats, oxen, camels, buffaloes, etc.

In addition, they developed the art of spinning mills, for the manufacture of wool and cotton textiles. They also worked metallurgy with materials such as copper, tin, and lead. Besides, they used gold, silver, ivory and precious stones to make their ornaments. Domestic and external trade in their products provided them with significant economic progress.

The culture of Indian civilization is a mixture of its customs and traditions of its people, fused over time and including their beliefs, architecture, literature, art, and their music.

As for their beliefs, the religion of Indian civilization originally included Brahminism, Hinduism, and Buddhism. Brahminism was a monotheistic religion and was the first among ancient Indians. This religion was based on the worship of the supreme god Brahma, considered the creator of all things, including the other gods, living beings and also their soul, which was believed immortal and, therefore, after the person died, his soul would reincarnate in another person, if he had been good, or an animal, if he had been evil.

Hinduism emerged as a mixture of other religious practices, mainly from Brahminism and encompasses a series of ritual practices such as prayer, meditation, pilgrimages, etc. Hinduism is based on the importance of the individual's behavior and how it affects their lives and that of others, since the consequences of these behaviors are represented by what is known as Karma, which argues that everything that is done in one life would be paid for in the next, for in Hinduism is believed in reincarnation, which is based on rebirth over and over again in different bodies, beings and environments, all conditioned by the life and behavior that we have led in the previous one. The sacred book of Hinduism is known as the Veda. For some of its practitioners, Hinduism is regarded as a philosophy of life. It forbids eating beef from cow, which is regarded by Hindus as a sacred animal. It also prohibits marriage between people belonging to different castes.

Buddhism is born from the character named Siddhartha Gautama or Buddha Gautama, who became a beggar with the firm belief that he had been chosen, so he adopted the name Buddha, which means "the enlightened". Buddha devoted himself to preaching his doctrines against Brahminism, condemning things like social difference and racism. One of his beliefs affirms that the soul can be guided to Nirvana, or paradise, through love, good, charity and other good virtues. Buddhism argues that lasting happiness can be achieved through our behavior in the present, regardless of past or future.

In the religious culture of India different gods are worshipped, among the most prominent are: Brahma, the creator god of the universe and is part of the Trinity Trimurti, together with the gods Vishnu and Shiva. Other Indian gods include Rama representing a protector, Indra who was the god of war, lightning, sky, storm, and atmosphere. And Agni who is the god of fire.

As for its architecture, India has impressive monuments associated with the religious aspect such as the Taj Mahal, Jama Masjid, Amber Fort and Qutab Minar. The Taj Mahal is without a doubt the most outstanding and fascinating monument in India. It was built between 1632 and 1653. It is considered a World Heritage Site. Jama Masjid is an impressive mosque, built between 1644 and 1658 on top of a small hill, which gives it the ability to be seen from many points in Delhi city. Fort Amber is a palatial complex located in the city of Amber. Qutab Minar is the tallest tower in the world and is located within the Qutab complex in Delhi. It has also been recognized as a World Heritage Site.

Indian literature is as old as its civilization and was written in the Sanskrit language, hence it is sometimes called Sanskrit literature. At first, literature was used to capture ideas about wisdom, religion, and worship with texts such as the Veda of Hinduism. Afterwards, other texts were written such as the so-called Mahabharata and Ramayana, two poetic works of great importance in this culture, which were written in epic Sanskrit. It is worth mentioning that the initial language of Indian civilization, was the proto-Indian or language of Harappa or Mohenjo-Daro, because it was in these first cities where this language originated.

As for their art, the Indians developed their paintings, sculptures, pottery, ceramics, tapestries, and yarns. As for Indian music it was made at first with wind instruments, like a kind of trumpet, and percussion, like a kind of drum called tavil.

Indian civilization, like the other civilizations of the world, made important contributions to science such as mathematics and medicine.

2. 4 CHINESE CIVILIZATION

Chinese civilization emerged a little over 5,000 years ago in the vicinity of the Yellow River or Hoang-Ho and the Blue River or Yangtze. Around these rivers that are born in the mountains of Tibet and flow into the Yellow Sea, the first towns were developing to later evolved in the first cities to make way for the emergence of Chinese civilization.

The social organization of this civilization was made up of the emperor at the top of the pyramid, for it was considered of divine origin. It was then followed by the nobles, who included the landowners and military chiefs in charge of the army. Down there was the bureaucracy formed by the emperor's trusted officials including governors, judges, police officers, tax collectors and agricultural supervisors. They were primarily responsible for monitoring agriculture and controlling irrigation. Then there were the peasants, traders, and craftsmen, who were the officials of the empire in charge of some agricultural, commercial, and artisanal functions. And finally, they were, at the bottom, the slaves that were the prisoners of war.

As for the political organization of Chinese civilization, it was characterized by being made up of emperor-dominated dynasties with absolute power and authority. This was succeeded by an heir, usually his firstborn male. Then, the Chinese bureaucracy of public officials was established. As for the dynasties we have those of the ancient stage of about 4,100 years ago that included the following dynasties: Xia the first Chinese dynasty, the Shang, and the Zhou. While in the imperial stage appear the dynasties of the emperors who subdued the people under a central government. Imperial dynasties include those of emperors: Qin, Han, Sui, Tang, Song, Yuan, Ming and Qing, the last Chinese dynasty to end in wars such as opium and the war against Japan.

The Chinese economy was mainly based on agriculture, primarily growing rice on the Yangtze River. They also raised animals for food and cargo, with which they transported the products to neighboring cities for marketing. Subsequently, metallurgy began to be developed to make weapons and work tools for agriculture and other tasks. The materials came from mining that developed in nearby deposits, where important minerals such as iron, copper, gold, and lead were exploited. The Chinese also developed porcelain and silk, products with which the Chinese increased their trade to the Mediterranean.

The religion of Chinese civilization is rather regarded as a philosophy of life for their people. These include Confucianism, Taoism, and Indian Buddhism. These forms of religion have had a major impact on Chinese culture. Confucianism represents the doctrine imparted by Confucius, an important Chinese thinker and philosopher. Among his teachings are the importance of good behavior, the preservation of tradition and the dedication to study and meditation. Taoism is a philosophy that arose from Tao Ching, whose fundamental pillar is the Tao or way forward to live in harmony.

As for the culture of their civilization, the Chinese also excelled in aspects such as their writing, painting, music, and architecture, which have great influence on traditional Chinese history passed down through time. Chinese writing represents one of the most characteristic cultural aspects of this civilization, because in addition to a means of communication, it is also considered an art. Chinese writing is composed of a system of characters that transmit ideas, anagrams, images and words. Chinese painting was developed thanks to calligraphy, which was made using the tools of Chinese writing: brush, ink, ink, and paper. After the development of Chinese calligraphy came the idea of using these techniques for painting such as portraits, flowers and birds, landscapes, and animals. Chinese music is based on the sacred, political, and popular aspect of Chinese traditions, using traditional instruments that produce a rhythm and tone very typical of their culture.

Its architecture includes important Chinese monuments such as the Great Wall, the Pagodas and the Terracotta Army or Mausoleum of Qin Shi Huang. The Great Wall was built to protect the northern region from attacks by other towns. It is approximately 7,000 km long passing through several provinces of China. The Pagodas are multi-story buildings with overlapping ceilings on top of each other. They were made for religious purposes, especially as part of Buddhism. Qin Shi Huang's Terracotta or Mausoleum Army is the compound where Emperor Qin built his and his family's tomb along with 400 other tombs, in addition to the impressive terracotta army he had built during his rule.

China civilization has made through its evolution great inventions such as printing, compass, and its porcelain.

The invention of the printing press arose after the writing paper, which at first was made using the mulberry bark and then made of bamboo and later made with of rice. With the appearance of the paper, Chinese ink soon appeared, which was used in the printing process for writing letters and documents. In addition to the writing paper, they also made paper money, books, cards, and calendars. The Chinese also devised a kind of compass to be able to predict future events, based mainly on art called Feng Shui. This was especially used to be able to decide which were the best places to live or to build. As for their porcelain products, the Chinese managed to make a lot of progress in the trade of this line due to its quality and its very striking designs.

2. 5 OTHER CULTURES AND CIVILIZATIONS

In addition to the first civilizations of Mesopotamia, Egypt, India, and China; other cultures and civilizations also emerged with the influence of early civilizations, such as Phoenician culture, Greek civilization, Hebrew culture, the Roman Empire, and those of American cultures.

Phoenicians

The Phoenicians were Semitic people from the Middle East possibly from the shores of the Persian Gulf that had settled in Asia Minor, on the shores of the Mediterranean Sea and to the west of Syria. There, around the 3rd millennium BC they founded their town which the Greeks called Phoenicia, because of the purple or Punic color that is spelled "phoniniks" in Greek. However, the Phoenicians called themselves: Canaanites or sons of Canaan as also mentioned in the Bible.

Phoenicia was located on the western side of Syria, in what is now Lebanon. Its territory comprised only a narrow girdle about 50 km wide by 200 km long, bordering on the north, with Syria; to the south, with Palestine; to the east, with the mountains of Lebanon; and to the west, with the Mediterranean Sea.

The territory of Phoenicia was very mountainous and unfit to develop agriculture, so the Phoenicians had to throw themselves into the sea and become great sailors, efficient merchants, and good colonizers. Given the mountainous characteristic of their territory, in Phoenicia the cedars grew in abundance, which provided them with the wood for the construction of their ships, with which they sailed the seas.

The Phoenicians were great navigators, so they managed to expand and colonize many places around their territory, spreading their economic and cultural influence through their colonies around the Mediterranean Sea. Given the great distances that the Phoenicians had to travel to market their products, they had the great idea of having bases along the shores of their area of commerce. Thus, the Phoenicians would create some colonies in foreign lands such as "Gades" in present-day Cadiz, Malaga, southern Spain, and Carthage in North Africa. However, sometimes it was only necessary to obtain some concession through negotiations with people from some civilized territory to settle there to develop deposits, public markets, or some other type of business to market their products. They also established factories in not-very civilized territories, to market goods through barter. In some cases, these factories had fortifications for their defense in the event of an attack.

As far as its mountainous territory, Phoenicia was divided into small city-States, on whose shores, the

Phoenicians established safe and important ports, such as Byblos, Sidon, Tyre and Arad. Byblos and Sidon were located on peninsulas, while Tyre was an island. By 3,000 BC Byblos was the most important city-State of Phoenicia, which maintained commercial relations with Egypt, exchanging its cedars with the papyrus of that country.

The historical evolution of Phoenicia was defined by the evolution of Sidon, Tyre and Carthage. The city-State of Sidon stood out as a center of naval and commercial importance of the Phoenicians between the fifteenth and thirteenth centuries BC. Ships from Sidon sailed through the eastern basin of the Mediterranean Sea to fill their warehouses with goods from Cyprus, Rhodes, Asia Minor, Greece, Aegean Sea Islands and Black Sea coasts. The Sidonians made concessions in civilized countries and factories in the not-very-civilized towns, where they obtained slaves, furs, and metals, in exchange for the products of their industry. However, the Sidonians did not form colonies. The importance of Sidon came to an end when the Philistines looted and destroyed the city of Sidon in the 12th century BC.

The city-State of Tyre, dominated by the commercial hegemony of the Phoenicians between the 12th and 7th centuries BC. Tyre inherited the adventurous and commercial spirit of the Sidonians. The Tyrians extended their maritime hegemony to the western Mediterranean basin, including southern Italy, the Islands of Malta, Sicily, Sardinia, Corsica, the southern coast of Spain and North Africa crossing the Strait of Gibraltar. They reached the coasts of England to the north, the Canary Islands to the south and the Azores Islands to the west. The Tyrians did not settle for trade relations; they also settled in some strategic locations, founding cities and colonies. But then the Assyrians, the Chaldeans, and the Persians subdued the

Tyrians, leading to the emergence of another merchant people like Carthage.

After the decline of Tyre, Carthage, North Africa, became one of the most important and prosperous city-States of the Mediterranean between the 9th and 2nd centuries BC. Its commercial dominance spanned from Sicily to the Spanish coasts. Its great rivals were the Greeks and later the Romans, who destroyed the city of Carthage, in 146 BC during the Punic Wars.

The social organization of the Phoenicians was made up of the royalty or class of the rulers, at the top, followed by the class of officials including the assembly people. Then followed by the class of free workers, made up of merchants, small owners, and craftsmen. Further down were salaried workers like peasants and servants. And finally, there were the slaves. It should be noted that in Phoenician women could participate in economic and social events.

Socially, the Phoenicians mingled more than any other town with people from other places where they settled. Phoenicians often married with natives from the places where they settled.

As for its political organization, Phoenicia was ruled by a monarchy like the rest of the western part of the world at the time. This monarchy was hereditary with highly important functions and had an assembly of notables that assisted the monarch in his duties. The noble elders of the assembly could make decisions in the absence of the monarch. However, as the Phoenicians became more affluent by growing trade, they could choose to form the government and thus turn it into an oligarchy, in which power was held by two magistrates called judges or *Shophets,* who, it is believed, were elected each year. There was also a Senate of 300 members for life and a Council with 104 members forming a public inspection tribunal, before which generals and officials accounted for their performance in office. Finally, a people's Assembly operated, whose relationship with the rest of the institutions was not very clear.

The eastern Phoenician city-States were politically independent of each other and their territories over which each of them exercised their dominance was quite small, except for larger city-States such as Tyre and Sidon.

The Phoenicians developed an intense economic activity in the industrial, commercial, transport and business sectors. In the industrial part, the Phoenicians developed three major industries: dyeing, glass, and metals. In the dyeing industry they made dyes, especially purple dye, which they obtained from the sea snail of the murex genus. With this dye they made fine purple fabrics, which were very well quoted by the nobility of the ancient world. In the glass industry, they created crystalline white glass, which could also be of other colors, depending on the combination of molten sand with metal oxides. As for metallurgical, they made brass and iron weapons; gold and silver jewelry; also, copper and bronze utensils.

On the commercial side, Phoenicia was a very mercantilist society, becoming a true world economic power for its time. They were creators of industrial, shipping, construction, and commercial companies. They developed the technique of international trade.

Among the products with which Phoenicians marketed were forest products, miners, agriculture, and their derivatives, marine, livestock and their derivatives, manufactures, metallurgists, etc.

Forest products included cedars and plant resins. Mining products include gold, silver, bronze, obsidians, gemstones, bitumen, tin, lead, malachite. Agricultural products and their derivatives included figs, dates, grapes, olives, barley, wheat, pomegranates, oil, wine, honey, etc. Marine products included fish, octopus, mollusks. Livestock products and their derivatives included horses, cattle and goats, milk, cheeses, wool. Manufactured products such as alabaster and stone cups, fabrics and clothing, chairs, tables, metallurgical products, ceramics, ornaments, textile products, purple dyes, iron products, perfumes, balms, tapestries, papyrus, glass products, boats, navigation technology, engineering and construction industry

As regards transport for the marketing of their products, the Phoenicians developed maritime transport and safe ports of course, as well as land transport. For maritime transport, they developed navigation with trade routes that crossed the Mediterranean in all directions, the Aegean Sea and part of the Atlantic. By sea, they brought from Europe silver, iron, lead, tin, amber, cereals and wool. While from Africa they brought ivory, gold, ostrich feathers and papyrus. As for land transport, this was used to bring in caravan wines, oils, spices, perfumes, fabrics, etc. from Arabia, Mesopotamia, Persia, and India.

For maritime transport they built their boats with their own cedar wood, which they waterproofed with bitumen. These boats were driven by oars and a square sail. As they did not know the compass by that time, they sailed closed to the shores during the day. At night they were guided by observing the position of the stars. Their ships were of two types: cargo and war. The cargo ones were wide for greater capacity but were slow. The warships incorporated a naval ram, a revolutionary invention for their time, with which they could damage enemy ships.

On the business side, the Phoenicians created large companies with people's labor and capital to produce in series and make common profits. For example, it is believed that it was Phoenician companies that, on behalf of King Solomon, built the famous temple of Jerusalem, over a period of 7 years.

Phoenician culture was a mixture of other cultures. It was a culture that had reciprocal influences with other peoples. For example, the Phoenicians had influence of Greek culture. However, they also had influence over Greek; as well as other cultures such as Egyptian, Assyrian, Etruscan and Roman.

The art of Phoenician culture that stood out most was craftsmanship, as its products were of high value for commercialization with other cultures or towns. They produced writing, ceramics, jewelry, etc. With regard to architecture they built temples such as Byblos. But the great legacy of the Phoenicians was their alphabet. The Phoenicians invented their own alphabet. However, at the beginning, at the end of the 3rd millennium BC the Phoenicians used cuneiform writing on clay tablets, because of the influence of Babylon. Subsequently, they used the hieroglyphic writing of Egypt. The Greek and Latin alphabets were derived from the Phoenician alphabet. The Phoenician alphabet was composed of 22 consonant signs or letters, representing elementary sounds of the human voice, with which any word could be written. Afterwards, it was improved by the Greeks, who added the five vowels to it.

The religion of the Phoenicians was polytheistic, for several gods were worshipped. Its main gods included Baal god of rain and war. Baal represented the sun. Another important god was Astarte representative of the Moon and goddess of Mother Nature and Fertility. These gods received other denominations according to the places where they were worshipped.

After all its splendor, Phoenicia went on to face serious difficulties, due to pressure from Egypt, Assyria, Babylon, and Persia. It finally fell to Greece in the hands of Alexander the Great in 332 BC. The first Phoenician city to be taken over by the king of Macedonia was Tyre, the other cities surrendered one by one. Subsequently, the great

Phoenicia became part of Rome with the exception of Carthage, which became a great power, which was fought on the island of Sicily with the Greeks and faced, in the Punic wars, Rome that would eventually annihilate it.

Greek Civilization

The first inhabitants of Greece were people from the Fertile Crescent and went into the Mediterranean Sea until they settled on the island of Crete in the Aegean Sea about 5,000 years ago. Over time Crete prospered to levels of a civilization about 4 thousand years ago. The civilization of Crete developed when the Achaeans, a town of warriors from the Balkan peninsula invaded and subdued the Cretan natives. The Cretan civilization is also called Minoan by the mythological King Minos of Crete.

The Cretans spread across the Aegean Sea and reached the Peloponnese, a peninsula in the south of the Balkans. South of the Peloponnese was located Mycenae, which over time also prospered until it became a civilization about 3.6 thousand years ago. This civilization ended when the Dorians from the north invaded it and destroyed it. In Mycenaean civilization came the first syllabic writing of the Greek language, which was called Linear B. This civilization is also called Crete-Mycenaean because of the influence of The Cretan civilization, and both are called Aegean civilizations.

Given the geographical location of Greece, in mountainous and arid lands, which made land communication very difficult, the Greeks had to master navigation to communicate with the rest of their territory and trade to survive. They also managed to expand their territory.

Greeks also expanded through Anatolia or Asia Minor, and southern Italy and Sicily. At that time apart from the Cretans and the Mycenaeans, Greece was also made up of other villages or towns such as the Achaeans, Dorians, Ionian, Aeolians, and Arcadians. These small villages were led by some patriarch and lived off agriculture and breeding. Over time, these small villages grew into independent city-states called Polis, which would transform Greek social and political life.

In the social organization of the Polis were at the top, the nobles who had political and economic power based on land ownership and agricultural activity; the bourgeoisie formed by officials of the political and economic authorities, some of whom were chosen at random by a sweepstakes, for which they designed award machines for these positions. Further down the social pyramid were merchants, craftsmen, and farmers; and finally, there was the class of workers or proletariat and slaves.

As for the political aspect, each Polis had its own laws, internal organization and also had its own government and armies. Government types ranged from monarchy to the creation of democracy. Sparta, for example, was ruled by kings and built great armies for which they educated and trained their people into the famous Spartan warriors, who fought until winning or dying. Athens, on the other hand, came to have a democratic government, the first in the world, and its people were more peaceful, allowing them to study to understand their world through their thinking. Athens became the symbol of Greek culture. The Athenians were the intellectuals. These two Polis: Athens and Sparta were the most important. Others that also highlighted were Thebes and Corinth.

The need to seek new land to meet the basic requirements of its people, due to their population growth, led the Greeks to the founding of independent colonies, which was an economic takeoff. This colonization was favored by the development of infantrymen called the

Hoplite; three-tier rowing boats called Trireme, which were similar to Phoenician vessels; and the introduction of the currency for trading transactions.

The Greeks fought many wars like the Medical Wars against the fearsome Persian empire 2,492 years ago. The Spartans formed an army under King Leonidas succeeded in successfully confronting thousands of invaders Persian soldiers and defeating them at the hands of their chief Darius I in the first medical war. Then came the second medical war 2,480 years ago under the command of the Persian king Xerxes son of Darius. However, Greece led by Sparta and Athens defeated them again in the Battle of Marathon.

Athens achieved a great boom, under the rule of Pericles, but Sparta wanted to free itself from the power of Athens, for these two Polis always rivaled for power. And having been allies, they began the long Peloponnesus war, which ended with the defeat of Athens. Then Sparta weakened after its war with Thebes and Athens resurfaced.

Then, some 2,323 years ago, Alexander the Great, son of Philip, king of Macedonia, northern Greece, wanted to prepare for combat, when he was only a young man of just 20 years old, and thus continue his father's work of fighting for then depressed Greece, until he ended the Persian empire. In his wars Alexander freed Asia Minor from the rule of the Persians, conquered Egypt and Babylon, and reached India. Alexander united the Western world with the Eastern world. He built an empire with which he managed to unite Greece. Alexander was taking Greek culture to all conquered places. After a dozen years in military campaigns, Alexander the Great died.

Greek civilization was greatly emphasized by philosophical thinking based on reason and knowledge. They were convinced to get to know the world through thought. Philosophical thought was widely developed in Athens by philosophers such as Socrates, Plato, and Aristotle. Socrates is considered the father of modern thought. His disciples Plato and Aristotle also stood out in the philosophical field.

With this kind of thinking, the Greeks opened the way to science: philosophy or art of thinking, mathematics, astronomy, physics, medicine, and politics. Among the most prominent Greek scientists we have: Tales of Miletus, Pythagoras, and Archimedes. Tales was a mathematician, astronomer and physicist who lived in the Miletus Polis. Pythagoras was a mathematician with great contributions in geometry and arithmetic. He is very famous for the theorem that bears his name. Archimedes was a mathematician, physicist, astronomer, and inventor. It is famous for its Archimedean principle, which states that every body submerged in a fluid experiences a vertical force or upwards thrust equal to the volume weight of the fluid displaced. This principle is still in force to this day. In addition, Archimedes formulated the laws of the lever, on which he pronounced the famous phrase: "Give me a foothold and I will move the world." The Greeks also exceled in medicine, with Hippocrates, the great Greek physician considered the father of medicine, who had his own and very analytical and intuitive vision for the discovery and advances of medicine.

Another character of Greek thought that also stood out was Homer, the author of epic poetry: the Iliad and the Odyssey. The Iliad narrates the destruction of Troy by the Greek hero Odysseus better known as Ulysses, using the famous Trojan horse. While the Odyssey chronicles Ulysses' return home from Troy. These two works constitute the two great pieces of Greek literature and the basis of Western literature.

Greek writing was based on its alphabet, which originated in Phoenician, with an improvement by adding the five vowels to it. To write they used sharp instruments on wet clay stones or tablets. On these tablets they could erase and rewrite. Later, they also wrote with ink on papyrus and parchment paper. With their writing they wrote their laws so that their citizens would be kept informed to reaffirm the concept of their democracy. They also wrote their own story.

Although all the Polis were different, however, they identified by their similarities: they spoke Greek and practiced the same religion, which was polytheistic, because they believed in a dozen gods who, according to Greek mythology, lived on Mount Olympus. The Greeks believed that King Minos was the son of the Phoenician princess Europe, from where the name came to the continent, and Zeus, the father of all the gods. They also believed that on one occasion Minos received a white bull as a gift from Poseidon, the sea god and brother of Zeus, for Minos to offer it in sacrifice, but Minos kept the white bull and offered another bull in sacrifice. When Poseidon learns what happened, he became enraged and decided to punish Minos, bewitching his wife, Pasiphae, to feel uncontrollable sexual desires for the bull. Pasiphae, in her undue desire to be possessed by the bull, turns to Daedalus, a Greek inventor who made her a cow-shaped armor. From this union was born a creature with human body and cow's head that gave rise to the minotaur. Other popular gods were Aphrodite, Apollo, Athena, and Ares.

Among the Polis were formed close and enduring associations of city-State groups called *amphictyonies,* whose inhabitants met periodically, around a common shrine in order to share in festivals and celebrations related to a common cult.

The Greeks lived off agriculture and breeding, metallurgical, handicrafts, trade, and export. From their agriculture they produced grapes and olives, from which they obtained wine and oil for consumption and export, they also raised cargo animals such as the horse, the products of their crafts included masks of the gold that they brought from

Egypt, from metallurgy obtained bronze weapons and later they got iron weapons.

They had a very Mediterranean diet based mainly on seafood, fish, grains, seeds, vegetables, and fruits. Their way of dressing was also very simple, as they only wore a pair of wool and linen robes mainly. In their moments of recreation, they enjoyed their theater plays called *Orquestras*. The theaters were built outdoors on top of a mountain. The stands of these theaters were semicircular, in which they took advantage of the natural inclination of the terrain to allow all spectators to see and hear the scenes unhindered. The theatres had exceptional acoustics and each spectator, even in the last row of the stands, could hear every word perfectly. The origin of the theater was religious; the first performances originated as ceremonies linked to the gods, especially the god of agriculture and that of wine Dionysus. However, they later served as the stage for the famous Greek comedies or tragedies.

Greek civilization was also noted for its architecture and the art of beautifying its works. As for the architecture they developed in the cities a sacred enclosure on top of a hill called *Acropolis*. In the acropolis of Athens, for example, was the treasure of the city, as well as large temples for religious rites such as the Parton, built by Pericles, the first democratic president of Athens in honor of Pallas Athena, the goddess of beauty and wisdom, protector of Athens.

In addition to the acropolis they built other sacred enclosures called the *Shrines* such as that of Delphi dedicated to the god Apollo where the oracle was located, which was a place to consult the gods. The consultants ranged from kings to poor people and met with a priestess to whom they made their queries, but before the consultants offered some sacrifice and paid for the consultation. It is believed that the priestess after contacting Apollo, received a message about the consultation, which was decrypted with the help of the priests and communicated to the consultants. The oracle of Delphi played a very important role in the affairs of wars and colonization. It became the religious center of the Greek world.

Another famous shrine is Olympia dedicated to the god Zeus where the Olympic Games were held every four years. The first Olympic Games were held some 2,776 years ago. In these games were participants from all the Greek cities and while the games were being held wars between the Greek peoples were banned. And the prize for the winner was an olive crown. But that filled the winner with glory.

As for the art of beautifying, the Greeks were lovers of beauty. That is why they managed to stand out so much in this art, especially in the elaboration of the statues of their gods and their heroes, with sculptures that represent human beauty with their correct proportions. Like the Hermes of Olympia, the Discobolus, the Doryphoros and the Venus de Milo. In terms of art, to beautify their most important buildings they could use columns with three main types of designs: the Doric, the simplest; Ionian; and Corinthian, the most sophisticated. To highlight the beauty of their pottery, they painted them with motifs related to literary epics and aspects of their daily lives.

Greek culture is considered to be the basis of Western civilization, which still holds dormant today. The Greeks invented democracy with the aim of representing the people, knowing their needs, and responding to their demands. Science developed by the Greeks is the main pillar of today's knowledge and teachings with what we study the world and space. The Greeks also developed the first maps of the world with longitudes and latitudes, discovering that the Earth was round. They also discovered the elliptical way planets do when they rotate around the Sun. They designed various inventions such as the steam engine, the water pump, the catapult, and the vest for the protection of their soldiers.

Greek civilization was the great European civilization. But all its greatness came to an end with the death of its great king Alexander the Great and a new empire arose: Rome.

The Greeks called themselves Hellenes and their territory Hellas. However, it was the Romans who called the Hellenes Greeks and their territory Greece. The Roman Empire that arose later was greatly influenced by the Greek civilization.

Hebrew Culture

To talk about Hebrew culture, we will have to resort to the most important source on its history: the Bible. And we will do so given the importance of the spiritual legacy of the Hebrew people in universal culture.

The Hebrews were nomadic Semitic people of The Middle East, who believed in one god, manage to survive on grazing and cultivation, lived in tents, and had flocks of sheep and goats. In addition, they used donkeys and mules as a means of transport and cargo. These people were originally from the Mesopotamia region and who, guided by Abraham, according to the Bible, left their homeland around 2,000 BC in search of the promised land, which, according to the Bible, God had promised Abraham.

Abraham was one of Tarah's sons, who was a descendant of Noah's tenth generation. Noah and his family were the survivors of the great deluge that occurred in the lower Mesopotamia region. Abraham was married to Sara and since she could not have children, Abraham had a son named Ishmael with Sara's servant named Agar. Then God granted Sara a miracle to have a son named Isaac with her husband Abraham.

The Hebrews with their flocks and belongings, together with Abraham and his family moved along the

Euphrates River until they reached Haran, north of Mesopotamia where they settled for some time. Haran was located in what is now Turkey on the border with Syria.

From Haran some of the Hebrew tribes crossed the Euphrates river and thus left their region in search of the promised land. To do this, they made their way south until they reached Canaan. When they arrived in the promised land, the Hebrews found the Canaanites, other towns which already inhabited the Canaan region. But over time they mingled with the other Canaanite peoples and both the Hebrews, and the other Canaanites adapted to each other and became sedentary farmers.

The Canaan region was located between the Mediterranean Sea and the Jordan River and included other regions such as Phoenicia in the north and Palestine in the south. It also comprised three regions: Galilee to the north with its capital Nazareth; Samaria in the center with its capital Samaria; and Judea to the south with its capital Jerusalem.

Canaan was crossed from north to south by the Jordan River, which originates on Mount Hermon and flows into the Dead Sea, 400 meters below sea level. Canaan is currently the territory occupied by Israel, Palestine, Gaza, and the West Bank.

The Canaan region, for the most part, was arid or desert; but it also had forest-covered hills, such as the Tabor Mountains, Nebo, and the Olives. Its climate was hot and dry. However, its soils were conducive to grazing and cultivation of vines, fig trees, olive trees and legumes. Its fertile lands were scarce and were located along the Jordan River. Here the Hebrews became more sedentary thanks to agriculture, living in more comfortable stone houses than the tents to which they were accustomed. There they formed their towns and their culture.

Over time, Abraham's sons gave rise to Arabs and Jews. Isaac Abraham's second son had twin sons named

Jacob and Esau. Jacob, also called Israel, had twelve children, who subsequently named the twelve tribes of Israel. One of Jacob's sons, Joseph, believed to be one of the first Hebrews to settle in Egypt.

According to the Bible, Joseph was Jacob's pampered one, which provoked the envy of his brothers, who ended up selling him to merchants and then took him to Egypt, where thanks to his ability to read the dreams, he became minister of the pharaoh. Joseph created grain reserves that saved the Egyptians from famine. Meanwhile in Canaan there was a great drought and his brothers, who had sold him, came to Egypt in search of grain. Joseph forgave them and invited them to stay with him, initiating the Hebrew presence in Egypt.

Apparently, in cases of famine, the population of Canaan migrated to Egypt in search of food, because in that country the crops were abundant and depended not on the rains, but on the flooding of the Nile.

It is also believed that there was an episode of mass emigration of Semitic people like the Hebrews from Canaan to Egypt in search of a better life. These people settled in the Nile Delta, a region that then dominated. It is believed that they were the Hyksos, who ruled Egypt. For this reason, they were known as the Egyptian sovereigns of foreign origin. Taking advantage of the fact that Egypt was ruled by the Hyksos, of the same Semitic race, some Hebrew tribes may have gone to settle in Egypt.

But since the Hyksos had as their chief god a foreign divinity, that caused a conflict with the Egyptians and the Hyksos were expelled to Canaan and the Hebrews were left in captivity and then enslaved until Moses came and freed them.

Moses was born in Egypt to Hebrew parents, his father being descendants of Jacob. He also had a brother named Aaron. Moses was part of the second generation of

Hebrews born in Egypt. He was also part of the Pharaoh's family, for it was a princess of this family who picked him up from a basket in which he was swept away by the waters of the Nile River. It was this princess, who gave him the name of Moses, who means saved from the waters. Moses' mother had put him in the basket to protect him from the Pharaoh's threat to kill every Hebrew male child.

As an adult, Moses could see how the Hebrew slaves were treated. Faced with a brutal punishment of one of the slaves by the pharaoh's people, Moses killed the torturer Egyptian and then had to leave Egypt and went to Midian, where he met the priest of the town, who adopted him as a son and gave him work as a herd supervisor. Moses later married Zipporah, the priest's eldest daughter, who gave him a son named Gerson. In Midian, Moses lived for forty years.

On one occasion when Moses had taken his flock to Mount Sinai, God spoke to him and told him to free his people. Moses obeyed and returned to Egypt and met with his brother Aaron to talk to the Hebrews about the plan. But the pharaoh was unwilling to let the slaves go until God sent him the ten plagues.

Moses then began the exodus with the Hebrews to the promised land, but they were persecuted by the pharaoh's army without success, for God separated the waters of the Red Sea so that the Hebrews would pass only, according to the biblical account. On his journey through the desert, god gave the ten commandments to Moses on Mount Sinai. Moses initiated and led the exodus to free the Hebrew people to Canaan. However, Moses died before entering Canaan and Joshua replaced him to complete the mission.

In Canaan, the Hebrews had organized themselves into twelve tribes that made up the United Kingdom of Israel and so the Hebrews were also renamed Israelites. The first kings of Israel were Saul, David, and Solomon.

Saul organized during his rule an army that allowed the Hebrews to live in peace and keep the Philistines and the nomads of the desert away from their borders.

King David established a powerful army with which he subdued his enemies. He was the creator of the Hebrew State and the founder of the capital of the kingdom he called Jerusalem, a city to which he brought the Ark of the Covenant, which was a cedar chest, where the Hebrews kept the ten commandments. David was famous for his courageous feat of killing the gigantic Philistine warrior Goliath with his slingshot.

His favorite son Solomon succeeded him on the throne, who during his reign achieved great economic development, mainly in commercial activity, with whose profits they built in seven years, with Canaanite and Phoenician artisans, the temple of Jerusalem where the Ark of the Covenant was kept.

After the death of King Solomon, some rivalries arose between the tribes of the United Kingdom of Israel, resulting in their division into the kingdom of Israel and Juda. The kingdom of Israel was made up of ten tribes with the names of Jacob's ten sons, having as its capital Samaria. The kingdom of Judah was made up of the other two tribes with the names of Joseph's children, having its capital Jerusalem. The Hebrews of Juda were also called Jews.

After this division of the United Kingdom of Israel, the two formed kingdoms were taken over by the great empires of the time. Israel was conquered by the Assyrian empire in 722 BC. However, Judah was spared the Assyrian conquest for more than a century, but in 597 BC the Neo-Babylon emperor Nebuchadnezzar subdued the kingdom of Judah and led the Jewish people into captivity in Babylon. Later, when Cyrus The Great destroyed the neo-Babylon empire, Cyrus allowed the Hebrews to return to their Judah.

But not all the Hebrews returned for fear of being enslaved and continued to disperse.

Later, in 70 BC, during the Roman Empire, under the rule of Emperor Titus, they destroyed Jerusalem and expelled the Hebrews, who on this occasion dispersed across the Mediterranean to the whole world. This dispersion is what is known as the diaspora. However, thanks to their beliefs and customs, especially their faith in their god, the Hebrew community survive and maintain their culture.

Hebrew culture had very particular characteristics in terms of its social, political, economic, and religious organization. The social aspect of the Hebrews revolved around the family group, which was patriarchal in nature, as the father adopted the figure of the highest authority. Abraham was the first Hebrew patriarch. There were also slaves in Hebrew society, which were obtained through the purchase or because they were taken as prisoners of war.

As for the political organization of the Hebrews, their tribes were ruled by the elders who were called patriarchs. The Patriarch was the chief and as such exercised the utmost authority over persons and their property. He was also the father of the tribes, judge, priest and chief of the army. Among the patriarchs, they stood out: Abraham, Isaac, Jacob, Joseph, and Moses.

Later, when the Hebrews first became a nation in the 12th century and established as the twelve tribes of Israel, each tribe was ruled by a military and religious chief named Judge. They adopted the sedentary way of life by forming towns and cities.

Subsequently, to unify and defend their nation against their enemies: the Philistines of the coast and the nomads of the desert, the Hebrews decided to be ruled by kings, following the example of the monarchies of Egypt and Mesopotamia.

As for the economic organization of the Hebrews, they had major changes when they settled in Canaan. From nomadic shepherds became sedentary and engaged in agriculture and livestock. In agriculture they excelled in the cultivation of wheat, barley, grape, olive, fig trees, legumes, and lentils. In the cattle ranch they shepherded herds of sheep and goats, with the help of horses, camels, and oxen.

The artisanal industry also thrived with ceramics and fabrics, both linen and wool. However, the most important activity of the Hebrew economy was trade, as the Hebrew peoples were located between Mesopotamia and Egypt, which was a must-see for the merchants passing through that area. The trade allowed them to export wines and oils and import precious metals, ivory and exotic spices, which they did not have. They marketed by caravans, by land and by boat with the peoples of the Mediterranean, following the practices of the Phoenicians.

On the religious side, the Hebrews were totally monotheistic. They believed in one God, who possesses attributes such as love, power, justice, and wisdom. This god had no visual representation, implying that the Hebrews were not idolatrous. Their beliefs are contained in the Ten Commandments.

As for art, the Hebrews exceled in music, with Samuel being the creator of a music school. They used musical instruments such as trumpets, flute, drum, harp, and animal horns called shofar. In the time of King David, music and dance were in charge of the religion. The dance was later excluded, but persisted in ceremonies, music, and hymns.

The contributions of Hebrew culture to universal culture include fundamental aspects of a religious nature, in force to this day. Among his contributions we have monotheism, the Bible, and the Decalogue. As for monotheism, the Hebrew people were convinced to believe in one god when the rest of the world for their time was polytheistic. This faith gave rise to the three largest religions in the world today: Judaism, Christianity, and Islamism.

The Bible was another of his great legacies. The word Bible comes from the Greek word Byblos, which means book and its plural is bible. Indeed, the Bible is the set of Holy Books. Due to its deep religious, philosophical, and literary content, the Bible is considered to be the most important work of humanity.

The Decalogue contains the ten commandments, the first moral code written to try to manage the emotions of the people.

Today, the Jewish people, having had different dominations, are established in part of the territory of Palestine, as a result of the effort made by the Zionists, to obtain a territory, which emerged in 1948; after World War II. Thus, they occupied the State of Israel, with its capital in Jerusalem, with opposition from neighboring Arab states. Since then they have had a series of war-fighting, with their neighbors, the Arabs, such as those of 1949, 1956, 1973, and they are now in conflict with the Palestinians who claim their territory, yet Israel has achieved appreciable political, social and economic development.

The Roman Empire

The Roman Empire has been the basis of the Western culture of our present civilization. In order to understand it better we will go back to its mere beginnings when Rome was founded. Then we will see its expansion, the beginning of the great empire, its rise and its fall.

The Foundation of Rome

According to mythology, Rome was founded in 753 BC. on the hill of Mount Palatine on the banks of the Tiber River, near the Mediterranean Sea on the Italic peninsula in southern Europe. Among the first settlers of Rome were the Etruscans, who were already in that region when Rome was founded. Other settlers had also arrived from the interior of the peninsula and very close to Rome such as those of the Albanian and Sabine mountains, and the Latin ones, coming from the town of Latina also near Rome. In addition, other towns such as the ancestors of the Greeks who had settled in the south of the peninsula arrived. There were also people from different towns around the Mediterranean. From the south-east of France and the northwest of Italian came the Ligures, as well as the Gauls, from what is now France that in the 6th century ransacked Rome, forcing the Romans to build walls around the city. All these peoples came together to form the city of Rome.

The Etruscans were inhabitants of Etruria, In Tuscany, a region in the center of the Italic peninsula. From Tuscany, they spread around Rome. In a region called Lazio, southern Tuscany, the Etruscans allied with the Latins and formed a Latin League. The Etruscans were a very prosperous, developed, and advanced town in the cultural, military, social, political, and economic aspects. The Etruscans had a very well-organized and trained army. They were the ones who had assimilated Greek culture and then introduced it to the Romans. They built walled cities and introduced the arch to build monuments and bridges. They were great artists in sculpture and painting. They developed metallurgical, as their region was rich in deposits of minerals such as iron, nickel, and copper, with which they made tools and works of art to be sold to the Greeks and the Phoenicians. On the political side, the Romans had a great influence on the Etruscans, so much so that some of their first kings were Etruscans, from which they learned a lot. The Romans also learned from the Etruscans, their organization, their architecture, and their military formation. Etruscan culture was the basis of the Roman culture.

Rome Expansion

Over time, Rome stretched to occupy another six hills for a total of seven and become a city-State with a monarchy as a form of government. And later, in 509 BC Rome had already been constituted in a republic and then an empire in 27 BC.

The Roman Monarchy began with the rule of King Romulus, its founder, according to mythology, in 753 BC and ended in 509 BC with the expulsion of King Tarquinius the Proud. During this period Rome was ruled by 7 kings who belonged to the Latin and Etruscan dynasties. In the monarchy, besides the king, there was also the People's Assembly and the Senate. The king was the highest authority with absolute power. He was also supreme priest, judge, and military chief. The people's assembly was convened by the king to debate the laws for approval or rejection. The assembly consisted of free citizens in the military age. The Senate advised the king and presented the candidates for the succession of the royal throne. The Senate was made up of 300 elderly patricians.

The Roman Republic began in 509 BC. During this period Rome became the first power in the world, with numerous colonies conquered in Europe, Asia, and Africa; thanks to its expansionist policy and the fact of having a powerful army, disciplined and very well organized. During the Roman Republic, their political institutions were also strengthened, and their culture spread. During this period, however, several social problems arose, such as the struggle between rich and poor and rivalries between ambitious warlords vying for power.

During the republic, the Senate of the monarchy was preserved, and other institutions were developed and modified. The Consuls emerged as authorities serving as government, military, and administration of justice. In this period the king was replaced by two consuls, who controlled each other. At the end of their government they had to tell the Senate about their duties. In the event of a national threat or danger, the consuls could appoint a dictator, with absolute powers, whose function could not last more than six months.

The assemblies were now of three types: the Curial Assembly, the Centurial and the Tribal. The Curial assembly was made up of upper-class people called the patricians and was convened by the king. The vote of the majority of the curials constituted the vote of the people.

The Centurial assembly consisted of military personnel, who met in groups of 100. The head of each group was called Centurion. These assemblies were convened and led by the consuls. With the majority vote, the laws were passed, and the consuls were elected.

The Tribal Assembly consisted of the plebs and were grouped by tribes. This assembly was presided over by a *Tribune,* or representatives of the commoners, who defended their rights before the Senate and the consuls. The tribunes' agreements were of legal character. The tribunes were elected in the Tribal Assemblies, in number of two.

In addition, magistrates in charge of watching over the operation of the government emerged, such as censors, quaestors, praetors, and councilors. The censors were in charge of making the census of people and their property. They also took care of the education and good customs of the people. The quaestors were the accountants who collected the taxes and administered the public treasury. The Praetors were officials who administered justice and they were the forgers of *Roman Law*. The councilors formed the municipal organization and were in charge of watching over the markets, cleaning the streets, maintaining the roads and highways, and organizing the Olympic Games.

One institution that played a very important role, especially during the policy of expansion of the Roman Republic, was the army. This was the main engine for wars and conquests. It consisted of citizens between the ages of 17 and 46, who formed the national guard. The army was organized into legions of 6,200 men each, and fought in a closed way, which was much more effective than the Greek army. With this powerful machinery Rome was able to conquer territories and impose its authority.

Roman expansion began with the conquest of the towns which were on the Italic peninsula, of which Rome was a part. Among these towns were: the Latins, the Samnites, the Etruscans and the Tarentines. The Latins were converted into settlers and then supplied men to the Roman army. The Samnites who lived in the mountainous regions of central Italy, that had formed a powerful army, with which they conquered the Campania region within the Italian peninsula and other territories south of the peninsula. However, this invasion led to war with the Romans, who ended up imposing and occupying in addition to Campania, other regions around it. The Etruscans, who lived north of Rome and who after the harassment of the northern Gauls and the southern Romans, were annexed to the Roman Republic. The Tarentines who were from the south of the Italic peninsula and from Greece, in the face of the overwhelming advance of the Romans hired a mercenary army of 25 thousand soldiers and a few elephants, with which they initially managed to crush the Romans. But after their initial victories they were defeated and Rome with this victory ended up dominating the entire Italic peninsula. The vanquished towns became allied colonies with civic rights, participation in the army and usufruct of the profits provided by the conquests.

Once the territory of the Italic peninsula was conquered, the Roman Republic launched to the conquest of the Mediterranean Sea, which they did in two parts: first they conquered the western part and then the eastern part. The conquest of the Western Mediterranean began with the wars of Carthage, also called *Punic Wars,* by the name given to the Carthaginians and their ancestors the Phoenicians for the purple red color they used to dye their fabrics. These wars were three, took place between 264 and 146 BC and were caused by Rome's interest in taking the island of Sicily in the hands of Carthage, after Rome had conquered the Italic peninsula. During the first Punic War, Rome defeated Amilcar Barca, commanded by the Carthaginian army, so Carthage had to cede Sicily to Rome. Afterwards, Carthage attacked the city of Sagunto, an ally of the Romans, thus initiating the Second Punic War. During this war, the Carthaginians were under the command of Hannibal, the son of Amilcar Barca, who, with some 26,000 soldiers and 40 elephants, crossed Spain, the Pyrenees, and the Alps. However, due to inclement weather and the rugged of the journey, half of the soldiers died. Despite adversity, Hannibal the great Carthaginian strategist, with the support of the Gauls annihilated three Roman armies, in Trebia, Trasimeno and Cannas. With this feat, Rome was besieged but not defeated thanks to its walls. But after several defeats, Carthage's army weakened, while the Romans reorganized and invaded Carthage. Faced with this situation Hannibal returned to Carthage to defend it; but was defeated in Zama, south of Carthage in 202 BC. With the victory of the Second Punic War, Rome gained supremacy over Carthage, the Western Mediterranean, Spain, France, England, and North Africa. The third Punic war was initiated by the Romans, who feared that the brave Carthage would be reborn, burned down and destroyed the city completely. After Sicily, Rome also took Sardinia and Corsica.

After the conquest of the Italic peninsula and the Western Mediterranean, the Romans embarked on the conquest of the Eastern Mediterranean taking Macedonia, Egypt, and later Greece in Europe; and Pergamon, Syria and Palestine in Asia. The rule of the Roman Empire encompassed the shores of the Mediterranean Sea, specifically: southern and western Europe, North Africa, and west Asia.

The expansion of Rome would have its consequences mainly in politics and social. Politically, Rome, after all its conquests, became the first power of the ancient world, owner of vast territories with great riches. The conquered territories became Roman provinces. Roman authorities and public officials became corrupted for lack of control in such a strong territory. Then the warlords appeared with a desire for power, which sparked civil wars. Socially, great inequalities arose between people. The wealth, power, and prestige that Rome had gained concentrated only on an elite of society. Most of the middle class had disappeared, as much of them died in the battles, and the few who returned sold their small estates to the wealthiest. Slaves increased because of the large number of prisoners of war, which intensified the business of selling them. The poor rose up against the rich and the Senate, leading to many social struggles.

The consequences of the expansion of Rome plunged the republic into a deep crisis. To solve this situation, the republic implemented from 60 to 43 BC a triumvirate, a form of government composed of three representatives. This first triumvirate consisted of Pompey, Julius Caesar, and Crassus. However, Julius Caesar, one of the greatest Roman servicemen of that time, was the most important character of all republican life in Rome. Julius Caesar conquered the Gauls, France, Belgium, part of Holland, Germany, and

Switzerland. In Alexandria, Egypt dethroned Ptolemy and restored Cleopatra, a young Egyptian woman of just 22 years with whom he had a son. Julius Caesar then went to Asia Minor and after achieving another victory, he returned victoriously to Rome where he was proclaimed as Dictator for life. But later, his enemies murdered him in the Senate in 44 BC. He was stabbed by a friend of his named Marcus Brutus. Julio Cesar as a warrior conquered many important regions. As a statesman, he managed to distribute land between his soldiers and the poor and arranged for a third of agricultural workers to be free. Also, he stabilized the currency based on the gold standard. And reformed the 355-day calendar of the lunar year, in 365 days of the solar year and named the month of July.

After the death of Julius Caesar followed about three years of disputes, followed by the formation of the second triumvirate with Marco Emilio Lepidus, Mark Antony and Octavian, who divided the government as follows: Lepidus had to rule Africa, but later retired to private life. Mark Antony was able to rule the East and Egypt, where he met Cleopatra and married her. Octavian, the heir nephew of Julius Caesar, went to rule the West including Spain and North Africa. Octavian wanted to be a dictator of Rome. Having defeated Mark Antony in Egypt and accused him of treacherous, both Mark Antony and his wife Cleopatra committed suicide. With the rule of Egypt, Rome became the largest empire in the world. And Octavian assumed all the powers of the Roman Empire under the title of emperor. This ended the Roman republic, and the Roman Empire begins.

The Great Empire

The Roman Empire began in 29 BC with the rule of Augustus Octavian and concluded with Romulus Augustulus in 476 AD. The empire encompassed territories in Europe, Africa, and Asia. These territories included: Britain, Gaul, Spain, Switzerland, the countries south of the Danube River, Italy, Greece, Turkey, Asia Minor and North Africa.

Octavian was the first emperor of Rome under the name of Augustus Octavian, assuming all powers. In addition, the Senate granted Augustus Octavian all the powers and he complied with Senate orders. As emperor, Augustus Octavian reorganized the empire, by introducing some reforms. Among political reforms, the emperor was the highest political, religious, and military authority. The Senate complied with the emperor's orders. However, he ceded some provinces to the senators, who were called Senate Provinces. He also created The Prefectures to ensure the well-being of the population.

After the death of Augustus Octavian, a series of dynasties followed in power, which can be grouped into two stages: the high and the low empire. In the high empire between 29 BC and 284 AD, Rome had a great boom. This stage of the empire runs from Augustus Octavian to before Diocletian. While the low empire between 284 and 476 AD, from Diocletian to Romulus Augustulus, is the stage that marked the decline of the empire until the crisis that brought its end.

Rise of the Empire

The Roman Empire stood out because of its great political, social, economic organization and the development of its culture. As for its political system, it was centralized, as the emperor was the highest authority and was part of the decision-making. After the government, there was the senate and then the assembly. The Senate was an adviser to the emperor with little or no decision-making authority. The assembly was rather a tradition, for it had no power either.

Its members were under the emperor's authority and were elected by the emperor.

The society of the Roman Empire was made up of patricians, commoners, and slaves. The patricians were a very privileged class that grouped members of the oldest and aristocratic families of Rome, including landowners; the commoners were peasants, merchants and craftsmen; and in the last in the social pyramid, where the slaves, who were owned by the people they served. They were engaged in domestic services, agriculture, mining, handicrafts, and construction. For the Roman Empire, within the family the most important role was that of the father.

The empire's economy was based on agriculture and farming, handicrafts, mining, trade, and tax collection. In agriculture they grew fruits, vegetables, cereals, vines, and olive trees. They built dams and irrigation ditches, plowed with an iron plow, and used compost. They raised cows, sheep, and pigs. Artisanal production was also part of its economy. In this area, they produced fabrics, perfumes, jewelry, leather, glass, and blacksmith products. Mining flourished thanks to minerals from the conquered provinces and the availability of large numbers of slaves. The Romans also exploited salt to preserve their food and later marketed it.

Trade was another of the economic bases of the empire, which increased with the exchange of products such as metals, precious stones, spices, silks and perfumes, with distant lands, thanks to the control they had of their maritime fleet and the network of roads. For their commercial transactions they used coins such as the gold aureus, the silver denarius, the bronze sestertius, the bronze dupondius and the copper as. And of course, the economy of the empire was also supported by the tributes or taxes of the Roman people.

As for the cultural, the Roman Empire also excelled in letters and philosophy, in urbanism and architecture and its customs. In letters and philosophy, poetry arose with poets such as Pablo Virgilio Maron, the best Latin poet, author of the works La Eneida, Las Bucolicas and Las Georgicas. The history stood out with Titus Livio, the best Roman historian, with his work: History of Rome. Other historians who also excelled were Pablo Cornelius Tacitus and the Greco-Roman Lucius Plutarco. In philosophy, stood out Lucius Seneca, the emperor and philosopher Marcus Aurelius, and the philosopher Epictetus, who was a slave to Nero. In the oratory stood out Marco Tulio Cicero, the greatest speaker in Rome, with his famous works Las Catilinarias and Las Filipicas.

As for urbanism, the Roman Empire had a great development. Cities were the political, economic, and cultural center. These cities were in constant progress. As time went on, they left their town appearance to become cities with grid structures, organized from two main streets: *thistle,* which was a street from north to south and the *decumano* that was a street from east to west. These streets were followed by the others. At the interception of thistle and decumano was located the forum and around it was the main public buildings. The houses of the empire depended on the economic possibilities of the people. The highest economical could live in individual houses called *domus,* while the humbler lived rented in multi-story buildings called *insulae.* For security, the cities were surrounded by walls.

The daily life of the Romans within the city was very different from their life in the countryside. In the city, people dressed in two or three clothes and wore shoes. Their diet depended on their economic level, but they usually made three meals a day: breakfast, lunch and dinner, the latter being the main one. In the countryside, people normally worked in agriculture and lived in the countryside in not as comfortable conditions as in the city.

Within the new cities, the architecture flourished thanks to the contribution of the Etruscans with the arch, the vault, and the dome with which they built harmonious buildings using bricks, stones, and concrete. Among these buildings were temples, amphitheaters, theaters, palaces, circuses, forums, basilicas, and thermal baths. The most important temples were the Pantheon of Rome and the temple of Vesta in a circular way. The Amphitheaters and Circuses were large circular works built to provide shows to the people. The most important were the Roman Colosseum and the Circus Maximus. The first was for gladiator wrestling and confrontation with beasts, with a capacity of up to 110 thousand spectators. The second was the Circus Maximus with sand track for horse-drawn carriage races with capacity for 300 thousand spectators. The Baths were buildings that had hot or cold baths, library, meeting room and concerts. The main thermal baths were Caracalla and Diocletian's in Rome. The Romans also excelled in the construction of other large works such as roads for communication and commerce between cities, bridges, and aqueducts to bring water to people.

As for the sculpture, the Romans sculpted busts and bronze or marble statues of their gods and emperors, such as the statues of Emperor Augustus and that of Marcus Aurelius.

With regard to their religion, the Romans were at first polytheistic, for they worshipped several gods as Jupiter, the one who was the most powerful of all, god of heaven and celestial phenomena. Mars, god of the army, Juno, goddess of mothers, Cares that of the harvest, Minerva the god of intelligence, Mercury god of the trade, Vulcan the god of fire and Neptune the god of the sea. In the temples, the Romans offered sacrifices, offerings, and prayers to solicit favors from the gods. Some temple priests called *augures* specialized in guessing the future. In their homes, the Romans had a small sanctuary. However, years later, in 313 AD the Roman emperor Constantine with the Edict of Milan turned Christianity into the official religion of the Roman Empire. In 391 AD Emperor Theodosius forbade polytheism and Christianity became the only religion of the Roman Empire.

Fall of the Empire

The decline of the Roman Empire began in 284 AD due to the weakening of the empire by internal crises and their divisions. The first division was that of Emperor Diocletian when in 293 BC he created a tetrarchy, a form of government with four rulers. from the period of the low empire. However, in this tetrarchy, power was still in Diocletian's hands. But the other division made by Emperor Theodosius before his death, in 395 AD, it did involve the marked division of Roman territory into two parts. Theodosius divided the empire between his two sons. Arcadian and Honorary. Arcadian, the oldest, ruled the Eastern Roman Empire: comprising the territories of Greece, Macedonia, Turkey, Syria, Palestine, and Egypt. The capital of this part of the empire was Constantinople in what is now Istanbul. Honorius the younger, reigned in the Roman Empire of the West; in the territories where Italy, France, Spain, Portugal, England, and North Africa are currently located. The capital of this part of the empire was the city of Milan, but in practice it remained in Rome. In addition to the previous division, there was also another event that precipitated the empire to its end. In 475 AD, his last emperor Romulus, a boy of only 15 years old, came to power from the Western Roman Empire, during whose inefficient rule, the great Roman Empire; characterized by its great political and military power, its territorial conquests and its victorious wars; rushed to an end.

The empire was losing territories and was later attacked and conquered by a barbarian emperor named Odoacer, ending the Roman Empire. Although the part of the conquered empire was the Western one, but this was the part where the great power of the whole empire was. This event started the Middle Ages in Europe. However, the eastern part of the empire lasted almost a thousand years further under the name of Byzantine Empire until it came to an end in the year 1453 of our era with the fall of Constantinople into the hands of the Ottoman Empire and with this event the modern age begins.

The legacy of the Roman Empire can still be seen today, especially the western part of our civilization. In the territories of their conquests, they left the mark of their culture: their language, their customs, and their constructions. Among the aspects of his legacy we have: Roman law, the Latin language, its constructions, and Christianity. Roman law is a set of written laws setting out the rights and duties of citizens in order to achieve a better coexistence between them. It was consolidated in 439 BC as the Law of the XII Tables during the time of the Roman Republic. Many of its principles are still in force today in Europe. The Latin language that was the language spoken by the Romans, began to spread due to the Roman expansion. Latin later became the basis of other languages such as Spanish, Portuguese and French. Another legacy of the Roman empire was its great constructions such as theaters, amphitheaters, circuses, temples, thermal baths, aqueducts, and bridges. Also, among its legacies is Christianity, which became the religion of the empire in the year 380 and then spread throughout the world.

American Cultures

The inhabitants of the Americas, who had arrived about 35 thousand years ago, developed several cultures, among the most important are the Mayan, Aztec, and Inca culture. However, this continent remained unknown until the arrival of the Europeans.

America, the New Continent

As the north pole froze, during the last glaciation, the Bering Strait Ice Bridge was exposed and thus humans, already converted into Homo Sapiens, from Siberia in the northeastern part of Asia managed to cross, about 35 thousand years ago, this strait into a new continent, which we now call America. However, it is also believed that after Bering, humans may have followed the Pacific Ocean coastal route to avoid walking the long ice-covered paths. It would take these first humans in America about 25 years to settle on this new continent from north to south attracted by a more favorable climate and greater abundance of food.

In the American continent there are all the climates and landscapes of the Earth. In addition to very important mountain systems such as the Rocky Mountains, the Sierra Madre and the Andes Mountains. There are also extensive plains on the Atlantic slope, where rivers flow as mighty as the Mississippi, in the northern part of the continent or North America, and the Orinoco River and the Amazon in the southern part or South America.

The first inhabitants of America were nomads and walked in small groups from one place to another in search of food. They hunted animals such as deer and mammoths and also fished and harvested wild fruits. In North America, the first Americans found resources for their survival, so they settled in places like Clovis and Folsom in New Mexico,

United States between 15 and 10 thousand years ago. Around these settlements were found some pieces that characterize these cultures as their stone spear tips, which were made with a degree of perfection and beauty not common for that time. These tips had channels carved with great precision.

In their quest for a warmer climate with more abundance in food, the first Americans continued to move south until they reached the central part of the continent, which is now called Central America, where they decided to settle down. There, over time, they learned how to cultivate the land, make fabrics to make their garments and develop basketry and pottery. Thus, they became more sedentary to develop in the southeastern region of the Mexican states of Veracruz and Tabasco, the first towns and their respective culture: the Olmec, the first of all advanced cultures of the American continent. The Olmecs built important ceremonial centers in several settlements such as La Venta in Tabasco State, San Lorenzo, and Tres Zapotes in Veracruz.

Olmec was an organized culture. Socially, the Olmecs basically had two social classes: the ruling class at the top and the commoner's class at the bottom formed by the peasants. As for their religion, they were polytheists because they believed in several gods, including the god of the feathered serpent. They also had sacred animals such as the jaguar, toads, alligators, etc. Their rulers believed to have supernatural powers, for they believed they were descendants of their gods, and in that same way they were regarded by the people. The government was theocratic, led by priests with a warrior elite and some commoners. As for their economy, this based on agriculture with the cultivation of maize mainly, although they also practiced hunting and harvesting wild fruits. In addition, they practiced trade by exchanging products with neighboring towns. As for their art, they highlighted the famous Olmec heads carved in stone of several tons of weight and up to four meters in height. These stones were brought from quarries more than a hundred miles away. These stones were also used in the construction of temples and other sculptures. The Olmecs also developed their own syllabic writing represented by hieroglyphs. They also had a numerical representation, which already used zero. And they also had a very precise astral calendar.

Over time, Olmec culture was giving way to other cultures. Around 2000 BC, the first urban societies emerged with various forms of organization such as the Maya and the Aztecs, in the Central America or Mesoamerican region, and that of the Incas, in the Andean region of South America.

These early urban societies were much more organized hierarchically, as they had economic, political, and social organizations similar to those that existed in the Middle East. For American cultures, their religion governed most of the acts of their daily life, and their art reached a high level of development. The North and Central American cultures developed writing and numbering systems.

In these societies, the construction of irrigation works, and the application of other agricultural techniques were used, which favored the steady growth of agricultural production and the population. This led to the development of cities with a hierarchical social organization.

Among these societies the warriors and priests formed the privileged group and exercised government. But most of the population was made up of peasants and urban workers, who had to pay taxes on goods and jobs. These societies were organized and governed by strong theocratic states, in which all authority resided in priests. The ruler was regarded as a god, and all revolved around him. The first cities were organized around the ceremonial center or temple of the town. The temples were buildings where religious functions were carried out, as well as economic functions, as they stored and distributed the products taxed by the peasants. This is how these societies further developed their cultures such as the Mayan, the Aztecs, and the Incas as the most important.

The Mayan Culture

The Mayans settled around 3000 BC in Mesoamerica and spread throughout the Yucatan Peninsula from Mexico to Guatemala and Honduras. In this region they built huge temples for their religious ceremonies and around them developed large cities with squares, palaces, pyramids, sports fields, aqueducts, and drains. The most important Mayan cities were Chichen Itza, Calakmul, Palenque and Mayapan, in Mexico. In addition to Uaxactun and Tikal in Guatemala. The Mayans came to occupy a third of the territory of Mesoamerica.

Mayan society was initially composed of nobles and commoners. The nobles were the ruling class with many privileges, which were transmitted by inheritance. This social class knew how to read and write. The commoners or the people made up the majority of society, who did agricultural, fishing, hunting, and building work. In addition, there were the slaves, who were prisoners of war or criminals. With the growth of the population over time emerged other social strata such as a middle class made up of artisans, some officials and priests, merchants, and soldiers. Priests engaged in government functions and religious ceremonies. In addition, they were responsible for the study of the calendar and knowledge of the cycles of agriculture. Priests were historians, astronomers, and mathematicians.

As for its political organization, power was handled by the monarchy, which was hereditary by family members descended from a common ancestor. The Mayan monarch was regarded as an intermediary between humans and the supernatural world. The cities-States of the Mayan were ruled by a local leader, who in turn reported regional officials.

The basis of the Mayan economy was agriculture with mainly corn and bean crops, as well as tobacco, pumpkin, cotton, tomato, cocoa, and cassava. In addition to agriculture they had other natural resources such as limestone for construction, the obsidian volcanic rock to manufacture their tools and weapons, and salt to conserve food. They could also obtain other products such as jades and quetzal feathers to adorn the clothes of the Mayan nobility, and seashells that were used as trumpets. Another activity of its economy was trade between city-States.

As for their religion, the Maya worshipped several nature-related gods such as sun, moon, rain, and corn. In addition, they believed in a supernatural world in which there were several gods, whom they had to satisfy with ceremonial offerings and ritual practices including human sacrifices such as beheading and the extraction of the heart to living people to praise their gods. The Mayan also believed that they were descendants on the gods.

The architecture of Mayan culture was basically religious, and, in that sense, they built buildings with limestone and with clay bricks cooked. Among its buildings were its temples and its palaces. The temples were built at the top of the pyramids for their centers dedicated to worship. The palaces were in the strata below and are believed to be residences of priests. The most important sacred centers were Copan, Tikal, Piedras Negras, Chichen Itza, Uxmal and Mayapan. Also highlighted were the buildings of the Governor's Palace in Uxmal and the Snail Tower in Chichen Itza. They created sophisticated statues and stone-carved reliefs.

Another achievement of Mayan culture was its writing, which used as symbols the Maya hieroglyphs with which they came to write on paper made of tree bark their own books known as codices. They also developed a system of calendars with which they recorded very accurately the cycles of the moon and those of the sun, the eclipses, and the movements of the planets. In addition, they achieved great development in mathematics and astronomy. In mathematics they developed a vigesimal or 20-based numbering system, which also included zero. Numbers 1 through 4 were represented with a period for each number value, number 5 was represented with a horizontal stripe for each value of multiples of 5. The rest of the numbers could be represented by combinations of dots and stripes. In astronomy the Maya made detailed observations of celestial bodies such as the Sun, Moon, and Venus with which they made numerous discoveries concerning the movement of the planets and came to predict eclipses and rains. But the main purpose of its observations was to understand the past time cycles and project them into the future to make their prophecies

Mayan culture began its decline at the end of the 3rd century and by the end of the ninth century had come to an end. At the beginning of the decline the major Mayan cities of the southern part of their lowland territory in Central America were mysteriously abandoned. It is believed that by then the Mayan had exhausted natural resources in that region to the point that it was no longer possible to maintain such a large population. It is also believed that the region may have been affected by some catastrophic environmental changes, such as an extended period of intense drought, which could have affected cities such as Tikal, where rainwater was necessary for human consumption, as well as to irrigate crops. However, in the highlands of the Yucatan Peninsula, some Mayan cities such as Chichen Itza, Uxmal and Mayapan continued to flourish until the year 1500, when the Spaniards arrived. The last Mayan city fell in 1697.

The Aztec Culture

The Aztecs, having traveled several places, settled permanently, in the early fourteenth century AD, in the valley of Mexico, where they founded their capital city Tenochtitlan, built on the waters of Lake Texcoco. Communication within the city was done through canals. In the center of the city were more than 70 buildings, including the temple, the lords' palaces, a ball court and abundant gardens and orchards.

In the region where the Aztecs had settled, there were other peoples, with whom they fought to seize the best lands and have control of the region. Over time, they dominated the entire region, showing their great power, thanks to their great army. The Aztecs dominated the entire territory of Mexico. They were a very warrior people, for from an early age, they taught children to be soldiers. Among their weapons were: shields, bows, and arrows.

The Aztecs expanded and conquered many towns and cities, which had to pay them taxes. The Aztecs became a powerful empire, so many of the cities under their rule rebelled against them. In fact, upon the arrival of the Spaniards in Mexico, some of these cities allied with them to defeat the Aztecs. However, the Aztec cities were united not only by a common language and by their customs, but, in the political and religious aspects, they depended on a strong central power whose headquarters were in Tenochtitlan.

The Aztec state had an important military force with which they practiced the war of conquest to achieve its great territorial expansion. The maximum extent of his domains occurred in the time of Moctezuma, the Aztec emperor until the arrival of the Spaniards.

In Aztec society there were basically two social groups: the nobles and the workers. The nobles were the privileged group made up of the emperor, priests, warriors, and government officials. They owned most of the land, paid no taxes, and controlled the state. The workers made up the majority of the population and formed the group of the unprivileged. It was the peasants, the merchants, and the craftsmen, who had to pay taxes and had an obligation to work on the construction of buildings and temples of the nobility. Slaves, who were mostly prisoners of war, also existed in Aztec society.

Agriculture was the basis of the Aztec economy. Among its most important products of the daily diet were corn and beans. They also grew tobacco, cocoa, cotton, agave, tomato, potato, cassava, onion, lemon, etc. In agriculture, irrigation and planting on terraces were widely used practices. But the technique of the chinampas was the most used. These were rafts of land that floated in the lakes and on which they cultivated. Trade was also a very important activity. The Aztecs exchanged products such as cocoa, gems, cotton, and precious feathers with towns from different regions.

Regarding its political organization, the Aztec State was theocratic, for it was ruled by an emperor, who was the supreme chief, military chief, politician and high priest regarded as a god. The position of the supreme chief was hereditary. In addition to the supreme chief, there were the priests, who were in charge of government functions such as the preparation of religious ceremonies and rituals. Priests were also responsible for monitoring compliance with standards and doing justice. The laws of the Aztec state were very severe, and the punishments varied according to the crime and the offender. In addition, the priests were the ones who possessed the knowledge. They knew astronomy, medicine, and writing. However, the majority of the population did not have access to this knowledge. There were also officials who were directly dependent on the emperor and who controlled and centralized the storage of the products collected as taxes.

The religion of the Aztecs was a big part of their lives. They believed in several gods, being Quetzalcoatl, the feathered serpent, one of their main gods. This was the god of life, light, fertility, and knowledge. The Aztecs used to make human sacrifices in the name of their gods. One of them was to take out a living person's heart with a flint knife to offer to the gods.

The beliefs of the Aztecs led them to develop certain omens and prophecies about their future. One of these omens heralded that the return of the god Quetzalcoatl would occur at the end of Moctezuma's reign and do so in the form of a white man. Indeed, the prophecy would have been fulfilled, according to their beliefs, with the arrival of Hernan Cortes in Mexico in 1519.

Hernan Cortes commanded 11 ships and 600 men arrived in the Aztec capital, Tenochtitlan, Mexico. Cortes and his people carried firearms and rode horses: two great novelties not seen by the Mexicans at the time: gunpowder and horse. This of course frightened the first towns with which the Spaniards came into contact. One of them was the Tlaxcaltecs, a town which had been subdued by the Aztecs. This town allied itself with the invading troops by discontent with the Aztecs, which favored Spaniards.

Moctezuma sent ambassadors to Cortes with gold and silver to stop the advance. But that, what it did was further increase the greed of the Spaniards. And Cortes took Moctezuma prisoner. A short time later, the massacre of many members of the Aztec nobility by the Spaniards in the Great Temple began. That led to the town's uprising, led by Cuauhtémoc. The Spaniards were besieged, and Cortes forced Moctezuma to speak to his people to stop the attack. But the Aztec warriors with arrows and stones wounded Moctezuma himself and Cortes himself fled. The other

Spaniards were stabbed as they fled and only a few of them, including Cortes, managed to escape.

Then the Spanish troops reorganized and with the support of the Tlaxcaltecs, they managed to crush the Aztec resistance in Tenochtitlan. Once the entire region was subdued, King Charles V of Spain rewarded the conqueror Cortes with lands and riches and appointed him Governor and Captain General of New Spain. Mexico has since become one of the centers of the Spanish Empire in America.

The assistant in the translation of the Spaniards, was a woman named Malinche, who was the daughter of a Mexican chieftain given to Cortes as a slave. She spoke the Nahuatl language of the Aztecs and the Maya. Among the Spaniards was a priest who spoke the Mayan language. This priest then translated into Spanish, which Malinche translated from the Aztec language to the Maya.

The Inca Culture

Before the Incas, there were other cultures in ancient Peru such as the Chavin culture in the village of Chavin de Huantar; Nazca culture famous for the Nazca lines made with great precision in the Pampas de Nazca to represent enigmatic figures including animals, mythological beings and some geometric designs, all made on a gigantic scale; the Mochica culture, which stood out for its ceramics, as well as for its architecture represented by "Huaca del Sol" and the Moon. There was also the Tiahuanaco culture, which developed in the Andean plateau or the Callao plateau of today, near Lake Titicaca, where we can see one of the most interesting architectural works of this culture such as "La Portada del Sol", as well as other very old buildings. Tiahuanaco culture is recognized as one of the forerunners of Inca culture.

The Incas settled in a place in the Andes mountain range, in what is now Peru, from where they dominated other towns of the region through the war of conquest. They established their capital in the city of Cusco, which, in their language, Quechua, meant the center of their world.

From its capital, around the year 1200; they began their expansion through the western region of South America, along the pacific ocean coast and the Andes mountain range and occupied the territories of what is now Bolivia, Chile and part of Argentina to the south, and Ecuador and Colombia to the north. The Incas became a powerful empire and as they expanded, they imposed their culture including their Quechua language, which is still used in native South American communities.

Manco Capac is believed to have been the founder of the Inca Empire in 1200; and that he was also his first emperor, who was succeeded by 13 more emperors including Atahualpa, the last emperor. The Inca territory in its entirety was called by them Tahuantinsuyo, which was divided into four regions called ""suyos", which were ruled by officials of the Inca emperor.

The domain of the Incas began in the thirteenth century and continued until the arrival of the Spanish colonizers in the sixteenth century. It is believed that their fall was partly due to the discontent of some Incas-dominated peoples, who in some cases joined the Europeans.

The Incas were one of the last native cultures to stand during the conquest of America by the Spanish. It was a highly developed culture in agricultural, weaving and engineering activities, despite not having known the alphabetical writing or the wheel. At its peak, the Inca empire was the most important regional power on the South American continent.

The Inca culture implemented advanced transport and postal systems. Its transport system consisted of a network of roads, the most important being the "Camino Real", as it was the central axis of the transport system that ran through the Inca empire from the imperial headquarters in Cusco. The postage system consisted of a very fast imperial courier, as it had brokers stationed on the different paths. These messengers passed messages or packets between posts located 1.5 km away from each other.

In Inca society, several social groups could be distinguished: royalty, nobility, and workers. The royals were the ruling class and was formed by the royal family with the Inca at the head and his wife the Qulla or Empress. The nobility was made up of priests, warriors, and officials. The workers were made up of peasants, fishermen, shepherds, and artisans, who paid taxes in the form of work to the Inca government. The working-class lived-in communities called ayllu. These communities were made up of people united by family ties, who had common ancestors and inhabited the same territory. The State delivered land to each community according to the number of its components for its subsistence. But the peasants did not own the land and these plots were worked collectively by all members of the community. The ayllu was to deliver strong product and work tributes to the state. There were also slaves in the Inca society, who were prisoners of war.

The Inca State was theocratic because the emperor, also called the Inca, was regarded as the son of the Sun, the most important god. The Inca State was also absolutist because it had all the power. In addition to the Inca, there was a council of nobles and priests, belonging to the royal family, who advised the Inca on the tasks of government. It was the great military force of the Inca State that made the expansion of the Incas. To facilitate the displacement of their armies, the Incas built a large network of roads with inns and post offices along these roads, which served to rest troops in the field and for the exchange of animals and weapons.

Agriculture was the basis of the Economy of the Incas. Their most important crops were corn and potato. The Incas applied different agricultural techniques that improved crop yields. They used the guano, which was seabird droppings as fertilizer. They also built irrigation canals and farmed on terraces on mountain slopes. In addition, they received tax payments on products that they did not have in their areas from the towns under their domain. Another important aspect of the Inca economy was the breeding of llamas and alpacas, as these animals provided wool and meat, and were also used as cargo animals. Trade with other neighboring towns was also important in its economy.

The religion of the Incas was also polytheistic, for they believed in many gods, but their creator god of their world was Viracocha. Besides, they believed in the god of the Sun, called Inti. Also, they venerated the Pachamama the goddess of the earth, Quilla the goddess of water, Illapu the god of lightning, among others.

However, their beliefs, as well as the Aztecs of Mexico, led the Incas to develop their omens and prophecies about their decline. These prophecies would be transmitted by oral language, for the Incas did not know the writing. It is believed that the Incas also awaited the return of Viracocha, their saving god. Therefore, when they heard about the arrival of Francisco Pizarro, many of the Incas believed that he was the saving god. But the Spaniard Pizarro had only arrived to take down the Incas.

In November 1532, Francisco Pizarro, with 200 men, arrived in Cajamarca, Peru, where 30,000 Incas were camped under Emperor Atahualpa. Pizarro planned to take advantage of the internal division between the Incas, faced in a civil war in which two brothers' descendants of the Inca,

Atahualpa, and Huascar, disputed the throne. Despite having a small troop, Pizarro convinced Atahualpa to speak and then took him prisoner. Although Atahualpa offered to pay a huge ransom in gold in exchange for his freedom and that Pizarro had accepted and received the ransom value. However, the Spaniards ended up eliminating Atahualpa, the last Inca emperor.

Atahualpa's order to kill his brother Huascar, who dominated the south of the empire, facilitated the alliance between Incas groups and the Spanish. Another factor that also influenced the fall of the Incas, as in the Aztecs, was the terror that the superiority of the Spanish's weapons caused in the Inca population. Firearms caused a lot of terror from gunpowder explosions and the presence of horses because they were unknown animals. Finally, in November 1532, Pizarro entered Cusco, the capital of the empire and placed as emperor a member of the Inca nobility. In this way, Pizarro gained the support of a sector of conquered society by making it easier for the Spaniards to conquer the Inca people.

In 1535 Pizarro founded Lima, in Peru near the coast to secure communications with the other lands of the Spaniards, located over the Pacific. In Peru, the Spaniards took large amounts of gold and silver, which made this region the most important of all the conquered by Spain in America. However, the indigenous uprisings and the struggles between the conquerors themselves, for their greed to enrich themselves quickly, cost Pizarro himself his life. This forced the Spanish crown to intervene and in 1544 created the Viceroyalty of Peru to control the Inca territory.

The European invasion had a tremendous impact on the Incas, as well as on the rest of the towns of America. Their entire organization changed economically, social, and political, their religious beliefs, their worldview and the customs of their daily life collapsed. For these societies that had built their own world, the invasion was catastrophic, for their whole life changed from conquest until they disappeared.

Some Incas, who still managed to survive the conquest, ended up falling victim to the devastating effects of infectious disease epidemics such as smallpox, against which the Incas had no developed organic defenses. However, those who also managed to survive the diseases became peasants between the 17th and 18th centuries.

Before the Spaniards, the Incas had been great builders and had developed great works of art such as their imposing buildings, by which we know their architecture and sculpture in the works that survived the destruction during the Spanish conquest as their huge temples dedicated to the sun god and other of its deities, as well as the construction of the Pukara or military fortifications , which occupied an outstanding place in the city. Regarding urban design, they developed irrigation and planting systems in the construction of their cities, demonstrating a culture with a high level of planning and technical capacity, which knew metallurgy, ceramics, textiles and goldsmithing.

A good example of Inca urban design is the construction of Cusco and Machu Picchu for religious and military purposes, at almost inaccessible heights. Cuzco was built in a valley located 3,400 meters above sea level. It is a monumental city, which was the capital of the Inca empire. 80 kilometers northwest of Cusco is the imposing Machu Picchu, which was an ancient Inca town built around the fifteenth century, in the Andes Mountains at 2,430 meters above sea level. Machu Picchu was found in the heart of the Andes, in the twentieth century. It is believed that this was one of the last refuges after the arrival of the Spanish conquistadors.

Arrival of the Europeans in America

In 15th-century Europe, most people believed the Earth to
be flat. Only a few scholars had begun to suspect it was
round. Some other Europeans had heard stories about a
Venetian traveler named Marco Polo, who talked of a distant
country referring to today's China. The only Europeans who
knew of the existence of other territories outside Europe
were sailors and merchants, who returned with fabrics, spices
and large shipments of gold and ivory. This would arouse
Europeans' curiosity to explore new lands in search of
treasures.

The first Europeans to go out to explore new sea
routes and lands were the Portuguese with Henry the
Navigator, who was entrusted for this purpose because of
Portugal's need to seek sea routes that would allow it to
obtain food. Portuguese explorers began the search for a
route to Asia bordering the African coast. In the year 1487.
Bartholomew Diaz arrived at Cape Of Good Hope, in the
far south of Africa. In 1498 Vasco da Gama following the
previous route arrives in Calicut, India.

Meanwhile, the Spaniards, after freeing themselves
from the moors' domain, decided to also go in search of new
routes and territories. From then on, they started putting the
journey together. The Spaniards wanted to find a new seaway
to the west that would allow them to trade with Asia and see
what new lands they could find.

At that time Spain was under the reign of the Catholic
kings, Isabel of Castile and Ferdinand of Aragon, who liked
the idea of going through new territories and decided to
accept a project that was in the mind of Christopher
Columbus, who had offered it to several governments
including that of Portugal. The reign took the project and
made available to Columbus three caravels or sailboats called

la Niña, la Pinta and Santa Maria, about 120 sailors and provisions for three months and thus undertake the journey.

Following the route to the ocean to sail the Atlantic Ocean, the Spaniards under Christopher Columbus, who apparently suspected that the land was round, arrived on the continent that Columbus assumed was India, to a small island called Guanahani, which Columbus named San Salvador, in present-day Bahamas on October 12, 1492. But as Columbus believed he had arrived in India, he called the natives Indians, when in fact he had reached a new continent. In fact, Columbus, it is believed, never got to know that he had discovered America.

Before the arrival of Europeans in America, many cultures already existed on the continent, among which were the inhabitants of the areas of Guatemala Mexico and Peru. They were the Mayan, the Aztecs, and the Incas.

At the end of 1492; the year of discovery, on December 24, Columbus and his group had settled on an island that Columbus called Hispaniola, between present-day Santo Domingo and Haiti. In January 1493 Columbus and his people returned to Spain and informed the Catholic kings of their journey. After his first voyage, Columbus made three more trips in 1493, 1498 and 1502.

With the arrival of Columbus to the new continent begins the conquest of America with Spain and Portugal at the head, followed later by the English, Dutch and French. The Spanish and Portuguese divided the lands of the southern part of the continent: the Spaniards took the western part, and the Portuguese took the eastern part.

Later, after Columbus, the Spaniards had two other important campaigns with Hernan Cortes and Francisco Pizarro in the conquest of the territory of the Aztecs in Mexico and the territory of the Incas in Peru, respectively.

After Columbus's travels, there were other travelers engaged in exploration and discovery. One of them was

Amerigo Vespucci, a cosmographer of Italian origin and naturalized in Spain, who made a couple of exploration trips to the territory where Columbus had arrived. Vespucci realized that this territory was not India, as Columbus had believed, but rather was a new continent. Later, a German geographer and cartographer published a map of the new continent in 1507 under the name of America in honor of Amerigo Vespucci. Another of these travelers was Alvarez de Cabral, who in 1500 discovered Brazil; Vasco Nunez de Balboa, who, in 1513; crossed Panama and discovered the Pacific Ocean; Juan Díaz de Solis, who, in 1516, discovered the Rio de la Plata; Fernando de Magallanes, who in 1520 discovered the Strait of Magellan, in which it was the first expedition to go around the world.

The Spaniards after subduing the Native Americans, imposed their culture, their language, their customs, and Christianity as a religion. They also took some of their gold, which is believed to make up half of the world's gold today. Over time, these peoples disappeared as original cultures. A large number of these natives died from diseases transmitted by Europeans. And to replace the labor of the natives, the Europeans brought millions of Africans to work in America as slaves.

After the European conquest of Central and South America, the first travelers to explore the territories of North America were the English with Juan Cabot, who under the English flag, between 1526 and 1529 discovered the coasts of Labrador and the island of Newfoundland in Canada in North America, which formed the basis of English colonization. Another of those European travelers to explore North America was Jacques Cartier, a French navigator and explorer who made three trips to North America in the service of the French crown and who in 1534 discovered the Gulf and San Lorenzo River in Canada, which was the first attempt at French colonization.

Later, in 1583 Queen Elizabeth I of England authorized the pirate Walter Raleigh to found a colony north of Spanish Florida in the United States, which would be Virginia, from which the other colonies would emerge. By 1733 the British had formed thirteen colonies in the United States along the Atlantic coast, from New Hampshire in the north, to Georgia in the south. The French, on the other hand, controlled Canada, and Louisiana in the United States.

Direct control of Europe in America began to decline on 4 July 1776 with the declaration of Independence of the United States to the British crown, an example that was then followed by the rest of the colonies of the continent.

3

WRITING AND SCIENCE

The Neolithic Revolution generated, from the region of the Fertile Crescent, the necessary push for settlements to achieve this great development towards prosperity to become the first towns and later in the first cities, living in an organized community and governing by their own laws and with central governments for the common good. The progress of the Neolithic Revolution would lead man into the invention of writing and the development of science.

With writing, one of the most fascinating inventions of human intellect, crucial changes were introduced in culture and society to give rise to civilization, which is the highest level of development that a society can achieve at a time of its evolution. With writing, prehistory ends, and the history of humanity begins. Thanks to the advent of writing and the progress of the Neolithic Revolution, humanity has been able to write its own history and give rise to early civilizations.

The invention of writing would take a long way. With the new economic model established by agriculture and breeding during the Neolithic Revolution trade developed. This meant keeping track of commercial transactions such as: knowing how many agricultural products and animals were held, how many were exchanged or sold, and how many were available in the hands of the owner, so he could count on to continue the operations of his business.

It felt the need to record commercial transactions in some way. This need led to the invention of writing in Uruk, in the Sumer region south of Mesopotamia about 5.3 thousand years ago. It can be seen that the origin of the writing is closely linked to the need to record business transactions. Then over the years, the writing evolved to this day: from Sumerian writing to Egyptian writing, and then to Indian, Chinese, and other types of writing until the invention of the alphabet.

As for science, we have been able to observe that since the origins of humanity our species has always been in the search, with great interest, of knowledge, which is that set of information about things, acquired through experience and research with their respective analyses. And to achieve it, humanity was developing a set of techniques and methods, which would later be called science. Science has its origins in prehistory and was established as such during the civilizations of the Neolithic period. Science includes a systematized set of knowledge about a particular subject matter, its experimentation, the explanation of its principles and its causes.

3.1 WRITING

Writing originated from the prehistoric man's need to record his business transactions. But before recording the transactions, the prehistoric man must have learned to count.

We can see then that before felling the need to write, the man of prehistory had first felt the need to count. Activity that he was able to learn, for perhaps, before developing the spoken language, he had already been able to observe and distinguish in the world around him, between a tree and a forest, a stone and a mountain of stones, an animal and a herd of animals, a star and a set of stars.

In other words, he soon drew the distinction between unity and plurality. From these simple and rudimentary observations, primitive man gradually obtained the idea of comparison and association of an object or a thing with a collection of objects or things.

Later, he established the notion of what a "pair" is as he watched on his body and that of other animals, his two feet, his two hands, his two eyes, etc. But perhaps the most surprising thing still was that he had also understood that the Sun always appeared every day and then hid and then went out on the same side again the next day. That is, primitive man had understood the notion of a cycle. This cycle is the solar day and with it, he had established the notion of time and could count the days as well.

There is evidence that primitive man 37,000 years ago already counted the days and had determined his lunar calendar from 29 to 30 days. As you can see in the Lebombo bone found in the Lebombo Range, in Africa more than 35 thousand years ago. This bone is a tool made from the fibula bone of a baboon monkey on which 29 scratches or notches were inserted. By the number of notches, it is believed that the bone was used to mark the days of a lunar month or perhaps also to mark the woman's menstrual cycle.

Man was driven to quantify the things of the world around him primarily to determine how many things he had: such as how many were the members of his family, clan or tribe, as well as knowing how many animals he had hunted. But even better, the count of the days led him to know which days were most favorable for hunting, one of the most important activities to get his livelihood.

Given the importance of counting, primitive man needed to develop a method to do so. At first men would start counting using stones, other small objects, and their fingers. The last counted object was the total or sum of all counted objects. So far, a great achievement had been made in learning to count. However, the next challenge would be to preserve that information over time. Initially, the man-made marks on a piece of stick, stone, or bone. He put a streak for every object counted and so he was always going to have the account information. In the same way it could also tie a knot in a rope for each counted object and thus have the information of the total counted.

Of course, if the number of objects was very large, a more practical method was needed for the account. The solution was achieved by creating a mark or symbol that represented a certain number of objects. For example, as the hand was usually held and as they could count to ten, then they would create a mark that would equal 10 objects in addition to the mark of each object counted as the unit.

Previously, counting 10 meant putting 10 marks of the unit, which could be a simple vertical slash. Now counting 10 was represented with a single mark of 10. To represent the 13; would be the mark of ten plus 3 units. These marks would be called numbers later. The vertical slash remains the number one representing the unit.

The new economic model established by agriculture and breeding during the well-known Neolithic Revolution in the Fertile Crescent about 10 thousand years ago, resulted in the development of trade. This involved counting crop products and herds to keep track of man's business transactions with his products. This allowed him to know how many agricultural products and or how many animals they had, how many were exchanged or sold, and how many were available in the hands of the owner so he could count on to continue the operations of his commercial activity.

It was then about keeping records of those business transactions. In this sense, the merchants in the city of Uruk, in Sumer, Mesopotamia in the Fertile Crescent began to mark the clay vessels of their products with a cylindrical seal, developed by them, which was a small stone roller with a relief that was marked repetitively when rolled on the clay still wet from the container of the products.

At first these seals contained nothing more than the property mark or the name of the shipper of the goods. Then, the number of products shipped began to be included, but without any sign indicating the nature of the products themselves. To overcome this limitation, they began to include drawings of the products and replace the seals with written signs.

Another important fact that occurred in the evolution of such records was that very soon they discovered that it was not necessary to make the marks on the containers, but that they could be done by marking clay tablets separately on both sides and thus keeping them as records.

On one side of the tablet, the name of the producer or sender could be marked, and on the other side of the table, could be marked the description or drawing, or the symbol of the product, and its quantity. These tablets were the first labels issued by the Sumerians. They depicted with drawings agricultural products such as wheat, barley, etc. And animals like cow, ox, etc. A number was added to these drawings indicating the quantity of the product. These simple forms of Sumerian registers constitute the first labels, which were tied with a rope to the product container.

Over time, these drawings became more complex until, in the face of the need to expand the possibilities of expression, they were derived into what would later be called pictograms or drawings to represent objects and thus transmit some written message. Thus, the sign to represent a cow resembled the head of a cow, the sign for wheat resembled a wheat spike and the sign for the day was a pictography of the Sun coming out of the horizon. These pictograms were the first steps towards writing in the Fertile Crescent, specifically in Sumer, Mesopotamia about 5.3 thousand years ago.

The development of writing in the world has been one of the greatest inventions of humanity since it has allowed us not only to achieve communication in written form but has also enabled them to capture fundamental facts of vital importance over the years for the human being.

3.2 THE FIRST WRITING SYSTEMS

After its invention, writing has gone through a long evolutionary process. Since its origin in Uruk, Mesopotamia many have been the contributions that different civilizations have made to the writing among which we include the contribution made by the Sumerians themselves, the Egyptians, the Indians, the Chinese, and the Phoenicians with the alphabet.

The Sumerian Writing

The use of drawings or pictograms used in Uruk in Sumer, Mesopotamia to transmit messages gave rise to Sumerian writing, in which, a drawing or pictogram of what was meant, represented just that: the object. For this reason, it was initially called *Pictographic* Writing.

Afterwards, the scribes, the people in charge of writing and interpreting the reading, improved this graphic system by using stylized images or metaphors to indicate concepts, this is what is known as ideograms and resulted in *Ideographic Writing*. For example, a sign representing a sun could also indicate the day.

When the Sumerians began to name the signs that represented things or ideas, they created a sound for each sign, giving rise to phonograms. Then they combined these signs and formed words, which they pronounced according to the sound of each sign. The use of phonograms was a significant and decisive advance, as the *Phonetic Writing* later appeared.

In the centuries that followed the Sumerians came to possess a writing capable of translating not only the images and concepts, but also sounds, represented by signs or incisions in the form of a wedge, which gave rise to *Cuneiform Writing* some 5,300 years ago. In this way, writing in addition to recording commercial transactions also allowed to preserve the thoughts and experiences of humans.

The writing was made on wet clay tablets that were then cooked to harden. To write they used a rod with an oblique cut, which represented one of the first styles or styluses used. These styles could be of different types of signs. The clay tablet was about 4 x 4 cm in size, which they held in the palm of their hand. But over time, the scribes preferred to use larger tablets that they had to hold with their forearm. In this way it changed the orientation of the signs and was written in horizontal lines, from left to right.

In conclusion, we can then say that the tablets of Uruk, in Sumer, Mesopotamia represent the beginning of the writing. The inscriptions on these old tablets consisted of brief business or accounting records. We can also say that the driving force for the continuous development of Sumerian writing was based on the demands of economics and public administration.

With increased productivity in the region, as a result of the development of new canal and irrigation systems to improve agriculture and breeding; excess accumulated agricultural production had to be conserved in deposits and silos in newly formed cities; which required accounting of the products that were produced and those that were sold and thus better manage the land and its products.

There was then a great need to record the trading accounts generated by the large number of transactions that were carried out due to the rise of domestic trade and also the external between distant lands. All those transactions needed to be recorded. Writing also served as a tax administration tool for Sumerians to record the tax that government authorities had imposed on the community.

Some 400 years later, after their respective adjustments, the Sumerians had an authentic form of writing: the cuneiform writing, in which each word was represented with a sign that, although at first it could have been a representation of its meaning, the practice had reduced it to a set of wedge marks.

Writing was then a rather complex technique, as the Sumerians had a sign for each word, which meant a huge inventory of signs that only priests mastered. This provided much power to the priestly class.

In the Sumerian language the words were mostly monosyllabic, meaning that each word represented a syllable, and the sentences were formed by joining words, so that many of them acted as prefixes and suffixes of others. However, cuneiform writing continued to have its limitations, which were overcome with the evolution of writing towards the syllabic system.

For example, drawing a cow's head to represent a cow made sense, but how to represent something about the cow, such as that cow was alive or dead? To communicate these things as efficiently as possible, it was necessary more than just drawing images or signs. They had to express ideas. That is, the writer had to be able to record the spoken language. To this end, the scribes used signs to represent syllables instead of words, giving rise to the syllabary, which in turn was later replaced by the invention of the alphabet some 1,500 years later, when letters were represented instead of syllables.

Some thousand years later, despite its limitations, writing at the time served many functions. It was used to make accounting, commercial, religious, literary, scientific, and other documents. About literary documents, the Sumerian script allowed the writing of literary texts such as myths, epics, fables, and even poems such as the epic Sumerian poem Gilgamesh, written with cuneiform writing on 12 clay tablets.

With cuneiform writing, documents such as letters, narratives, business contracts, memos, manuals for important activities, religious and scientific records were written in Mesopotamia. Texts on scientist aspects related to medicine, astronomy and mathematics were also written.

The collection and storage of written documents by the authorities led to the emergence of libraries, in which it could also see other types of documents also written on clays with the meanings of the words of the Sumerian language. These documents are so-called dictionaries.

The Sumerian language is the oldest known written language. Given the urban, social, and commercial development of the region, the Sumerian cuneiform writing expanded rapidly throughout Mesopotamia. Over time, the writing was adopted by other towns on the way to civilization such as the Akkadians, Hittites, and Persians.

It is important to note that while in Sumer, Mesopotamia developed cuneiform writing about 5,300 years ago, around the same time, some 1,600 km away, in Egypt, about 5,100 years ago another type of writing was also developed. And later, writing began to appear also elsewhere such as the Indo Valley and China.

The Egyptian Writing

The writing that developed in Egypt almost the same time as in Sumer, was the so-called *Hieroglyphic* writing, which was initially composed of about 700 hieroglyphics. These hieroglyphics are symbols or figures for reproducing words and could be engraved in stone, carved in wood, or later written with ink on *papyri* or *ostracon*. The papyrus was a support of hieroglyphic writing consisting of a kind of sheet of paper or foil obtained from the stem of the papyrus plant that was used by the Egyptians to write on it. The papyrus plant grows in the Nile River area. This kind of papyrus paper was obtained by soaking the stem of the papyrus for a couple of weeks and then cut into very thin strips and pressed with a roller to remove some of the liquids they contained. Then the strips were placed horizontally and vertically on a flat surface and pressed again so that the sap left in the strips would stick them together. Finally, the foil was rubbed with a firm object with a soft surface to leave it ready for use. The writing was always done on the face with the horizontal strips exposed, on the other side it was rarely written.

To make a papyrus roll, they stick these sheets together. At the end of the writing, another piece of papyrus foil was stuck to the roll to name the work. These rolls could be about 20 sheets with a size of 5 meters long on average. However, a 42-meter papyrus roll has been found, the largest known. This scroll deals with religious and historical themes during the Ramesses period and is written with hieratic writing. These works written on the papyrus scrolls were read holding the scroll with the right hand, while it was unwrapped with the left hand, in which once read the scroll was rolled again. The writings on these rolls were stored in cases made of parchment.

To write with ink on the papyrus they used a kind of brush or calamus, which was a hollow reed, cut obliquely at its end. The calamus was obtained from the stem of a cane plant or a bird feather such as ducks, turkeys, and swans. In fact, the hollow part of the pen that is inserted into the bird's skin is called a calamus.

The ostraca were fragments of clay or ceramic vessels on which some writings were made. Hieroglyphic writing was written in both rows and columns, almost always framing symbols. For example, if they wrote the name of a god or king, they put it first and placed the rest of the signs based on this name. One of the first examples of hieroglyphic writing was Narmer's palette, about 5,000 years ago.

Hieroglyphic writing is a kind of sacred scripture, used in temples, tombs and monuments. Egyptian hieroglyphic writing was a highly organized writing system that was used for more than 3,600 years. It later became *the hieratic writing,* which was a type of italic writing used to write letters. Hieratic writing was faster because it was a kind of shorthand of hieroglyphics, widely used among priests to express themselves quickly when the drawing was not used, each hieroglyphics had its corresponding hieratic abbreviation, dominating the phonetic element and writing from right to left. The hieratic writing was simpler than hieroglyphic writing and was for a long time used throughout the Pharaonic period to write, with calamus and ink on papyrus, administrative documents, accounting, legal, letters, scientific documents, and religious documents. Around the year 860 hieratic writing becomes the *demotic* or popular writing, which consisted of signs taken from the hieratic, with almost complete exclusion from hieroglyphics, becoming in a short time the dominant writing of Ancient Egypt and was written in stones and wood, as well as papyri with calamus and ink. This type of writing was italic and was used for all kinds of documents, although religious documents continued to be made with hieroglyphics. Hieroglyphic writing was used for monumental inscriptions, where only priests and scribes knew its meaning. In this hieroglyphic writing there were about 24 alphabetic signs equivalent to loosen letters or complete words separated from a single consonant, 136 syllabic signs, but next to these were more than 3 thousand figures much more complicated. The demotic writing disappeared over time and replaced with the Greek language.

Egyptian writing has been understood since the 19th century of our era, after the Frenchman Jean-François Champollion in 1822 deciphered the inscriptions recorded in 196 BC in a basalt stone found in the city of Rosetta, Egypt, in the Nile Delta, near Alexandria in 1799 and brought by English troops to the British museum. This stone contained the same text engraved in three different alphabets: hieroglyphics, demotic and Greek. Champollion was able to decipher hieroglyphics as he could read the Greek language and by deduction, he was able to come to the meaning of the writing in the other two languages.

The Indian Writing

As for the writing of India or the writing of the Indo, also called the proto-Indian language, it is important to indicate that this writing could not be legitimized as such, because it does not appear in the sites excavated until now. This writing was what it is supposedly developed at the beginning of

Indian civilization, in the first towns of Harappa and Mohenjo-Daro.

The Chinese Writing

The Chinese writing is estimated that it is more than 3 thousand years old. This writing system is based on three basic elements: pictograms, ideograms, and phonograms. It has a kind of alphabet with thousands of characters, which were drawn in wooden or bamboo tablets until the invention of paper by the Chinese in 150 BC. On the paper, made of the pulp of tree fibers, they used ink and brush to write documents and books.

The Alphabet

The great contribution to writing was the development of the alphabet by the Phoenicians more than 3 thousand years ago. The Phoenicians were a town of sailors and merchants who lived in what is now Lebanon, and who by then had an alphabet. This consisted of only 22 consonant signs, so the writing was greatly simplified. They were signs of purely phonetic value and allowed any word to be written.

The Phoenicians spread the alphabet throughout the Mediterranean and many towns adopted it and made some modifications to it. For example, the Greeks added the vowel signs to it. The Etruscans bequeathed it to the Romans, and they propagated it among the towns of their empire.

The other important factor in the evolution of writing is obtained from the Greeks about 800 BC. Greek culture introduced alphabetical writing, which is what is currently used, with some variations, of course. This writing consisted of a 24-letter alphabet, coming from the Phoenicians.

The invention of the scroll in the West was also important for writing. The parchment has been in use since 1500 BC. Its name comes from Pergamon, a Greek city. In this city is where a high-quality material was produced to make scrolls. It was used a lot, in many years. But it was not, until 200 BC, that the parchment began to replace the Egyptian papyrus. The parchment is usually made of sheepskin, to achieve a smooth surface.

3.3 SCIENCE

As human beings carried out activities to achieve their livelihood, they accumulated knowledge about how to do things. The first thing to learn was to collect wild fruits and take some animals. Eventually they learned to make containers to load their fruits and then by incorporating meat into their daily diet to continue surviving, they invented hunting. To do their hunting they needed tools and made them of sticks, bones, and stones. These human beings were the Homo Habilis, who began to accumulate knowledge.

Then, the successor to the Homo Habilis, the Homo Erectus with his development of group life, introduced hunting technology. In addition, he invented fishing nets and was the great master of fire. Homo Erectus lived in groups on the banks of the rivers where they obtained some supply of water and food, but during the glaciations they had to take refuge in caves to protect themselves from the cold and make the necessary changes to survive, because these ancestors of ours were very organized.

However, Homo Erectus evolved about 200 thousand years ago in Homo Sapiens, who had well developed language, which allowed to transmit knowledge from one generation to another. Some 40 thousand years ago, Homo Sapiens had perfected the manufacture of weapons and tools, thus entering the Upper Paleolithic by developing rock art to boost its culture.

During the Neolithic period, Homo Sapiens discovered the agriculture with which arose the knowledge of plants, fruits, soils, ploughing, and irrigation. As for plants and fruits, our ancestors came to know the plants from which they could eat their fruits and those that did not. They differentiated edible plants from poisonous ones. Of the edible plants they managed to gain extensive knowledge of them. Over time they also came to discover medicinal plants. As for soils and ploughing, farmers were able to obtain an accumulation of knowledge giving rise to the development of agronomy. In terms of levees, dams and irrigation channels, engineering would also emerge. In Sumer agriculture became systematized and developed on a large scale with advances in agricultural and irrigation techniques. Large irrigation systems were implemented.

Later, the irrigation system also included equipment to draw water from a river, canal or well to irrigate crops and for domestic consumption as well. In addition, plowing emerged as an evolution of the weed to sow the seeds. With the appearance of the wheel in Sumer, it was also adapted to the plow to improve its handling and efficiency. Plowing was an instrument of a breakthrough for agriculture. It made the field work easier and was one of the first man-made sophisticated instruments.

With the knowledge that human beings were acquiring about the workings of things, science began to emerge. Thus, with the knowledge gained from the observation of the cosmos arose astronomy, with the knowledge of the plants arose agronomy, with the knowledge to make levees and irrigation system came engineering, with the knowledge to make bricks and buildings, came construction and architecture, and with the knowledge of metals arose metallurgical, and so on to develop a wide range of disciplines. Science developed in being abstract thought. As people carried out the activities to meet their needs and that of their environment, they also accumulated knowledge to which their respective technical rules were applied.

Science in ancient times arose in Mesopotamia, then came to Egypt and eventually passed on to the Greeks, who established the concept of science to encompass all kinds of knowledge. The Greeks then transmitted science to the Western world, where in the sixteenth century of our era, the science of antiquity came to an end when Galileo Galilei the great Italian scientist demonstrated that, if two stones of different weight were dropped simultaneously, the two would reach the ground at the same time. This experiment gave way to classical science, which clarified the relationships between people and things in the visible world, thus emerging a stage of changes in the human mind.

Modern science began in the early 19th century with discoveries such as X-rays, electron, and radioactivity. With the theory of relativity and quantum mechanics, a whole new world was shown, to which our senses are not in the ability to see or feel it. Modern science made it possible to understand the atom, the sun, and the stars. It changed many of the parameters used by humanity until then. We started talking about the speed of light and nuclear fusion. With modern science, biology also experienced great progress, as it was to cover subjects of matter initially visible to deal with matter at the cellular level and now studies vital processes at incredibly small molecular dimensions.

Science is now defined as all knowledge consisting of principles and laws that derive from the observation and reasoning of a cluster of information and data, which are systematically structured for understanding. Science encompasses several fields of knowledge and study, in which scientific theories and methods are developed, after which objective and verifiable conclusions can be drawn.

Astrology and astronomy closely related in prehistory arose from the observations of our ancestors. However, the former was based only on beliefs. While the second, it did turn out as science. Astronomy resulted from observations made by early farmers in establishing a cause-and-effect relationship between the seasons and the pace of harvests. Observation of the behavior of nature and plants allowed to know the edibles and those that were not, as well as medicinal plants, which would later lead to the birth of medicine.

The importance of celestial bodies in the behavior of nature on Earth led people to the study of cycles, which resulted in the lunar calendar in Mesopotamia and the solar calendar in Egypt. To continue with the knowledge development, sometime later, urban cultures established a set of calculations, weights, and measures.

With writing comes literature with its early classical works: "The Book of The Dead", "Gilgamesh's Epic" and the "Bible". These works establish man's passion for his transcendence and his relationship with his god. However, science began with the first observations that our ancestors would make from the cosmos in ancient times.

3.4   FIRST OBSERVATIONS

Human beings have always been intrigued by the cosmos: that great order that exists among all the components of the universe. And of course, they tried to find explanations for the things they saw, but they always ended up with more questions, as they believed that the heavens exerted supernatural influence over life on Earth.

However, our ancestors made their maps with figures in the sky and transmitted them to us intact as the constellations of the zodiac with astral signs, which could exert a mystical influence on our lives. Faced with the supreme of the universe, the human beings began to feel fears about the influence of the universe and began to weave their conjectures on it. It was thought the full moon would bring chaos to Earth. People were panicked by the alignment of celestial bodies or eclipses, among which the moon and the solar are the most frequent. It was believed that strange situations like these could exert some force or influence on the Earth.

The human being has been observing the heavens of the cosmos in antiquity, since the dawn of history, trying to decipher so much mystery, as the appearance and disappearance cycles of the Sun with its light and heat, the Moon appearing in the cold and dark nights and the brightness of the distant stars showing before his eyes. For prehistoric humans, anything explained by the primitive science of that time was taken as a result of the supernatural, usually as a divine force. This way of perceiving the sky gave rise to the superstitions.

Our superstitions and supernatural connections between heaven and Earth are rooted in ancient celestial events. But the human beings who feed superstitions condemn themselves to live in a world of concerns. Although sometimes they try to seek some explanation, but do not always use logical thinking and fall into more superstitions and false beliefs that can later limit their ability to think logically. Attributing to the heavens the guilt of how bad it happens on earth. They even come to blame the heavens or their gods for their misery.

The events of the sky that most caused people terror were eclipses, which are the result of cosmic alignments when the Sun, Moon and Earth are precisely in line. A total solar eclipse results when the Moon stands between Earth and the Sun. This is a spectacular event. The sun seems to disappear from the heavens. To witness one of these events is to experience an extraordinary feeling.

Lunar cycles have long generated all sorts of strange beliefs, especially stories about the full moon. Once again it is the human mind that seems to be programmed to make an order from the world of the chaos of heaven. It is said that the full moon induces strange behaviors about humans and our brains want to seek some explanation, but they do not always use logical thinking and fall into superstitions and false beliefs. Other heavenly disaster carriers were comets with their trails crossing the skies. Fear of comets as disaster carriers is a recurring theme throughout history.

Stars, however, were perceived a little differently. The Egyptians searched the stars for signs of well-being and prosperity. They managed to identify one of these stars and called it Sothis or Sirius as we know it today. And they would ask their gods looking up to the sky that the Nile would bring enough water to fertilize their land and thus secure good crops. Today, some poor people in the Third World still ask their god to send them food from heaven and wait. After some time, what turns out is a huge frustration, causing them to lose even their faith.

From his first observations in the heavens, man has always been intrigued by the Sun. The sense of admiration of primitive man for the powers of the Sun has naturally led him to believe in it as his god. As we can see in different forms of this manifestation left by ancient cultures. Our ancestors began to weave all the countless legends we still hear today about the Sun, Earth, Moon, and Stars.

The admiration of the sun god would continue later when Pharaoh Akhenaten, around 1,400 BC, embarked on a struggle with the priests of the time claiming that he had a direct alliance with the mighty sun gods of Egypt. Akhenaten was a threat to the established priesthood by trying to place it as a direct alliance with the Sun. Akhenaten proclaimed the sun god as all powerful and forbade the worship of any other god. Since then in Egypt the Sun god was called Aton, for the name of Pharaoh Akhenaten meant friend of the Sun. Akhenaten closed all temples that did not pay tribute to Aton and removed all the names of the other gods from public buildings. Influenced by priests, people resisted changing their beliefs in their other gods.

After Akhenaten's death the old gods were restored when the new Pharaoh, a boy of only 9 years old came to the throne. His real name was Tutankhamun in honor of the Sun, but with the problem of the former pharaoh his father, the young king for his love of the god Amon became Tutankhamun. The most famous of the Egyptian kings in history. But for the ancient Egyptians the Sun was more than an object to worship and to the foundation of religious sects. The Sun provided people with the basis of understanding of the seasons and then would also create the basis for religion. A legacy that is still with us today.

Our ancestors had begun the process of observing the cosmos carefully, thoughtfully, and systematically during the stone age. Observing the heavens before they were able to start recording the facts. The first thing they observed was the power of the Sun. Some came to believe that the Sun had to be flattered to reappear after the cold, dark night. And as a natural step for our ancestors, who had very little knowledge of science, they began to attribute supernatural answers to the most basic questions about nature. But they were sure of something and very convinced: the enormous power of the Sun, which gave them life and while lighting they could obtain food and defend themselves from other predators. The period of light is what we know as day and the period of darkness as night. These would be, after observing the great power of the Sun, their first astronomical observations: day and night, with which they later developed the concept of the week.

The Day and The Night

For primitive man, the Sun was supreme. His recurring cycle of light and darkness formed the basis of the first principle of organization of our natural world: day and night. This was the first astronomical observation and man's first attempt to explain what was going on down here as he observes what was going on up there. And so, the primitive man began to seek his connections with the heavens and the earth. The Sun also provides the most basic and natural daily clock. So, they used in Egypt the first sundial. As early as 1724 India had created the world's largest sundial, with precision of 20 seconds. Sundials were used until a century ago when they were replaced by modern clocks. However, it seems that the human body is always in tune with the daily rhythm of the sun clock cycles. In addition to the day and night cycles, in ancient times they had also invented the concept of week.

The Week

Ancient men also observed the 5 celestial bodies visible to the naked eye that twinkled in the night sky. The Sun and Moon served the ancient man of inspiration to develop his ideas. The Babylonian gained from their observations to celestial bodies, such as the planets, the Sun and the Moon; the inspiration for the next division of the natural order: the

7 days a week. Then the Greeks continued the work. Using the 24-hour Egyptian notion in one day, it occurred to the Greeks that every day it was ruled by a planet. And as a result of this new order we have: Sun, Moon, Tuesday, Mercury, Jupiter, Venus, and Saturn. After a combination of languages and mythological influences, the days of the modern week were formed: Sunday, Monday, Tuesday, Wednesday, Thursday, Friday, and Saturday. After the week, they concentrated on the month.

The Month

The next challenge of our ancestors was not in the Sun but in another celestial body: the Moon. They came to determine the cycles of the moon between 29 and 30 days. The 30-day period we use today is the month, which is derived from the moon's name. By adding all these cycles, they got the year.

The Year

Grouping all these cycles, days, weeks, and months we have as a result the year. Our ancestors were also able to determine the seasons of the year, which served as guides for their crops. And to have all the information of all these periods, they developed the calendar.

The Calendar

In ancient times, the Sun was a source of scientific study in early cultures, in addition to its religious part. In Egypt, they had already devoted to the study of the movements of the Sun. The Egyptians knew it would take the Sun about 360 days to complete a full lap. By then they had divided the circle into 360 degrees. Each degree representing the distance traveled by the Sun, on the background of those of the stars in a day. Moreover, the ancient Egyptians were well aware that the actual year was 365 days and not 360. And to further complicate the thing, they also used a 12-month calendar of 30 days each. And when adding everything up nothing matched, they decided to take 360 as their official year and ignore the other 5 days.

Through the ancient Greeks, and then the Romans, modern Western cultures inherited Egyptian and Mesopotamian calendar and astronomy. But even the 365-day year was not perfect either. To be, it should have 365 days plus a quarter of a day or 6 hours. Every year a quarter of a day was lost. The Romans developed a calendar in which every four years an extra day would be added to the year to recover the quarter of a day lost per year. In doing so, it arose the leap year. This calendar worked well until the 16th century when the seasons of the year were misaligned again. Finally, the cycle of the Sun's seasons gave the world a simple and unified calendar after 32 and a half years.

3.5 FIRST OBSERVATORIES

The Sun offers the fundamental principle of organization of the modern world. Ancient civilizations created monuments with an incredible ability to accurately track the cycles of the Sun's seasons. Among these early observatories we have Newgrange and Stonehenge.

Newgrange was the largest prehistoric monument built in Ireland, Europe around 3,200 BC, before the pyramids of Egypt. This was the most striking ancient work built on the surface of the Earth. It consists of a group of burial mounds designed and built to mark the shortest day of the year; the winter solstice, when the days begin to get longer and hotter, which indicated to primitive farmers when it would be time to plant again. Newgrange was an immense circular tomb about 250 feet wide with a long passageway made of stone that stretched from the entrance to the large, vaulted chamber where the ancient bones of its dead were preserved. Above the entrance is a rectangular stone box, which was a tomb aligned so that a flash of light from the rising Sun on the winter solstice would enter the box, travel through the stone passageway, and illuminate the back of the camera wall. It is likely that Newgrange also had a religious or ceremonial significance.

Hundreds of miles from Newgrange, on the Salisbury Plains in southern England is the Stonehenge Monument built in 2,500 BC, some 700 years after the Newgrange. Stonehenge is perhaps the best-known solar observatory in the ancient world. When these huge solid rocks were erected in place, the Egyptians were only beginning to build their pyramids and yet the extraordinary structure of the Stonehenge was able to accurately trace the cycles of the Sun, Moon and stars, suggesting a great understanding of the cosmos far from the primitive. Stonehenge aligns with birth and sunset. On the summer solstice on the longest day of the year, the Sun is born on the marker known as the heel stone. In mid-winter it is placed directly at the opposite end of the monument. In all these monuments from the Newgrange, Stonehenge, to the pyramids, the worship of the sun god continues to bring the testament of the power of heaven on earth: the worship of the Sun.

With the flourishing of civilization, the Egyptians had inherited their understanding of the heavens, from the oldest Mesopotamia civilization. With this knowledge, the Egyptians were among the first to make their maps of the night sky and engrave them on the stone. They managed to sculpt in the stone the zodiac that had originally been invented in Mesopotamia and passed through the ancient Egyptians to modern days.

It is important to note that Mesopotamia was a stoneless land, in which the first clay bricks were made as those still used today. With these bricks were built the first towns with large monuments in the form of pyramids called Ziggurats, which were also used as observatories.

It was at these Mesopotamian observatories that man first tried to track the stars in the firmament, it was there that the two great paths of understanding the heavens began to emerge: the science of astronomy and the belief of astrology. It was also the Mesopotamians who imagined patterns and designs of the star-filled night skies. Thus, they filled the heavens with all kinds of creatures and characters. Some mythology and some others of real life. These patterns and designs were passed down from generation to generation and are still maintained today.

Then came the so-called signs of the zodiac of the modern world. These formed bands around the sky through which the Sun, moon, and planets passed on their journey through the firmament. Modern astrology has its roots in the belief that originated in the ancient world. Thus, came ideas such as that if someone was born when the Sun appeared to be in front of a sign of a particular star, that person was born under the influence of that sign.

Today astrology can be explained as a cosmic illusion. Every day in its orbit around the Sun, the Earth moves a little further into space, creating the effect of the Sun moving a little towards the stars in the background. Mesopotamians also noticed 5 particularly bright stars that seemed to move towards the bottom of the zodiac constellations. Today we know that these were the 5 planets visible with bare eye.

4

WEALTH AND POWER

During the beginning of prehistory, some 2.5 million years ago, in the Early Paleolithic period, humans were nomadic as their ancestors and lived off the harvesting of wild fruits and some animals they ate. This was a job with which they got their livelihood. Since then work has become their *capital* to survive. Everything we acquire in life will be based on this basic principle. To achieve a better life, we will still strive for more profit. The accumulation of profits would give rise to wealth. By that time, the fruit of his work was only the worker's.

The human is a social being, like the animals from which he evolved, so he has generally always needed other humans, not only to feel better, but also to do better the things he needs in order to survive. As a group they can do a better job by helping each other and at the end they will have a higher production, with more profit and more wealth. We see how the being with his work managed to get his daily livelihood and working in groups all managed to get their livelihood as well. Which stimulated both the individual and the group. Wealth was then distributed among the members of the group.

Later, during the beginning of the Neolithic, some 12 thousand years ago after glaciation, came the discovery of agriculture with which trade and wealth would later arise, which is linked to the abundance of things of value as goods or money.

With the rise of civilization in Mesopotamia, economic activities had increased, making some families richer than others thanks to trade among the inhabitants of the towns. At some point, one of these families would take control of the town, becoming the economic power and authority of the town with the support of the church. Then the authority of the town created the first local institutions such as the council of the elders and the first assembly formed by the important people of the town. So that power was constituted by the religious, political, military, and judicial sectors. However, religious power was closely linked to the other powers.

Later when the towns became cities with larger economies, the first kingdoms emerged with kings considered gods with absolute power over all aspects of society with the support of the council of elders and assembly. With the kingdoms came the wars and the formation of armies to defend against invasions. Then the culture of war appeared, used to conquer lands and form empires.

After originating and being configured in early civilizations, power and its structures spread into the Western world. In Greece in the city of Athens arose the democracy with which power first passes from kings to the hands of the people.

In this chapter we will be talking about the details of wealth, capitalism, power, religion and power, and the struggle for power.

4.1 WEALTH

With the discovery of agriculture and breeding, especially with its surplus of production, arose later trade with which, in turn, wealth began. In addition to the surplus of agriculture and breeding, property also emerged as another element that would also contribute to wealth. With the efficient use and management of resources, the economy was developed, and finance was later developed to control profits. All these practices ended in the creation of an economic system known as capitalism, the best producer of wealth.

Agriculture and Breeding

Agriculture and breeding were discovered by Homo Sapiens in the Middle East during the Neolithic Period. However, it was with the surplus of agricultural products and breeding that prosperity and wealth began.

With the surplus of agriculture, other people engaged in other activities such as breeding could be fed. So, the farmer changed part of the surplus of his crop to the shepherd for some of his animals, giving rise to the commercial exchange in the form of barter.

Subsequently, the internal organization of the first settlements became more complex. The cultivation of land and the rearing of animals could produce enough food and even with much more surplus to solve the problem of food supply. As a result, the population increased considerably, forcing humans to expand farmland extensions, introduce irrigation and establish trade with surpluses. These new economic practices, unsurprisingly, further increased the growth of the population, leading to the emergence of a new class of workers: artisans.

Once again, with the surplus of agriculture and breeding they could feed the artisans. So, the farmer traded the craftsman food for handmade products.

These new economic activities further accentuated the concept of property as the land where they planted or raised his animals. Their lands were considered by humans as part of their belongings and would be willing to protect and defend them. It was with this idea in mind that they formed villages and small towns with huts or houses very close to each other.

The Property

From the beginning of the existence of the human being there has always been the concept of property, for he from the moment he harvested the fruits of nature or taken another animal to feed himself, those fruits or animals became a property of the human being, who obtained them to meet their feeding needs. When he invented hunting, the weapons he developed to hunt were also considered his property. Sometimes, if someone else tried to snatch his resources from him, the owner would try to defend them, because he considered them his property.

Later when he discovered agriculture, it already represented a higher cost for the human being than that of making a hunting tool. In both cases, both to make the tools and to produce the fruits, the human would use his work. Now with even more reason, he would try to defend his property, because besides of the land being his property, so were the products he obtained from it, such as agricultural products or the animals he raised on his land.

With sedentary lifestyle due to the development and evolution of agriculture, ownership could be shared by family, clan, or tribes. In other words, in addition to personal property, collective property also emerged. The property can be exchanged or sold, which constitutes another element of wealth.

Trade

With agriculture during the Neolithic period, trade also emerged, which is the fundamental element of wealth. Initially trade was done through the exchange in the form of bartering of agricultural products and breeding by other local artisanal products such as basketry, pottery, ceramics, yarn, and weaving. Subsequently, emerged more complex networks of exchange of specialized goods between villages or regions, such as the obsidian and bitumen trade.

With trade also emerged the first means of transport, including wagons and navigation; as well as the manufacture of better tools to perform, maintain and protect all the activities that allowed them to achieve sustainment.

Traders were always looking forward to having more new products to market, which would appear as new techniques and technologies were developed to improve the production of existing products or to create new products.

During the Neolithic, clothing also emerged, for which techniques were developed to obtain wool and linen fibers. With the invention of the loom were made fabrics to make the clothes, which was no longer only to protect from the cold as in the Paleolithic, but by then it was given an ornamental and decorative use, with which fashion also arose.

When the clay was discovered, pottery arose and a wide variety of clay objects began to be made such as statuettes for religious purposes, containers for transporting grains and liquids, and mud bricks for the construction of houses. Later the ceramic appears with techniques to decorate it with figures and colors.

After trading in the form of barter and before the use of the money, the payment of goods with the cattle was implemented. However, it was in Mesopotamia that payment with money to obtain the goods was implemented during the metal age, based on the first pricing system using sales of various products. This would result in the emergence of the commercial and market economy, as well as finance.

With trade, means of transport by land and rivers arose. By land they used the first wagons and by rivers they used rafts. Over time, the manufacture of the first wagon pulled by animals to transport goods and people were very favored with the appearance of the wheel. While the rafts would be transformed into canoes.

The Economy

During prehistory, humans lived in groups among which they exchanged, apart from the food they collected for their livelihood, their ideas, tools, and some resources to do the things they used in their daily lives. However, realizing that their resources were limited, they would try to make better use of them. This simple observation would give rise to what we now call economics. That is what the economy is all about: using the available resources as efficiently as possible.

As we have already seen, the first activities that provided human beings with resources to be used, it was agriculture and breeding, which gave rise to another activity such as trade, with which human beings could obtain prosperity and riches. When a person traded part of his crop for an animal, he was doing an economic activity, as agriculture, breeding and trade covered the basics of the economy such as production and consumption.

The purpose of the economy is to manage the resources available to meet human needs and to avoid resource scarcity, so the economy must include good planning in any social group, which in turn requires the incorporation of the raw material production process. The orientation of the economy must always be to improve the living conditions of individuals and society.

Since its inception, the economy has continued its pace of progress. Already in ancient civilizations such as Mesopotamia, Egypt, India, China, Greece and the Roman Empire, the economy had made great progress. Plato and Aristotle in Greece excelled in the economy. Plato made a definition of an economy that included resource management and trade. Aristotle was the first analytical economist, who dealt with various economic issues, which are still maintained today, such as his economic definitions and monetary and value theories.

In the Middle Ages, the feudalist economy emerged in Europe, as well as the contributions to the economy of scholastic philosophy. The feudal system was based on the tenure of territories or fiefdoms in a society divided between lords and vassals, in which the former owned the land, and the latter were responsible for producing it. As for the contributions of scholastic philosophy to the economy, these were a series of economic regulations of agreements to religious doctrines, led by St. Thomas Aquinas.

Later, mercantilists and physiocrats stood out. The formers were characterized by favoring economic intervention, while the latter regarded agriculture as the only source of wealth for nations.

At the end of the 18th century, economics began to be widely regarded as a science, since the publication of Adam Smith's book, "The Wealth of Nations". The theories posited at that time are known as classical economics, in which economists Adam Smith and David Richard stood out with their theories of comparative advantage, the law of declining returns, and theory of income distribution.

The study of economics includes prices of goods and productive factors such as land, production, capital and technology, the behavior of financial markets, the law of supply and demand, the consequences of state intervention on society, income distribution, economic growth of countries and international trade.

The study of economics can be divided into two major areas. The macroeconomics that studies the overall functioning of the economy as an integrated set and the microeconomics that studies the economic behavior of companies, households, and individuals.

An economic system is a set of rules governing the economy of a territory. These economic systems can be of two types mainly: those that give greater power to the state as in socialism and those that attach more importance to the freedom of choice of individuals as in a republic. In socialism there is a regulation of the market, and property is in the hands of the state. In addition, companies are state-owned, prices are set by legal laws. In the republic, on the other hand, the economic system is capitalism, there is private property, there is freedom of enterprise, prices are set by the law of supply and demand, and there are competitive markets.

An economic system, as a mode of organization, is composed of a number of elements such as goods and services that meet our needs; also economic agents such as business, families and the State; and productive factors such as land, labor and capital. Each of these three elements is organized in different ways and gives rise to economic activity, which according to its nature can be part of the primary or agricultural sector, the secondary or industrial sector, or the tertiary or services sector.

Finance

After trading in the form of barter, the payment of goods with livestock was implemented. Subsequently in Mesopotamia the trade was implemented by paying with money to obtain goods. These commercial transactions were based on the first pricing system in the sale of products. This would result in the emergence of the commercial and market economy, as well as finance, the term of which still refers to the study of the movement of money between individuals, companies, or states.

Finance corresponds to a part of the economy that studies the obtaining and administration of financial resources such as money or capital for the purchase of raw materials, acquisitions of machinery and equipment, payment of wages among others to carry out production operations. Finance also studies and analyzes investment and savings of financial resources.

The rise of finance took place in the 15th century, with the rise of capitalism. During this time commercial banks began to develop by offering intermediation, lending, and savings services for the investor. Over time, in addition to banks, other financial institutions emerged with products that have evolved and modernized. By the twentieth century finances are considered as an area of study of a new discipline, which has been perfected over time with the development of theories that try to explain the optimal determination of the price of assets, the expected profitability, decisions in scenarios of uncertainty, etc.

Finance can be divided into four important groups: personal, corporate, public, and international finance. Personal finances refer to the study of obtaining and managing the resources of families or individuals for the optimal management of employment income and indebtedness, to make investment and savings decisions, and to finance a career or a profitable profession or the purchase of a car or a house. Corporate finances are oriented to the study of obtaining and managing the resources of companies to carry out their productive projects with optimal financing to be able to distribute dividends among their partners. Public finances focus on the study of obtaining and managing the financial resources of state institutions to obtain resources through taxes, invest in profitable public projects, choose optimal mechanisms for resource redistribution, and properly manage the government deficit/surplus. And finally, international finance refers to the study of international financial transactions for investment and indebtedness abroad considering the effects of exchange rate fluctuation on country profitability and risk.

Finance provides for its study, accounting, which is a resource to determine expenses and income to know the situation and condition to be able to establish the necessary strategies in order to improve the economic performance of a person or family, company or state, depending on the accounting group being used.

In finance there are a number of concepts that allow us to understand even more about the study of money and how finances are organized. These concepts include risk and profit, the value of money and the interest rate. Risk and benefit refer to the minimization of investment risk. However, the benefit may be greater at a higher risk. The value of money refers to fluctuating the value of money over time, i.e. the change that represents investing money in the present compared to the future. Devaluation and inflation are key to the concept of the value of money. The interest rate is the value that is paid for borrowed funds to financial intermediaries, which are the agents dedicated to contacting both parts of the finances, the savers and those in need of financing.

Economic agents such as individuals, families, businesses, or states should use finance to make the best decisions to invest, save and spend in uncertain conditions. To do this, agents can opt for various types of financial resources such as: money, bonds, stocks, or derivatives, including the purchase of capital goods such as machinery, buildings, and other infrastructure.

4.2 CAPITALISM

After the fall of the Western Roman Empire and the fall of Charlemagne's empire, a form of social and political organization called feudalism emerged in Europe during the 10th and 12th centuries, which consisted of a relationship that created and governed obligations of obedience and service from one part of society called the vassals and the other part called the feudal lord or owner of the fiefdom, who would give protection to the vassal in exchange for his loyalty to the feudal lord. The relationship also established that the feudal lord had all the rights of the fiefdom, while the vassal had to end up producing the fiefdom with the peasant labor and paying a portion of the production to the feudal lord. The feudal economy was based on agriculture and breeding.

Feudalism was characterized by its basic aspects such as social, political, and economic. On a social level it had a society made up of a privileged class, including royalty formed by the king and his family; the nobility where the warriors were, who also served as the vassals. Then followed by the unprivileged class made up of peasants. At the political level, feudalism had a decentralized power, with a Catholic church having a very influential role in the power of the nobility through relationships of loyalty and protection that offered the king in exchange for noble domains and titles. And on the economic level it had an economy based on subsistence agriculture and breeding with a small trade based mainly on exchange.

The source of wealth was in the ownership of the fiefdoms, which were in the hands of the feudal lords. There was no industry, as the products were made by artisans. However, after the 11th century the trade of the Middle Ages increased thanks to the work of the merchants, who left the fiefdoms to initially sell some agricultural products and later some other artisanal products. This is how the bourgeoisie originated, which would later give way to capitalism.

Feudalism began its decline due to the depletion of farmland with the subsequent lack of food for the population, resulting in famine with a large number of deaths and to finish also appeared epidemic diseases such as pests. However, feudalism came to an end in the 14th and 15th centuries.

When a stronger commercial activity began to form and current money began to be used, then the strengthening of capitalism began and always since its inception, this economic model has been constantly evolving. Modern capitalism emerged in the second half of the 18th century, when the industrial revolution appeared and political thought was moving towards a new scheme of individual freedoms, both political and economic. The industrial revolution gave a new impetus to the economy with the massification of production and consumption. This also required the massification of jobs under a salary scheme. This is how the working or proletariat class emerged.

Today, capitalism is an economic system that is based on private ownership of the means of production, as well as on the principle of free market, whose objective is the accumulation of capital. Capitalism is therefore based on ownership of the means of production and resources, from which trade profits are extracted.

Capitalism presents free market as its basic principle. The market, according to the traditional capitalist model, is regulated by the law of supply and demand, aimed at meeting consumer needs. In this sense, competitiveness among producers is a key aspect of this economic system.

Capitalism uses capital and labor as its fundamental factors, which increase competition in the supply and demand of goods and services. Capitalism also uses the free market with minimal state participation, recognizes the right to enterprise as an individual right, so that any person or group that possesses the necessary economic resources can open a company and employ others.

Capitalism has been spreading in many parts of the world. At the end of the twentieth century one of the phenomena of capitalism was observed as globalization, which is a process of expanding economic integration driven by low prices of means of transport and communication among the countries of the world.

However, the definition of traditional capitalism may be affected by the country in which it develops, especially by the type of political system or government that the country has, especially socialist or communist systems of government. This usually ends up modifying the factors of capitalism such as the production, marketing, distribution and price of the goods and services produced. For socialism is a sociopolitical doctrine based on the ownership and collective administration of the means of production.

4.3 THE POWER

Power as the capacity, faculty or ability of one or more persons to exercise control and dominance over others living in a certain territory or political unit; it has its origin in the process of socialization of the human being, since due to our character as social beings we have always felt the need to live with other people and thus we began to form social groups from which the family would later emerge, made up of a father, a mother and children. The family then became the first nucleus of society and the need appeared to have a person in charge of directing and organizing the members of the social nucleus, who was generally the father.

Subsequently, several families were grouped into larger groups and when they began to settle, they formed the first tribes and villages and thus help each other in food collection and also to defend themselves. This constituted our first society and to lead it, it was also necessary to choose someone who took charge of the affairs of the village and who had the capacity to keep society together. This would give some power to that person, who was normally chosen from the fittest. The relationship between power and authority is necessary for power to be able with its authority to achieve the obedience necessary to impose itself.

During early civilizations, the villages developed even more. Already in the south of Mesopotamia, in the villages that lived from agriculture and breeding, there was the institution of the church about 6,500 years ago. The church exercised organizational functions over the relations of the people of the villages, in addition to some commercial functions, which was indisputably a type of power so that some families wanted to have it and for this they would seek control of the temple, which by then resided in a building of very good construction as a sign of power.

Over time, economic activities and trade increased and some of the families in the villages would become richer than others thanks to trade among villagers. At some point, one of these families took control of the village to represent the economic power and authority of the village with the support of the church to justify its social position and the accumulation of its wealth.

The village authority created the first administrative offices with local institutions such as the council of the elders and the first assembly formed by important officials of the village, including military chiefs. Finally, religious, political, military, and judicial power were constituted. However, religious power was closely linked to the other powers.

Then, due to the continuous development of the villages, they became towns and cities with a greater economy based on agriculture, livestock, pottery and metallurgical, thanks to the important role of the merchants, who were also closely linked to the church. Cities became more important with the increase of their economy to become city-States, which were economically self-sufficient. However, some clashes had already begun to form over control of the cities, leading to the walling of the cities. To defend the cities came the idea of forming a military power giving rise to the first kingdoms with kings, who also exercised religious functions with progressive control of the temple until they came to assume central power. However, the elder's council and assembly continued to support the king.

The city-States had their own laws and were governed by a governor named Lugal, who regulated the activities necessary for the proper functioning of the city such as the distribution of water, the conservation of the canals, the defense of the city and the administration of justice. Over time, these rulers became kings or monarchs with absolute reigns or monarchies, as they controlled every aspect of the social, economic, and political life of the people of the city-States, which also had centralized institutions.

To become king of one of these city-States, the candidate was usually a leader with very close ties to the church and as ruler was regarded as a god on earth and his power was hereditary thus forming the first dynasties. These governments exercised all authority, administered justice, and handled the city's resources absolutely as well, forcing people to work and pay taxes. These governments also had a very well-trained army.

However, with the armies wars would be carried out, not only to defend their territories, but for the conquest and domination of others, giving way to empires as a form of political organization constituted by the power of one state that dominates another. The power of the empire was exercised by an emperor, who had all kinds of authority. The world's first empires were Akkadian, Babylonian, and Assyrian in Mesopotamia.

With the emergence of empires, the former form of government of Mesopotamian city-States underwent some modifications. Under the emperor's rule, the position that kings once held became as city administrators.

On the other side of the Fertile Crescent, in Egypt power as such began to originate after the villages were grouped together and formed the kingdoms of Upper and Lower Egypt about 5 thousand years ago. These kingdoms were ruled by a king-god, named Pharaoh. Pharaoh's power was hereditary, forming dynasties for nearly three thousand years.

Egyptian territory was divided into nomos or provinces administered by nomarcas or governors, which obeyed the pharaoh. There were also officials to control food and treasure, collect taxes and defend the territory. Among the most important officials were the prime minister, priests and chiefs of armies. The prime minister called "vizier"" was in charge of leading agriculture and presided over the supreme court. Priests were a very powerful group that usually took care of temples and organized the worship of the pharaohs and the gods. The priests of the great temples had many privileges and some of them could own property and did not pay taxes. Army chiefs protected the territory and even conquered new territories.

In addition to Egyptian civilization, it is interesting to address the origin of the power of Indian and Chinese civilizations. As for India, we see that, at first, its territory was also made up of a group of villages ruled by chiefs, priests, and feudal officials. Then, as the invasions of foreign towns increased, the Indians, to defend themselves against the invaders, developed their city-States with walls around and in the center of the cities stood the king's palace, whose authority was greater than that of the village chiefs.

However, the invaders ended up dominating the native Indians, forming empires with monarchs of absolute power. After this, the power remained in the hands of the warriors, until the priests managed to take it and imposed their Brahman religion. Thus, India's power was composed of a king, as the highest ruler; priests, who administered justice and imposed laws on spiritual principles; and feudal officials, who owned large latifundios.

As for China, power in ancient times was made up of an emperor, who was considered of divine origin. Then they were followed by the nobles who included the landowners and military chiefs. In addition, there were the emperor's trusted officials including governors, judges, police officers, tax collectors and agricultural supervisors.

These emperors later began to form dynasties dominated by emperors with absolute power and authority, who were succeeded by an heir, usually their firstborn male. Chinese dynasties ranged from ancient times to imperial era. The ancient dynasties begin with that of Xia, which was the first Chinese dynasty since 2100 BC; followed by the Shang and Zhou dynasties. During Zhou dynasty the Chinese kingdom was organized into provinces and states. In the Chinese imperial era appeared the dynasties of emperors that unified the Chinese people under a central government. Imperial dynasties included those of emperors such as Qin, who made China an empire; Han, who promoted the economy; Sui, who reformed the country and expanded the construction of the great wall; Tang, who achieved the growth of culture and art; Song, who established his capital Kaifeng and conquered the southern region; Yuan, who was dominated by the Mongol empire and had a lot of social instability; Ming, who had Nankin and then Beijing as capital, developing maritime communication and used silver as a monetary system; and finally we have the Qing dynasty, which was the last Chinese dynasty that ended in wars like the Opium and the war against Japan

After originating and configuring in the first civilizations of Mesopotamia and Egypt, India, and China; power and its structures spread all over the world. From the Middle East they continued to the east of the Mediterranean Sea and moved to Greece, which was made up of villages and tribes, which would later become Polis or city-States.

Greece around 1400 BC had as its form of government a monarchy where power was exercised by a monarch or king with divine right in some cases and his office was hereditary. The monarch had military functions, but also performed religious and judicial duties. The monarch was assisted by other military chiefs who, like him, also owned land. Around 1000 BC the last king of the Polis or city-State Athens, was replaced by a magistrate.

Greece also had an oligarchy, a form of government in which power was exercised by a small group of people as some family or affluent group. Subsequently, there was an aristocracy in which power was exercised by the nobility and its office was also hereditary.

Around 750 BC, major changes in the political sector were already taking place in Athens, such as the time-limiting of the ruler's mandate. Then other reforms arose, including the elaboration of the first written constitution with the rights and duties of the people, as well as the laws to be followed in the lives of citizens. Other reforms such as the elimination of debt slavery also emerged. These early reforms would open the way to a political system that would lead to democracy.

Later, more reforms would arise, such as the participation of citizens in the assembly and in the courts. A new political organization of four classes according to their resources was created, each with different military and political obligations. The poorest did not participate in the council, but neither did they pay taxes. The council of 500, made up of 50 members from each of the ten tribes of Athens, was also created to replace the previous council of 400. This new system would give political rights to the majority of citizens.

All these reforms gave rise to democracy as the government of the people, in Athens by 461 BC. This first democracy was of a direct type, as power was exercised directly by the people in an assembly where the people were involved in electing laws as well as public officials.

The political transformation of Athens was revolutionary for its time, for as we saw from the beginning in both Greece and early civilizations, power had always been in the hands of an elite of society, who exercised it absolutely. However, it was in Greece that power for the first time in history passed into the hands of the people, giving rise to one of the most important forms of governments in the world: democracy, the government of the people.

After Greece, power and its structures came to Rome. In ancient Rome there was a monarchy from its foundation between 753 and 509 BC, which included 7 kings from Romulus its founder to Tarquinius the Proud. During the monarchy, the king was the highest authority with absolute power and was also supreme priest, judge, and military chief. In addition to the king, there was the Senate and the People's Assembly. The Senate consisted of 300 elderly patricians, who advised the king in making decisions and complying with laws and healthy customs. The popular assembly was made up of patricians and was convened by the king to discuss issues of the king for approval or rejection.

After the monarchy, Rome became a Republic in 509 BC, which lasted until 27 BC. In a Republic, the ruler was elected to represent the interests of citizens for limited periods of time. At the beginning of the republic Rome was ruled by the nobles or patricians, who formed an oligarchy.

During the Republic, Rome became a world power with several colonies conquered in Europe, Asia, and Africa, thanks to its expansionist policy and powerful army. As for the political aspect, the Roman Republic had as its main institutions the Senate and the Assembly. The Senate was inherited from the monarchy and consisted of an elder's council advising the government. However, it was later modified to include the participation of the commoners, in addition to the patricians. The Senate became the Republic's main governing body. It could declare war, peace, establish alliances with foreign states, seek public finances, etc.

With the emergence of consuls as authorities exercising government, military and administration of justice, the ruler of the republic was replaced by two consuls, who controlled each other and at the end of their rule had to account for the Senate about their duties.

The Assembly was a representative body with legislative functions, as well as judicial and executive functions to vote on laws and elect consuls or magistrates. The assemblies became of three types: the Curial Assembly, the Centurial and the Tribal. The Curial assembly consisted of upper-class or patrician people. The vote of the majority of the curia constituted the vote of the people.

The Centurial assembly consisted of military personnel with a chief called centurion. These assemblies were convened and led by the consuls and with the majority vote the laws were passed and the consuls were elected.

The Tribal Assembly was made up of the poor and grouped by tribes. This assembly was presided over by a Tribune, or representatives of the commoners, who were elected to the tribal assemblies to defend the rights of the tribes before the Senate and the consuls. The tribunes' agreements were of legal character.

In addition, there were judges in charge of ensuring the functioning of the government such as censors, quaestors, praetors, and aediles. The censors were responsible for censusing the people and their assets. The quaestors were the accountants who collected taxes and managed the public treasury. The praetors were officials who administered justice and they were the forgers of Roman law. The aediles formed the municipal organization and were responsible for the monitoring and cleanliness of the town, as well as the maintenance of streets and roads.

During the period of the republic there were constant clashes between the most important social groups in Rome: the patricians and the commoners. The commoners called for the same rights as patricians, as well as better land-sharing and the abolition of debt slavery. All these difficulties led the Roman Republic to a deep crisis until it collapsed.

However, something could survive from the great Roman Republic as its great cultural legacy: its law and institutions. Roman laws that, although initially unwritten, were transmitted orally. But given their importance, ten men were chosen from among the patricians to collect them in the so-called law of the XII Tables. Likewise, Roman institutions of legal principles of justice such as courts, are also part of that Roman legacy. For a long time, it was only the Roman code and its laws endured for so many centuries that many of the laws we use today are based on them. In fact, the Europeans after their conquest of the American continent also introduced them to it.

After the fall of the Roman Republic, the Roman Empire began in 27 BC with Octavian as its first emperor under the name Augustus Octavian. In the empire, the emperor was the highest political, religious, and military authority. In addition to the emperor, there was the Senate and the Assembly, both at the service of the emperor. After the death of the first emperor, a series of dynasties were followed in power that ended with the 15-year-old Emperor Romulus Augustulus. The empire came into crisis because of its weakening due to its divisions and its inefficiency until it came to an end in 476 AD.

With the end of the Western Roman Empire ends the Ancient Age of the universal history of Western civilization and the Middle Ages begins. Today's Europe has its origins in the fall of the Western Roman Empire at the hands of the barbarian peoples who were entering the territories occupied by Rome. However, before the fall of the Roman Empire, during its weakening, the empire had already lost many of its territories since year 386 after incursions by the barbarians or Germanic towns such as the Goths of northern Europe. These towns over time had developed some relations with Rome and managed to learn a lot about the Romans, which made it easier for them to enter territories formerly occupied by the empire.

Later, the Goths were divided into Western Goths or Visigoth and Eastern Goths or Ostrogoths, from which other towns would later emerge and form the Germanic kingdoms. The Ostrogoth kingdom from the Heruli of Scandinavia, one of the Germanic towns under its chief Odoacer, is known to have deposed the last Western Roman emperor Romulus in 476. This ended the Roman Empire and Odoacer became the new king of Italy.

Although the part of the Roman Empire conquered by Odoacer was the Western one, this was the part where the great power of the whole empire was and with its fall began the Middle Ages in Europe. The new Germanic kingdoms were established almost throughout Europe in the new states formed in the territory formerly occupied by the Roman Empire with the help of the church of Rome.

Among the other important Germanic kingdoms, we have: the Visigoth kingdoms, the Franks, and the Lombards. The Visigoth kingdom from year 414 came to dominate the entire south of France and much of the Iberian Peninsula until it disappeared as a result of the Muslim invasion of 711. The Visigoth kingdom was a friend and ally of Rome.

The Lombards, another Germanic town, arrived in 568 and settled in northern and central Italy, and also converted to Catholicism. In 572 the Lombards formed their kingdom, but as early as 774 their dynasty had been dethroned by the Franks at the hands of Charlemagne, for the Lombards had apparently dared to defy the power of the pope.

The kingdom of the Franks from its inception expanded to dominate the north of present-day France, Belgium, and western Germany. This empire also converted to Catholicism with a good approach to the pope. Eventually, the kingdom of the Franks under the command of the Frankish king Charlemagne, who was crowned by the pope of Rome in the year 800, gave rise to the Carolingian Empire, the greatest and most powerful Germanic Empire of the Middle Ages.

The Carolingian Empire extended its dominance throughout almost all of Europe, in which it came to cover France, Austria, Holland, Belgium and northern Spain. Charlemagne turned his court into a great administrative and cultural center. He ruled his extensive territories by confiding them to counts, marquises and dukes, as they did before in the Lower Roman Empire. He also established a monetary system based on the silver coin that dominated Europe for centuries.

Given the great expanse of the Carolingian empire to hold it together, its emperor always had to travel with his court from one place to another and face continuous wars to ensure that he was obeyed everywhere. In addition, Charlemagne and his successors maintained a habit of dividing the rule of empire as an inheritance among the sons. This caused Europe to be divided into many territories and kingdoms, and in each of them the power also ended up divided. However, the idea of a Catholic empire allied with the Pope of Rome remained throughout the Middle Ages and beyond as an ideal of political unity.

Charlemagne had his subjects from northern Europe also converted to Catholicism. In return, the Pope recognized him as emperor as part of the power of Rome and supreme lord of all Europe. This would make Charlemagne think of creating a new Roman Empire. But all this manipulation of the papacy of Rome, would give immense power to the Catholic Church, which would use its indulgences for the forgiveness of sins its sudden ones to create religious wars as the crusades and then the inquisition as can be seen in greater detail in subchapter 3.3 on wars.

Meanwhile, Charlemagne's attempt to create his new Roman empire was not possible due to his death in 814; after which, all its power fragmented throughout Europe. After the fall of the Carolingian empire, feudalism, whose system of government was exercised by a king and his family along with a Catholic church that played a very influential role during the Middle Ages and beyond, emerged in Europe during the 1000s and 1200s. In addition to the king, there were also the nobles and peasants. The nobles were loyal to the king, so they were also called vassals, the nobles were also warriors and provided that service to the king, because he had no army. The king's power was weak, yet he was the owner of the lands, which under the feudal system were divided into sections and called fiefdoms. These fiefdoms were given by the king to the vassals to put them to produce with the work of the peasants.

During the feudalism, some of the people who worked the land in the fiefdoms managed to free themselves from their relationship with the Lord of Fiefdom and began to bring the agricultural products that they produced to some collection centers to sell them. With sales profits continued to invest in agricultural production, then in livestock and later in handicrafts. Since this activity was very profitable later, they would also include a variety of products, becoming these people very good traders. Eventually these merchants moved to urban centers where they became very prosperous. They were known as the bourgeois, who later came to form a social class composed of merchants and craftsmen, owners of the means of production and trade with land, fabrications, machines, and money. It was the bourgeoisie that originated capitalism and its great power in Europe, as well as the great changes in economic, political, and social on that continent. Changes that would contribute to the demise of the feudal system.

Feudalism began its decline mainly due to the depletion of lands with dire consequences for Europe as periods of famine, which was also joined by the plagues that spread throughout Europe killing millions of people. Finally, feudalism came to an end in the 14th and 15th centuries and gave way to capitalism when strong commercial activity and current money began to form.

Modern capitalism emerged in the second half of the 18th century, when the industrial revolution appeared thanks to more advanced thinking, giving way to a new scheme of individual freedoms, both political and economic. The industrial revolution gave new impetus to Europe's economy with the massification of production and consumption. Thus, a new global economic system had emerged with great participation of the bourgeoisie. This also required the massification of jobs under a wage scheme resulting in the emergence of the working class or proletariat. With power, dominant nations emerged in Europe, which began to devote themselves to the exploitation and colonization of other poorer nations or regions.

Unlike these dominant nations, slower development emerged in other nations such as China and Russia, as their class of traders was weak in the face of the authoritarian state bureaucracy that led these nations to socialism.

After the 15th century, stronger kings emerged with better-trained and equipped armies, so that their nations could concentrate on acquiring political hegemony abroad. To carry out this strategy required a lot of resources, which could be obtained by these nations through the development of public finances through tax collection. Modern states had arrived, and urban life flourished with better economy.

On the other hand, the eastern part of the Roman Empire made up of the southern Middle East, North Africa and part of the Iberian Peninsula, under the name of the Byzantine Empire had come to an end in 1453 with the fall of Constantinople in the hands of the Ottoman Empire, after almost a thousand years after the fall of the Western Roman Empire. With the fall of the Eastern bastion of the Roman Empire, the Modern Age began in Europe.

During the Modern Age, the Renaissance period arose in Italy, which then expanded throughout Europe making much progress due to a change in attitude and a better way of thinking. Art and sciences such as medicine, astronomy, geography, etc. emerged. Some inventions were made such as the printing press and the telescope. This was the time of Leonardo Da Vinci, Michelangelo, Lorenzo Medici, Nicolas Machiavelli and many more.

There were also many political changes during the Modern Age, such as the French Revolution, which was a political, social, economic, and military movement that emerged in France in 1789 with the leadership of the bourgeoisie. After clashes with king Louis XVI's troops, and the revolutionary troops managed to take control of the Bastille, a fortress of Paris used as a state prison, where France's great revolutionary thinkers were imprisoned. This would add a lot of pressure to the conflict and the French people decided to form a Constituent Assembly, in order to sign in 1791, the first Constitution, which proclaimed national sovereignty and the separation of powers. Then the Legislative Assembly was formed, which laid the division of political power into two large groups. After abolishing the monarchy in 1792, the popular classes stormed the king's palace and apprehended it. Elections were called for with victory for the revolutionaries and the assembly decided to execute the king in the guillotine, ending the absolute, unjust, oppressive, and unequal monarchy among the predominant social groups in the country. As the old regime collapsed, it was settled in its place by a democratic republican government, which would later have its influence in several European nations. However, the king's act of execution would spread terror among some European countries, to the point that Britain, the Netherlands, Spain and Austria came together to end the French revolution for fear that the same thing would happen in their territories. After this, the French were afraid that the revolution would end, which took advantage of the opposition to take command and arrest the revolutionary leaders. Finally, the revolutionaries would return to power in 1794; but after several uprisings against the government, it would be overthrown by a coup in 1799, under the command of Napoleon Bonaparte, who established a centralized and authoritarian regime and restored relations with the church, which in 1804 proclaimed him Emperor of France, which started Napoleon's imperial stage until the end of his empire in 1815. The French Revolution enshrined freedom and equality before the law as the foundations of the current rule of law. Their ideals of freedom, fraternity, popular sovereignty, and fundamental rights of citizens spread throughout Europe and the world. One of the consequences of the French revolution was the awakening of nationalist and democratic ideas that spread throughout the world especially to the United States, a country that would become independent of the English, which was followed as an example by the rest of the countries of the Americas.

Meanwhile, in Europe during the Modern Age, some of the dominant nations were consolidated as world powers, because their navigators and explorers came to conquer other continents such as America and Australia. The Modern Age was also the era of great explorers, such as Christopher Columbus, Vasco da Gama, and Hernando de Magallanes. These explorations would lay the foundation for the colonialism of European imperialism in dominant countries such as France, Germany, England, Spain, Italy, the Netherlands, and Belgium. These countries divided the American, African, Australian, and Asian continents.

During the Modern Age, the global market emerged with the capitalist system, the consumer society, and the industrial revolution as great economic changes with its consequent growths of cities especially those of Europe and

America. The most important religious change of the Modern Age was Martin Luther's Protestant reformation to the Catholic Church.

Scientific thinking also emerged at this time to boost the sciences with discoveries, theories, and the manufacture of new instruments. Among these thinkers were: Nicholas Copernicus, Galileo Galilei, Johannes Kepler, Isaac Newton, and many others who laid the foundations of contemporary science.

However, some of these great scientists like Galileo were attacked by the famous Catholic Church inquisition when Galileo tried to expose Copernicus's model on the solar system. The great scientist Galileo was a victim in the seventeenth century of the holy inquisition, because the church accused him of attacking its institution by defending the heliocentric model, that is, that the Earth was the one that revolved around the Sun and not the other way around as the church held. However, it would take more than three and a half centuries for a good pope named John Paul II to come and ask forgiveness on behalf of the church for what it did to Galileo.

4. 4 RELIGION AND POWER

Prehistoric man associated the devastating and threatening forces of nature with events of supernatural powers, that is, as something beyond his control, to which he became accustomed to fearing the threat of his own survival, until he felt immense respect for those supernatural powers to the point of calling them gods, to whom eventually began to worship them, have faith and offer them tributes to obtain favors and even offer them sacrifices.

With the development of belief, rituality and spirituality emerged the first manifestations of shamanism and then primitive religiosity. Thus, religious worship appeared as a way of showing veneration, devotion, and respect for something that is believed and considered powerful and divine.

To communicate with and influence the spirits of the almighty gods, the primitive man used rites, thus leading to the emergence of rituality, one of the important aspects of shamanism and what would later be called religion.

When the prehistoric man tried to represent the spirits of the gods in the form of symbols to ask them for help, he believed that, if he could have the representation in the form of paint or figure of something, then he could also interfere with the spirits of that thing at his convenience. In trying to physically represent several of his gods, polytheistic belief arose.

What we now know as religion is based on primitive beliefs and originated with the advent of shamanism, which was a type of beliefs conducted by a Shaman. Religions and the shaman later emerged from shamanism, today's religious authorities.

Religion as an institution originated during the Neolithic revolution, with the discovery of agriculture, when our ancestors settled down and formed the first human societies. Religion can be defined as a system of beliefs, customs and symbols around a divinity, something considered sacred or something of some spiritual value. Its basic function is to consolidate a series of values to hold together a social group with a certain degree of spiritual satisfaction through faith.

At first, religion was polytheistic, as it included belief in various gods as in the ancient civilizations of Mesopotamia and Egypt. Today, the polytheistic religion still practiced is Hinduism in India, within which there is a great diversity of philosophical and spiritual tendencies with two aspects in common: belief in the supreme god called Brahma and belief in reincarnation.

After Abraham's appearance, he introduced the concept of monotheistic religion or the worship of a single god. This type of religion includes Judaism, Christianity, and Islamism, which have a sacred book containing the doctrines, codes, and traditions on which their faith is based.

It is important to note that both polytheistic and monotheistic religions believe in a supreme god who created everything, so they are called theistic religions. However, there are other religions called non-theistic, which do not believe in a supreme god who created all things.

Among today's monotheistic religions we have Judaism, Christianity, and Islam. Judaism is the oldest religion of the monotheistic religions of the world and its origin is based on accounts about Patriarch Abraham. Judaism preaches the existence of one God, creator of the universe. In this religion, the family is very important and much of the Jewish faith is taught at home. The sacred book of Judaism is the Torah. Jewish cults are performed in synagogues and are led by a rabbi. Some of its sacred symbols of Judaism are the Star of David and the Menorah or the seven-armed chandelier. The star is on the flag of Israel and the menorah on the shield. Judaism now has about 14 million faithful worldwide.

Christianity is the religion that recognizes Jesus Christ as the son of God. It is a messianic religion, for it believes in the messiah or envoy of God. The holy book of Christianity is the Bible next to the new testament, whose teachings are preached in Christian churches. Preachers are called priests, bishops, or pastors according to the denomination of Christianity. Today, Christianity has about 2.1 billion faithful worldwide.

There is a denomination closely related to Christianity called Catholicism, which is a religious doctrine representing the Catholic Apostolic and Roman Church, whose supreme authority is the pope, who resides in the Vatican, which is why its history is closely linked to Europe, a region over which the Catholic Church exercised great power during the Middle Ages, to the point of keeping all the kingdoms of that time together. The Catholic denomination has some 1.214 million faithful worldwide.

Another denomination of Christianity is Protestantism, which began with the reform promoted by Martin Luther in 1517. Over the years, however, many Christian Protestant movements have emerged, such as Pentecostal evangelicals, Baptists, etc. Protestantism proposes to eliminate the mediation of priests for salvation and obtain it in return only by the declaration of faith. Currently, there are around 700 million Protestants in the world.

Islamism is also a monotheistic religion that arose with the preaching of its chief prophet Muhammad in 622 in Mecca, Saudi Arabia. The believer of the faith of Islam is called a Muslim and his holy book is the Koran, where the word of Allah was revealed to the Prophet Muhammad. The Koran also admits other prophets such as Abraham, Moses, and Jesus. The place where the Islamic faith is practiced is the mosque. Islam currently has about 1.9 billion faithful. Like Catholicism in Europe, Islamism united the tribes of Arabia to form a kind of empire that stretched from India to part of Europe.

The non-theistic religion, which is still practiced today is Buddhism, which is a philosophical, religious, and moral doctrine founded in India, during the 6th century BC by Buddha or Siddhartha Gautama. Buddhism believes in reincarnation as a means to free human beings from their material suffering. That is why Buddhism is oriented for the liberation of being through spiritual beliefs and practices, which seek to develop in the individual positive states such as calm, concentration, awareness, and healthy emotions. Buddhism has a large presence in all countries of Asia. Currently, it is spreading almost all over the world.

Religion has exercised over the centuries many functions as in the social aspect, which includes the moral principles or values associated with spirituality, but its use for political purposes has been the function that has always kept it linked to power, which has always been very ambitious by all, so that people use any means to achieve it.

Since the organizing of religions, the priests emerged, who, it was believed, were intermediaries between men and the gods, which granted great political power to the religious and every official that religion legitimized. For example, when the pharaoh of ancient Egypt spoke to his people about the problems of the water low level of the Nile and droughts, the effect on people would not have been as effective if people did not see pharaoh as a god.

Thus, in ancient times kings, emperors, and pharaohs to justify their absolute power considered themselves gods, eventually removing the boundaries between politics and religion, for by mentioning God or what is proclaimed in his name nothing was questionable. That is why almost all religions have been linked to political power and have become machinery of dominance.

Religion and power when they come together to gain the dominance of some territory are able to create up wars like the one that arose in ancient Egypt when Pharaoh Akhenaten tried to change the worship of the god Ammon-Ra to that of the new god Aton-Ra. The priests of the ancient god in the face of the threats of losing their power waged war on those of the new cult until they went against pharaoh himself. Another example of these wars were the crusades between Christians and Muslims over disputes over control of Jerusalem. The Inquisition of the Catholic Church with the persecution and burning of heretics was a religious war full of horror. We can also cite the war of the European conquerors to forcefully impose the Christian religion on the new American continent.

However, power must also have the capacity to unite society and for this nothing better than to have any ideological or religious justification. Society has always accepted power when it is legitimized by an institution such as the church. Moreover, when there are strong tensions between opposing tendencies to power, they can be resolved through the relationship between power and religion. That is why in almost all societies power and religion have always been closely united. However, when we have tried to change this bond of legitimacy of power with religion and replace it with that of the people, that has almost never worked because the people can also be manipulated by religion. As a result, the link between power and religion still stands and we can see it in Christianity and Islam. In the case of Christianity, especially the Catholic denomination, religion and power has been maintained over the centuries from the Vatican in Rome. In fact, the power that emerged in Europe and America from the Roman Empire always had the legitimacy of the Catholic church. This religion is perhaps the one that has had the most power, for it has always held the power of the Pope. This religion enjoyed many benefits during the feudal era in Europe. In the case of Islam, power and religion even become confused in one.

In Christianity and Islam, political and religious power has always helped each other. In Christianity, political power helps the religious with laws, donations, tax exemption and other fiscal exceptions, etc. While religious power legalizes political power. In Islamism, many Muslims have fervently whished for some kind of revenge by invoking ancient Muslim prophecies to take revenge on the peoples of

Europe and the United States for what in the past these countries did to their Middle Eastern region when they conquered them and altered their borders to take some benefits. Many of the Muslims, from what is called the Islamic State, are stroking these concepts and ideas to establish a kind of Islamic empire to carry out their revenge.

4.5   THE STRUGGLE FOR POWER

The struggle for power arose from the origins of the human being with the first disputes. During prehistory, since the concept of property arose, human beings have been involved in disputes to defend their property or to take over that of others. During the dispute, anyone who was the winner would get the power.

Throughout history we have made up wars and then governments to take and manage power, even the people themselves have been involved in the struggle for power. As for the power of the people, it is worth noting that the people have in some specific cases come to distribute some of their power with the so-called power groups to achieve some special benefits.

Origin of the Struggle

In humans, from their origins, some disputes may have arisen over some of their resources, especially if they were scarce. If the humans who were in possession of the resources could not defend them, then the aggressor would take them by force by exercising power.

Over time, as humans became sedentary and settled on some batch of land where they stored their food, some other humans who were still nomads, when they reached that batch, they likely had a tendency to take from those foods and some other things or take the whole batch of land. But those who had taken that lot of land before felt it as their property and everything in it so they would be willing to defend it even with their lives. If the sedentary failed to defend his property, he would lose it and the aggressor would keep everything as a result of his power.

As the towns more developed and prospered, they could be more attractive to other people to try to obtain food and shelter without any effort. Consequently, peoples would have to prepare to defend themselves with sticks and stones or with any kind of weapon they had.

Later, with the emergence of cities and early civilizations there were disputes or wars even to take land with certain improvements such as some kind of irrigation. This would be the case with the wars between Lagash and Umma in Sumer, Mesopotamia. These wars were the first documented in human history.

With the development of cities and the discovery of metals, better weapons were formed to defend themselves, resulting in the formation of the first armies armed with spears, axes, daggers, knives and swords, and in addition, protected with helmets and shields. Armed armies would start wars to defend themselves in the first place. However, over time wars would often be used to obtain, in addition to better lands, other people's lands to expand the territories of the aggressors. After the cities had grown and progressed, some of them had to build a wall to avoid invasions by those who practiced wars for the struggle of power.

Wars

In order to seize power, the practice of war became a major military culture allowing one state to dominate others to form the first empires such as Akkadian, Babylonian and Assyrian that emerged in Mesopotamia. In the empire, power is exercised with all kinds of authority by a king, monarch, or emperor.

With the emergence of early civilizations, the war became more organized and even the horse and carriage were incorporated giving more importance to the military class. As time went on, other components for war were added such as gunpowder to make firearms, which would revolutionize war forever. Thus, artillery sprang up, strengthening the military armies. Afterwards, new techniques for war and military with better training were also developed, as happened during the heyday of the Roman Empire that developed highly professional military systems. In this case, the purpose of wars was to expand the empire and thus gain more power, clearly.

Throughout the history, many things related to wars have been changing, weapons, tactics, strategies, logistics and above all communications, due to technological advances, of which we know so far. Some innovations are likely to still remain in testing periods.

Currently war is defined as any armed struggle or bellicose conflict between two or more towns, nations, or regions, in which there are usually wounded, dead and property damage. Normally, war involves undermining the state of peace. Depending on their goal, wars can be of different types such as religious wars, world wars, civilian wars, etc.

A war is called religious when it is promoted for religious reasons. Of these we can cite the crusades and the holy inquisition of the Catholic Church in Europe during the

Middle Ages. The crusades originated due to the great power that the papacy of Rome already had. Based on its power, the Catholic Church began to administer its indulgences about the penalties for the sins of its followers. To grant these indulgences the church could impose some kind of penance or sacrifice in return. Thus, it came to ask its followers to go to fight to regain the Holy Land of Jerusalem, which gave rise to the crusades, which were 8 wars that occurred in almost two centuries between the years 1095 and 1291. They were called crusades because the followers of the church that participated in these wars used the symbol of the cross. The purpose of these wars was to go to Jerusalem to reconquer the Holy Land that had been taken by Islam. To organize these wars the church began to recruit people among its followers using indulgences.

After the first crusade, the order of the Knights Templar was founded in France in 1119 with the purpose of protecting Crusader Christians when they were going to Jerusalem. At first, the Templars, since they did not have many financial resources, survived thanks to donations. And they managed to settle in the ancient temple of King Solomon. In 1129 the order of the Knights Templar was approved by the church. The order of the Templars would end up becoming of a great prestige structure with political and economic power within the Christian community. Politically in 1139 the Pope of the church at that time declared them exempt from obedience to local laws, except that of the Pope. They also did not have to pay taxes. Economically, they developed financial techniques that would emerge like those of today's banks. They also acquired large tracts of land in Europe and the Holy Land and built large buildings. They formed the first international import and export manufacturing companies. After almost two centuries, the crusades began to weaken due to internal conflicts. Furthermore, the Muslims had developed better leaders like Saladin, whom the Templars managed to defeat in 1177 with an army of 26 thousand Muslim soldiers. Finally, the order of the Knights Templar came to an end in 1306 after being dissolved by Pope Clement V, after the harassment of the French King Philip IV, ending the Knights Templar accused of heresy and some were killed and even burned alive.

However, in its eagerness to retain its power, the Catholic Church began the intolerant stage of the inquisition regarding any idea or thought of its followers that the Church considered contrary to its interests. By labeling these ideas as heresies, the Catholic Church began to inquire about the alleged heretics, which would give rise to the famous inquisition. In an attempt to end heresy for fear of losing its power, the Catholic Church began to establish inquisition institutions or courts during the Middle Ages to persecute and punish with torture and even death all those who opposed the designs of the Catholic Church. The first court of inquisition was established in the south of France in 1184. Later, the state-level inquisition of Spain was established in 1249. The disastrous practice of the inquisition, had the support of governments such as that of Rome, Spain, Portugal, France, Germany, etc. Perhaps the most ruthless part of this practice was the burning of living people.

In addition to religious wars, there are other wars involving the whole world such as world wars, which take place on a large scale. Among these we can cite the first and second world wars. The first world war between 1914 and 1918; it was the first major war to involve countries on five continents of the world. However, most of the fighting took place in Europe. The initial cause of this war was the assassination of Archduke Franz Ferdinand of Austria, heir to the Austro-Hungarian Empire, on 28 June 1914. The archduke was killed by a Serb, so Austria-Hungary claimed Serbia and declared war on it. Then Russia came out in defense of Serbia and, in response, Germany, which was an ally of the Austro-Hungarian empire, declared war on Russia and France. During the first world war Europe was divided into two sides: Italy, Germany and the Austro-Hungarian empire formed the Triple Alliance, while France, the United Kingdom and Russia formed the other side called the Triple Entente. As the war progressed more countries became involved. This war had been one of the biggest wars in history to this time, with a high cost mostly in human lives calculated in more than 15 million among soldiers and civilians, something never seen before. A year after the end of the first war fighting, its official end was sealed with the signing of the Treaty of Versailles in France.

However, it seemed that the lesson of this first catastrophe was not learned and 20 years later World War II occurred between 1939 and 1945. Like the first one, the second world war also involved many countries in the world, only that this war was worse than the first one. It was a catastrophe in every way. More than 50 million people between the military and civilians are believed to have lost their lives. The cause of the Second World War began when in 1939 Adolf Hitler's German army invaded Poland, as he wanted to extend his Nazi regime throughout Europe. After the invasion of Poland, the United Kingdom and France declared war on Germany, but still the German army continued its military campaigns with which it managed to conquer much of Europe. In this war, in addition to Europe, fighting spread to various parts of the world. Japan joined Hitler's Germany in 1940 as the Japanese wanted to conquer part of China and Asia. However, their attack on Pearl Harbor in Hawaii in 1941 would complicate their cravings for power by causing America's entry into this war. The Second World War had many technological advances, which played a decisive role, but definitely the most important of all advances was the atomic bomb, which was developed by the United States and used it against the Japanese cities of Hiroshima and Nagasaki on August 6 and 9, 1945. As a result, more than 200,000 people died from the bomb explosion and the subsequent effects of radiation. After that first, atomic weapons have never been used again in a war. But perhaps the darkest side of world war II was the Holocaust, in which Adolf Hitler and his Nazi regime carried out an ethnic, political, and religious genocide in Germany and the territories they conquered. The German authorities pursued and locked up in concentration camps where a total of 11 million mainly Jewish people died.

There are also other types of wars such as the so-called civil war, which is an internal war between the inhabitants of the same town or country without the direct interference of other countries. Examples of civil wars are many in the world.

There are also the so-called preventive wars, which are initiated by one nation on the grounds that another country prepares to attack it. An example of this kind of war could be the Iraq war.

There was even a cold war, as an updated type of war that occurs when two or more nations try to undermine their enemy's political regime through economic influence, propaganda, and espionage, but without direct violence.

Human history is full of wars that normally begin to take or retain power or make some profit as has happened since prehistory, during early civilizations, the ancient age and that continue to happen to this day.

The Government

The government is the representative of power. The governing authority of a political unity such as the State, with the aim of directing, controlling, and administering the institutions of that State, as well as regulating political society and exercising authority and sovereignty within the State. The government is also responsible for collecting taxes on all members of the state. This money serves to create, develop, and maintain utilities and build infrastructure for the well-being of citizens.

The government, in order to respond to its society, must also create a social protection system for its citizens that includes different areas as important as health, labor, education, livelihood and housing. This social security system must be self-financing, safe, corruption-free and of very good quality.

For its part, the State is a socio-political organization constituted by a territory, a population, and a government. The State enjoys internal autonomy and sovereignty to perform political, social, and economic functions within its territory. In addition, it has its own bureaucratic institutions, laws, and economic system, in which power is exercised over a population that is in its territory.

There are two types of states, depending on the political structure of their governments: the Unitary State and the Federal State. The Unitary State is one in which there is only one centralized political power for the whole territory, while in the Federal State the power is decentralized, because it is divided among the different regions that make up the political territory. The power of each region usually has the same level of autonomy and representativeness in power or federal government.

In order for the government to be more efficient in meeting its objective, power must be structured into units with specific powers and functions such as the executive branch, the legislative branch, and the judiciary. The main function of the executive branch is to coordinate and pass laws; while the main function of the legislative branch is to create the laws; and the main function of the judiciary is to enforce the laws.

The executive branch is represented by the head of government, which is the highest level of authority and is generally recognized as the leader of the State. In addition to the head of State or president, the government also includes executive directors, such as the prime minister or vice president and the other ministers representing the legislative and judicial branch.

Depending on the position and relationship between these powers, there may be several types of systems of government: a presidential, parliamentary system, or an assembly system. In the presidential system as in the United States, there is a separation of powers between the legislature and the executive and each of them, congress and the president, is elected by separate elections. In the parliamentary system there is a close relationship between the legislative branch and the executive in which the first or parliament chooses the candidate of the second as the head of government, as is the case in Spain. However, there may be a hybrid system between the presidential system and the parliamentarian, such as the French system. In the assembly system, the legislative power is above the executive branch, and it is the assembly that elects the president.

According to its political forms, government can be of different types, among the most important we have democracy, monarchy, and dictatorship. Democracy is the form of government in which people through political parties elect the president and officials to administer the state.

Political parties are in theory public interest associations that follow certain principles and ideas for the fulfillment of their objectives: first, channel and convey the interests and demands of the population to be considered in the decisions of democratic government; and secondly to enable the participation of the population in the democratic political process by choosing the people's representatives to exercise political power.

Democracies in turn can be of various kinds depending on how the people wield power. Among them the most important ones we currently have are representative democracies and Republican democracies. In representative democracy, the government is in the hands of representatives elected by the people for a certain period of years. In a Republican democracy the head of state or president is elected by the people through their representatives. The republic ensures that there is a division of powers within the State, such as the executive, legislative and judicial power. It also guarantees the temporality of the mandate of the rulers and respect for national law.

In other forms of government such as monarchy and dictatorship, unlike democracy, power does not reside in the people. In the monarchy, which was very common in the past, the administration of the State is in the hands of a monarch for life and its power is hereditary. In the past, monarchies were regimes of absolute power. Even during the Middle Ages, this was a widespread form of government in Europe, but it began to lose power after the French Revolution. Later appeared the constitutional monarchy, in which its members have symbolic value and without any real power over the administration of the State. This is the kind of monarchy that basically exists today in Europe.

In a dictatorship, power is exercised by one or more people, usually with the help of the military sector. In a dictatorship there are no citizen freedoms and mechanisms of control are established against citizens in the education, media, and censorship of positions contrary to those who govern.

Democracies and dictatorships are now the most common types of government in countries where early civilizations such as Mesopotamia, Egypt, India, and China emerged in ancient times, but without the glory of the former.

In Iraq, after the departure of Saddam Hussein, after his two-decade dictatorship, a Federal Parliamentary Republic was installed in the country, whose government is chaired by a president and a prime minister, although it is the latter that governs. The country has a constitution, which was approved in 2005. The President is elected by the Council of Representatives by a majority of at least two-thirds of the Members. Otherwise, it would have to go to a runoff.

In Egypt, there is a socialist democratic system with a 1971 constitution. The system has several political parties in theory, as one is the dominant one. The head of the State is the president, who in turn elects and dismisses the members of his government, including the prime minister. The assembly of the people elects, for a period of 5 years, its members, among which the workers and the peasants must be at least half.

In India, long after the empires stage, in 1858 India was colonized by the British and its territory became under the king of Great Britain as Head of State. But, after its independence from the British, in 1947, India would lose Pakistan, a part of its State. Three years later, India adopted a democratic, socialist, and secular system with free elections and proportional representation. Currently, India's political organization consists of an executive power, composed of the President and the Prime Minister. The president is elected every five years by the state assemblies and the national parliament, however, it is a symbolic authority with few powers, for it is the Prime Minister, who truly holds the command. There is also a Council of Ministers.

In China, after the fall of the Qing dynasty, China's last dynasty, the country plunged into civil war from 1927 to 1949 for the confrontation between the Chinese Nationalist

Party and the newly formed, for that then, the Chinese Communist Party, which under the leadership of Mao Tse Tung, took full control of China and declared it by the People's Republic of China. China has a communist and socialist government with many restrictions on freedoms.

The People

The town is the group of people who live in the same place that can be given various denominations such as tribe, village, city, nation, region, etc. People of a town may be of different race, gender, religion, or social or economic level. Together all of them are called we the people.

From the origins of power, the people had always been below the ruling elite, even in Ancient Greece, especially in Athens, which previously had governments of monarchy, oligarchy, and tyranny. However, in the 6th century BC, when Athens had consolidated itself into a city-State thanks to its political independence and good economic situation, a form of government called democracy or government of the people emerged. Athenian democracy was a real revolution, for power for the first time passed into the hands of the people. This first democracy was directly, as the people exercised their power directly in a kind of public assembly to participate in the approval or repeal of matters or laws that would govern their society, as well as to elect public officials. The people were already exercising their power.

Moreover, many years later, the other great definition of democracy would emerge as the government of the people, by the people and for the people. This concept was uttered by the American President Abraham Lincoln in 1863. We see that also in this concept of democracy, the people is the great protagonist, because it has the power to choose and be chosen to govern its own destiny in its citizen life.

Since its inception, democracy has been the best political system that people has had to this day. Democracy, by establishing that the will of the people is the basis of government authority, makes this political system compatible with human rights. In addition to contemplating freedom of thought, expression, and religion. By all these characteristics, democracy is the political system used by more than half of the world's countries. In fact, democracy has now become a way of life.

However, democracy has been nothing perfect, even when it originated in Athens, since at that time it did not include all citizens such as women, but with subsequent reforms they always manage to solve their problems.

Democracy now faces many other problems and threats. Among them the strongest is corruption, which creates great crises of governance. Corruption goes so far as to finance election campaigns and then demand the chosen one's payment as a return on investment by awarding juicy contracts. Corruption also buys votes to win elections, and corrupt institutions and even voters bribe for that.

Another threat of democracy comes from some legally elected populist leaders, who after having the people on their side and taking the media, take over the state's businesses and resources to expand their powers and thus stay in government through fraudulent elections. All this fraud is possible with the help of the political opposition, which is made allied by these supposed leaders.

Moreover, among other problems that democracy faces are the interferences of other states with undemocratic regimes such as Russia and China, which conspire for the collapse of democracy.

In established democracies, trends have emerged from some groups with some defined agenda to undermine the democratic system. These groups defend certain political ideologies such as communism, socialism, or progressive movement. These enemies of democracy are usually associated with some political party in the country, from where they will try to play with nationalist sentiments focused on some minority sector of the population to achieve their goal.

But the fulminant threat of democracy is a coup, which is to take the government surprisingly and violently by some power group. The most frequent coups are usually military coups with members of the country's armed forces normally supported by civilians, who are also responsible for ensuring the support of the official media. After the coup, a dictatorship is installed in which government officials are immediately replaced, and institutions such as the police, national guard and army are turned into repression agencies.

In addition to the military coups, there are other types of coups, depending on their characteristics, such as institutional coup, autocoup, etc. But whatever the case may be, democracy is the overthrown one and the people lose their power. However, sometimes democracies can be overthrown without any coup, revolution, or reform. We have seen the enemies of democracy to use new ways to topple a democratically elected government, just because that president is uncomfortable for them. This is what they call an impeachment.

Perhaps the worst of all the problems of democracy is the apathy of the participants. In recent years, there has been a decline in people's participation levels in elections, which could call into question the legitimacy of elected officials. To break with apathy, people must participate in elections and thus defend the power of democracy.

People can also be seen with some reluctancy to participate in their democracy because of the widespread demagoguery used by politicians in their election campaigns.

Moreover, most politicians are not adequately prepared to the point of being unaware of their duties. By not seeing solutions to their problems, due to the deceptions of politicians, people get frustrated, and their apathy grows. However, politicians seem never to learn. President Lincoln said that a part of the people can be deceived all the time; the whole people can be deceived a part of the time; but they all cannot be deceived all the time.

In addition, there is another type of apathy in democratic participation, which could be the kind of religion of the people. Religion in some regions of the world sees it as more important that government be based on the will of God and not on the will of the people. For certain kinds of people with this kind of religion, democracy may not be of much importance.

What is also a fact, is that all the problems and threats of democracies can be increased by the media in all their denominations: written, spoken and television press, because this can serve as a platform and even worse if the media sympathized with the ideology of these people. Today it is almost impossible to find free and objective media. It is impressive the excessive distortion of journalism to manipulate society with its articles so that it follows the interests of the media.

Social media with their "fake news" are also part of this problem. The information that some people send without verification on social media against democracy is disseminated around the world with great ease and speed. In election periods, social media rumors achieve their goals especially in vulnerable countries by negatively affecting democracy.

To put an end to these problems and threats, citizens must better prepare themselves to defend their democracy's power. Democratic countries must include the study of democracy, human rights, forms of government, the state, the republic, the rule of law, the Constitution, etc., so that their citizens know the scopes that their political system, especially the role that democracy has played in their lives and express their ideas without fear to confront the enemies of democracy at the political level. In addition, citizens must be involved in the politics, economy and history of their country and the rest of the world. With the preparation of the citizen, there will be more possibilities to choose better representatives and to be a better representative if elected. It is very important when choosing to consider the intellectual and moral capacity of the candidate. Finally, we can ensure that all the problems and threats of democracy can be solved by people and always with more democracy.

However, it would be good and convenient to remember Aristotle's reflection, which basically establishes that a very democratic democracy can generate its own problems and threats. Coincidentally, Carlos Andrés Pérez, president of Venezuela, used "democracy with energy" as a political slogan, really aiming to make a firm government without licentiousness. With this slogan he comfortably won his first presidency. However, President Pérez was overthrown by a coup in his second government by his political enemies to later give way to a dictatorship which has still been in power for more than twenty years.

We must always remember that democracy is the power of the people, so the people must defend their democracy so as not to lose their power.

However, it would be good and convenient to recall Aristotle's reflection, which basically states that a very democratic democracy can generate its own problems and threats. Coincidentally, Carlos Andrés Perez, President of Venezuela used as a political slogan "democracy with energy", with which he comfortably won his first presidency. However, President Perez was overthrown in his second government by his political enemies and then gave way to a dictatorship that has still been in power for more than twenty years.

We must always remember that democracy is the power of the people, so the people must defend their democracy so as not to lose their power.

Power Factors

The power that had always been in the hands of kings and the elitist class, passed for the first time into the hands of the people with the rise of democracy in Athens, Greece in 461 BC. Later in the 18th century with the French Revolution and the American Revolution emerged the first modern democracies with a new structure of political power divided into three: legislative, executive and judiciary. These three branches of power had mechanisms and systems to control and balance each other.

In democracy, citizens can delegate quotas of power to certain groups to act on their behalf. Over time and as these groups did a good management, they developed some prestige until they gained power. A power factor is a group of people organized with an interest and purpose to achieve some benefit for the people they represent.

There are many of these power factors, however, we will only talk about the most important ones for the democratic societies of today's world, because even though these organizations have emerged for the legitimate purpose of helping people, today we see them corrupting themselves and given their importance to society we have to rescue them for the good of the people. Among these power factors we have the media, religion, trade unions and some non-governmental organizations.

The press arose from the need to know the development of the environment where one lives. However, after the nineteenth century with the Industrial Revolution the mass press emerged with the ability to create public opinion and shape it, which certainly played a very important role in the development of democracy. But then the press acquired the power capable of balancing or unbalancing central political power. At first, the press began using political scandals to get people's attention and sell their newspapers more. But these scandals would have their respective impact on the election result.

With the advent of other media such as radio, television, as well as the internet and social networks today; information can reach more people and the power of the media increased further. So much so that today they are the ones who practically elect the rulers: people only vote for whoever the media tells them.

Religion, which as we have already seen, has always been linked to power. However, in 19th-century Europe when different political ideologies emerged, the Christian church began to lean towards democracy and resumed its influence in society with support for human rights and freedoms. The Christian church also emphasized the important role of the family. Today, however, the Catholic Church with its pope at the helm is using its great influence in society to go against the values it enacted before, even the pope has been accused of persecution of the Christians and promoting values contrary to those of democracy.

The unions originally consisted of groups of workers organized to defend the labor-related economic, professional, and social interests of the people who composed them. Among these interests were the terms of the contract such as wages, vacations, training, etc. The trade unions were democratic organizations dedicated to negotiating with the employer the conditions of recruitment. Each union grouped and represented workers with similar activity or industry and with the power they had acquired negotiating with the companies to reap their benefits. However, that power increased so much that it is now being used for political purposes for their own benefit.

Non-governmental organizations (NGOs) are social initiative and humanitarian entities, independent of the public administration and that do not pursue any profit. NGOs can address issues such as: health care, environmental protection, promotion of economic development, promotion of education, technology transfer, etc. Its importance has been recognized by the UN since 1945. These organizations may be local, national, or international. The participation of NGOs in politics, before corruption devours them, can serve to defend the interests of organized citizens over any idea or objective, which can serve as a mechanism for expanding democracy.

In order for these power factors to function as efficiently as possible without deviating from their objectives or not being corrupted, their efforts must be monitored by the political powers of the State and by the public itself to avoid, for example, seeing the media ideologization the people against democracy, trade unions controlled by political parties, complacent judges elected by Congress Etc. If proper surveillance is exercised, it can largely prevent the system from being corrupted.

What we should not do in any way is to remove the power from where we have already put it, for that would cause power to pass again to the one who has taken it away: to the ruling elites. We must be vigilant of the democratization of power so that we can put it in the hands of the people.

5

CURRENT WORLD:
A DANGEROUS TREND

Today's world focuses its attention on the coronavirus pandemic, as we can see when we take a look at geopolitics. However, we must know about our current world, its political systems as well as the institutions for world peace, in addition to its economics systems, and later adhere to the solution of its problems, which today show a dangerous trend.

Today, the main political systems in most countries of the world are democracy and dictatorship. The basic difference between these two political systems is that in democracy there are freedoms and respect for human rights, whereas in dictatorship there is no such a thing, since the power of the dictator is absolute and with no opposition to his actions, thoughts and ideas are allowed.

As for the main economic systems of today's world are the system of market economy or capitalism typical of democratic countries and the system of state planning of socialist countries. The basic difference between these two economic systems is that capitalism is based on private ownership of the means of production and the principle of free market, whereas state planning or socialist economy is one in which the State owns the means of production, that is, where private property does not exist. In socialism or communism there is usually a State planning economy, although there are now exceptions like China and Russia that had to go to a market economy. China to solve its economic problems, as did Russia after the collapse of communism in the Soviet Union.

Our world today already presented some problems under normal conditions of its development and evolution, with clear signs of a dangerous trend. However, the arrival of coronavirus would only make things worse, for besides causing diseases that could be fatal in some cases, it is also accelerating political decline and economic collapse. This coupled with existing social problems, complete a daunting picture. However, there are still solutions to prevent collapse.

Perhaps the most important problem in society has been the loss of its moral and ethical values, as they have led it to widespread corruption to the detriment of all social structures.

Democracy for example, already presented its own problems, which usually come from politicians with socialist or communist ideas supported by the media. And to make matters worse, the institutions that were created to maintain the peace and well-being of the world, such as the United Nations (UN) mainly, have fail to fulfill their purposes, and have instead failed democracy and the people.

The political decline could lead to an economic collapse, which would make it more difficult to solve people's social problems in any country. However, this seems to be the goal of socialist or communist politicians along with the media to impose their ideology.

To avoid the collapse of civilization, all the difficulties that threaten our civilization must be addressed, starting with the pandemic that currently plagues us, the lack of morals and ethics, corruption, political decline, economic chaos, and social problems. In addition, the State can develop reasonable social welfare for its people, as long as it can afford it and maintain it without falling into debt.

But in order to help the people, the State must ensure that its country has sustainable economic growth capable of creating reasonably paid jobs so that people can meet their fundamental needs. This is possible with private participation and society itself.

In this chapter we will be discussing in detail the geopolitical situation and the issue of coronavirus, political decline, economic collapse, social problems and how to prevent the collapse of civilization.

5.1 GEOPOLITICAL SITUATION

To see what is happening on the international scene, we will take a look at the events and their consequences in the vast geography of today's world, using geopolitics.

Before the arrival of coronavirus, in today's world attention was focused on political, economic, and social problems, usually and as always. However, now with coronavirus have emerged other kinds of events, which are occupying the attention of the whole world.

In China, the propaganda machinery of the Asian giant rolled heavily against the United States, after this government imposed new tariffs for more than $ 200 billion on Chinese products.

In Turkey, President Erdogan sought Brussels for European support for his policy in Syria and insisted that he has every right to send his army to Northwest Syria, for which he sought the support of both NATO (North Atlantic

Treaty Organization) and from the European Union. Meanwhile, in Russia, Putin paved the way to stay in the Kremlin until 2036, for which he should amend the constitution. We see that the world was focused on the struggle for power. However, during the first quarter of 2020, the event that most caught people's attention was the outbreak of the coronavirus.

To see some world events with their details, we will go to the regions that are on the news today around the world such as America, Europe, Africa, and Asia.

In America, a former United States national security adviser condemned China for its handling of the coronavirus outbreak and called on the rest of the world to "act" and hold the Communist government accountable for damage caused to people around the world. According to this former official, China would have silenced those who tried to speak, expelled some journalists, and destroyed samples, so they should be seen as responsible for the pandemic.

During the pandemic, we also have, in another order of ideas, that the United States carried out attacks against an Iraqi militia with ties to Iran in Iraq, in response to the deaths of two Americans and a British soldier. In addition, the United States penalized the Russian firm Rosneft, with financial sanctions aimed at forcing the dictator of Venezuela to end his dictatorship.

The most important press headlines at the moment, all related to the coronavirus, among which the following appear:

America, Mexico: *Mexican drug cartels fight during coronavirus, prices rise as China's laboratory supplies run out*. The onslaught of the coronavirus has not only caused the fall of the world economy, but it has also affected the black market where it hurts, and the Mexican cartels are no exception. The virus outbreak has skyrocketed the price of heroin, methamphetamines, and fentanyl, as the Sinaloa cartel, and its main rival, the New Generation of Jalisco, struggle to obtain the chemicals necessary to manufacture synthetic drugs. , which generally come from China and now have a minimal supply. A former agent with the Drug Enforcement Administration (DEA) Division of Special Operations in New York told Fox News.

Europe, UK: *UK coronavirus blocking rules must be followed or exercise may be banned, says health secretary.* As sunny, warm weather sent many outdoors and to parks in London over the weekend, the UK's top health official warned that officials can ban outdoor exercise if people drop the rules to stop the spread of the coronavirus. Several parks in London were closed after the warmest weekend in six months sent thousands outside to the parks, with plenty of places to sunbathe and in large groups. Fox News.

Africa: *Coronavirus closures prevent African elite from seeking medical care abroad.* Africa's ban on coronavirus travel is making it harder for rulers and the wealthy to fly abroad for emergency medical care, as they have in the past. For years, leaders from Benin to Zimbabwe have received medical care outside of Africa, while their own poorly funded health systems are limping from one crisis to another, The Associated Press reports.

Asia, China: *The Chinese Physician who first raised the alarm on COVID-19 disappears.* The Wuhan-based doctor who gave the first alarm about the coronavirus outbreak in China has reportedly disappeared. Ai Fen has not been seen for days and some fear he may be the last high-profile person critical of COVID-19 management to disappear without a trace, "60 Minutes, Australia" reported. Ai rose to fame as the first doctor to notice a group of patients with intense flu-like symptoms in Wuhan, more than a month before Chinese officials were forced to confirm the outbreak. Fox News.

Asia, China: *China joins the UN Human Rights Council panel despite a troubling record, response to the coronavirus.* China has been named to a panel on the controversial United Nations Human Rights Council, where it will help search for leading candidates despite its history of decades of systematic human rights abuse that the United States has said fueled the coronavirus pandemic. Fox News.

Asia, Israel: *How China can be legally responsible for the coronavirus pandemic.* A cover-up and crackdown by the Chinese government in the first few weeks of the coronavirus emergence is raising questions about whether the communist superpower can be held legally responsible. "In general, countries like China have sovereign immunity, and governments cannot be brought to ordinary courts or held liable regardless of their conduct." An expert Israeli lawyer who has long specialized in suing terrorist regimes and sponsors of human rights abuse, she told Fox News.

The coronavirus has overshadowed other issues such as global warming or climate change and terrorism, which were the focus of world attention before. However, we can see that all three of these themes have had the characteristic of spreading around the world with lightning speed, something that normally occurs with any threat to humanity.

Geopolitics indicates to us, as we have seen, that all humanity is immersed in the pandemic caused by the coronavirus. The entire world is focused first on solving this problem and then dedicate itself more fully to the economic crisis. The pandemic is believed to be under control in about 5 months. The truth is that humanity will learn from this crisis and will better prepare to give an immediate response in the future, if necessary.

The Covid-19 coronavirus that is currently affecting humanity belongs to the extensive family of coronaviruses that are common among bats and other animals. These viruses can cause disease in both animals and humans.

In humans, the Covid-19 coronavirus can be spread between people when they are close to the person who carries the virus as someone else or some object where the virus still lives. Symptoms of infection can be fever, cough, shortness of breath, or difficulty breathing. The incubation period, or the time between infection and the appearance of disease symptoms, is an average of 5 days.

The virus can cause respiratory infections that can range from the common cold to more serious illnesses. Although no one is exempt from catching the virus, those most likely to contract the virus are the elderly or those with pre-existing medical conditions such as high blood pressure, heart disease, or diabetes.

The World Health Organization (WHO) has declared the spread of the coronavirus as a "public health emergency of international importance", something that has only happened very few times in history. International health authorities in several countries have taken measures, such as closing their borders or imposing isolation on their inhabitants.

This virus originated in Wuhan, China towards the end of last year, however, it began to be known at the beginning of this year 2020; after the virus had spread to the rest of the world. During the first quarter of the year, the virus has infected more than 2.5 million people and killed more than 200,000 worldwide.

After starting to see the ravages of the coronavirus, a debate has opened today about the cause or reason for not disclosing the information beforehand, because that way the world would have been better prepared to face the problem.

Some people have condemned China for its handling of the coronavirus outbreak and have asked the rest of the world to act and hold the Chinese government accountable for damage caused to people around the world. According to these people, China would have silenced those who tried to speak when the outbreak of the epidemic began, and that it would have expelled some journalists and destroyed samples of the problem, so China should be seen as responsible for the pandemic.

There was even a journalist from the Asian continent who assured that China may be legally responsible for the coronavirus pandemic. According to this person, the cover-up and repression by the Chinese government in the first weeks of the emergence of the coronavirus are raising serious doubts about the attitude assumed by China, for which he thinks that this country may be legally responsible. Although countries such as China generally have sovereign immunity and governments cannot be brought to ordinary courts or held liable regardless of their conduct, but this person thinks that it is possible to bring them to trial for terrorist acts and against human rights.

However, the case might be, the great lack of knowledge and uncertainty about the Covid-19 coronavirus pandemic has also affected the stock markets and economies around the world by causing a huge crisis. Today, with the pandemic and its risks known to the world population, governments have been forced to apply extraordinary measures such as closing public buildings, companies, and shops, in addition to limiting the mobility of people. This as a consequence has reduced the levels of production, consumption, as well as travel in most countries with all the economic consequences that this implies. According to international institutions such as the Organization for Economic Cooperation and Development (OECD) and the International Monetary Fund (IMF); the pandemic may reduce world economic growth in this year 2020.

To alleviate the situation, some governments such as the United States have injected large amounts of money into people who have temporarily lost their jobs so that they can pay for their most urgent expenses. Other governments, like France's, have suspended the payment of rent and other people's services. All these measures are aimed at reducing the adverse effect on the economy.

During the coronavirus pandemic, there has been a drastic drop in the world's capital markets, mainly in the Wall Street exchange in the USA, the London stock exchange in Europe and the Nikkei in Japan. The stock market crash was due to extreme measures taken first by China and then by the countries of the rest of the world to try to stop the spread of the Covid-19 virus through social distancing.

And last but not least, there was also a collapse in the price of oil as a result of a price dispute between the main oil-exporting countries. Oil prices fell immediately after the pandemic was known by as much as 30%; from $ 45 to $ 31.52; the biggest drop in oil in a day, since the Gulf War in 1991; 29 years ago. This drop was due to the failure of a meeting in Vienna of the group known as OPEC +, made up of the 14 members of the Organization of the Petroleum Exporting Countries and other producers, among which Russia is the largest. The strong man in Russia is believed to have chosen to drop oil prices to favor his Chinese friends and harm the United States. As a consequence of the Russian option, Saudi Arabia decided to lower the price of oil.

However, after the first quarter of this year, oil prices continued to fall until they reached negative values, which has been their biggest drop in all of history. But all these measures as explosive as the stock market and oil drop, taken at this precise moment it could lead the world into a great economic recession, according to some experts.

5.2 DECLINE OF THE POLITICAL SYSTEM

The main political systems in most countries of the world are democracy and dictatorship. Democracy is the form of government, in which power is exercised by the people, through legitimate mechanisms of participation in political decision-making. The fundamental mechanism of citizen participation is universal, free, and secret suffrage, through which representatives of society are elected for a certain period of time.

Elections are held by majority, proportional representation, or a combination of both. However, the existence of elections is not a sufficient indicator to affirm that a government is democratic. It is necessary that there is a constitution, which is respected and obeyed by that government along with everything established in it such as respect for human rights with equality of citizens before the law; freedom of thought, expression and religion; and the presence of political parties.

There are several types of democracy, among which direct, representative, and participative democracy stand out. Direct democracy is one in which citizens participate directly in matters related to the functioning of society, such as the approval or repeal of laws, or in elections to elect their representatives by direct vote, as when democracy was first formed in Athens. At that time Athenian society was small and everyone could vote directly, but today societies have a large population, which would make the application of direct democracy very difficult.

Representative or indirect democracy is one where citizens exercise their political power through representatives, who themselves have previously elected by vote, in free and periodic elections. Representative democracy is the most practiced system in the world.

Participatory democracy is one that, as its name implies, gives citizens greater direct participation in decision-making on matters of society. In this type of democracy, citizens can assume a more leading role in politics, both at the community, regional and national levels, through the use of some consultation mechanisms, such as the referendum or the plebiscite for the approval or repeal of laws or even for the revocation of the mandate of a ruler. Participatory democracy could be considered as a modern evolution of Athenian direct democracy.

Democracy can also adapt to different forms of government organization. For example, to a republican system in which the leadership falls on a president like in the United States of America. It can also be adapted to parliamentary monarchies in which the figure of the prime minister exists, with powers similar to those of the president as in various countries in Europe. In fact, Western Europe and the United States were the cradle of modern democratic systems inspired by liberal or equality principles.

As for the dictatorship, it is defined as a system of government where there is no division of powers as in democracy, since all the power of the State is concentrated in the dictator, who exercises it with absolute authority and does not allow any opposition to his actions, thoughts and ideas. It is an undemocratic and autocratic regime, where there is no participation of the people. When all power is in the hands of one person, the dictatorship can be confused with a totalitarian regime. In the case of a monarchy, power is also in the hands of a single person. Dictatorships are generally implemented through a coup d'état, which is frequently carried out by the military, which is why dictatorships are generally military in nature. This type of dictatorship has been very common in Europe, Latin

America, Africa, the Middle East, where they still exist in some countries.

However, a dictatorship can also be for illegal occupation of a government, in the face of a power vacuum or in the face of resistance to abandon power. This is the case, in which a democratically elected leader can become a dictator if, at the end of his term, he resists calling elections or handing over power to his successor. Dictatorships, because they are regimes of force, are always viewed with a certain skepticism by the people and some political tendencies, however, with all that, they come to find support not only on the left but also on the right. From the side that they come; dictatorships always threaten the power of the people because they all have the characteristic of being totalitarian regimes. All of them are "de facto" governments, that is, governments that exercise power without being recognized or endorsed by any legal norm, so they do not have political legitimacy and are generally not legally recognized by the international democratic community.

Of the de facto governments, there are many examples in Latin America such as that of Augusto Pinochet in Chile in 1974 after overthrowing Salvador Allende by force; or that of Hugo Banzer in Bolivia in 1971 after establishing a military coup with which he overthrew the government of Juan Jose Torres Gonzalez.

However, there are also other political systems in the world with another type of dictatorship such as the so-called failed dictatorships such as the case of Venezuela; the dictatorships of socialist or communist countries like China with a single party, as well as absolute monarchies like in Saudi Arabia.

As we have seen, the two types of political systems that are still in practice in most of the world are democracy and dictatorship. To evaluate them, we will consider the most important thing for people living in society, which is respect for their human rights. As is well known, in dictatorship the government exercises absolute power over the population and prevents the most elementary human rights such as liberties. Accordingly, it undoubtedly immediately jumps out that the best political system is democracy, so we will focus on determining the best type of democracy and then see the problems that are causing its decline and how we could solve them to see it flourish.

There are different types of democracy as we have already seen. However, the best type of democracy is representative or indirect. In it, citizens exercise their political power through representatives, who themselves have previously been elected by vote, in free and periodic elections.

Until now, the type of democracy that has been most solid is representative democracy as in the case of the United States, in which the power of the State is in the hands of a president, for what is also often called presidential democracy. It is also important to note that the United States is a Federal Republic. By being a republic, its regime must be democratic. And because it is a federal republic, the functions of government are divided between the central government and its 50 associated states.

The federal government's own powers include the minimum and essential powers to guarantee the nation's political and economic unity, in matters such as foreign policy and defense. The rest of the competences correspond generally to the federal states, although some of them are exercised in a coordinated manner at both levels of government, as in the case of Education policy. In addition to the federal and state governments, there is also local government like that of counties that function as a basic administrative unit. To fulfill its management, each state has a governor elected by the people and its own legislature.

The United States' political system is based on the rule of law and on the equity of all citizens with an emphasis on equality before the law, the impartial application of justice, and the pursuit of the common good. The American political system is very attached to its constitution, written in 1787 and consisting of 7 articles and 27 amendments, of which the first 10 were adopted in 1791, and make up the so-called Bill of Rights, which include and guarantee freedom of expression, religion, of the press, the right of assembly, the right to file lawsuits against the Government and a series of individual rights in procedural aspects and judicial procedures.

In the United States there are two main political parties: Republican and Democrats. There are also three powers: the executive, the legislative and the judicial, with a clear separation and very balanced.

The executive power rests with the figure of the president, who is directly elected by the people in universal suffrage for a period of 4 years with a possible re-election for one more term. The president is responsible for the appointment of his cabinet or administration made up of secretaries, whom only he can remove. The legislative power is in the hands of Congress with two chambers: that of Representatives, which has a number of delegates from each state, chosen according to the population; and the Senate, which has two senators per state.

The judiciary is made up of the Supreme Court, the courts of appeal, the federal district courts, and special courts such as the Court of Accounts, the Court of Claims, and the Court of Appeal for ex-combatants. Federal judges are appointed by the President of the Republic with the approval of the Senate, and they hold the position for life, unless there is an impeachment in the House of Representatives and with the approval of the Senate. The American courts use the two legal systems of law: the so-called "Common Law" or Anglo-

Saxon common system and civil law. Under the American system of law, much consideration is given to jurisprudence, that is, the preceding cases in court decisions. Federal courts have exclusive jurisdiction to interpret the law, determine the constitutionality of the law and apply it in individual cases.

Something that can be seen in this political system is that both the executive and legislative branches need to work together in order to govern. Congress controls the president's policy by voting on the budget annually. The President can veto a law proposed by Congress but does not have the power to dissolve it. Congress cannot remove the President and only in extremely serious cases can it apply the "impeachment" procedure and remove him.

So far, we have made a description of the democratic system that looks most attractive for the benefits it provides to citizens. From now on, we will focus on the problems that are causing the decline of the best democratic system and then try to find the solution.

Among the real problems that we have detected in representative democracy, as in the case of the United States, we have, first of all, an excessive interference of the media in the government. This interference can go for or against, depending on the government's ideology. If this is in tune with that of the media, then those media would let the government do what it wants as long as the government follows policies that are in the interest of the media. Otherwise the media would try to impose their ideology.

Today, some democratic presidents have tried to deal with the coronavirus crisis in the most effective way possible as public officials really trying to help the people financially so that they, at least, could bring food to their family while the emergency of the coronavirus last. However, the media is only trying to interfere with the management of those governments, just because these presidents are uncomfortable with these media because they have different ideas or because they are not of the same political ideology.

Regardless of the damage it may cause to democracy and the people, the media have done everything possible and continue to try by all means to remove presidents from their offices, even though they were democratically elected, and they have followed through on the promises that they did to the people during their electoral campaigns such as to lower taxes and unemployment mainly in the neediest sectors. Even when all its measures are for the benefit of the people, which is framed in the essence of the Republic and Democracy.

However, it has been seen how those same media have allowed other presidents to do whatever they want, up to taking measures to the detriment of friendly countries and other measures very in favor of their enemies. It is also interesting to understand that it was the people who gave it all the power that those same media outlets have today and that sometimes use it against the same people. Those same media that have put themselves at the service of governments that have ended in dictatorships, have then been put aside once the dictators take power. It is in a democracy where the media can operate freely, and it is in a democracy where the people have the power even to defend their media.

The role of today's media is not healthy for democracy, which could accelerate its deterioration, which had already begun more than 30 years ago with governments of presidents involved in political scandals as in the United States with the famous Lewinsky scandal. in 1998 as a result of a sexual relationship between the president at the time and a White House employee. The investigations into this extramarital affair by the President, resulted in the causes of this case being real and confessed, which is why they brought the President to impeachment. But the president was exonerated in 3 weeks.

Despite the fact that this scandal has remained in the past, it is important to understand that this type of scandal has its socio-political repercussions. As we have seen, the American people have always been very attached to their constitution and their religion. However, in the face of that abuse of power and without anything happening, the morale of the people went to the ground, as well as confidence in the justice system. Swearing on the Bible was a sacred act before this scandal. This president lied to the people with his hand on the Bible and the worst thing is that after that anyone can do it. It is important to note that the intention of this exhibition is not to harm any president, but to avoid any type of scandal to avoid the decline of democracy.

Another event that could be very negatively affecting the democracy of the countries of the world is the role that some of the international institutions such as the United Nations (UN) especially, are currently playing. Some of its members and observers are very concerned that the UN has been taken by socialists and communists to implant their own world view including their ideologies. This institution must represent all the countries of the world with citizens with updated concepts and ideas, so that they can be able to understand that the organization is oriented towards the benefit of all its members such as full freedom, human rights, the right to private property etc. The UN is today questioned for having changed its original principles. There are cases of despotic, authoritarian, corrupt governments, and violators of human rights, which are not sanctioned by UN. Some of those governments may even become part of the UN Human Rights Council. Many see this institution in decline.

In addition to the UN, there are other international institutions designed to safeguard world peace. Among which the following stand out: Organization of American

States, European Convention on Human Rights, Emergence of international relations, Indigenous Parliament, Association of Southeast Asian States, The Arab League, Organization for the African Union, International Federation of Human Rights.

The *United Nations* (UN) is an international organization founded in the United States in 1945 after World War II, through the signing of a document known as the Charter of the United Nations, in which 51 countries committed to maintain international peace and security, foster friendly relations among nations, and promote social progress, the improvement of living standards and Human Rights. Today the UN has 193 member countries around the world and has its main headquarters in New York and an office in Geneva. To fulfill its core objectives, the UN has specialized bodies and commissions such as the General Assembly, the Security Council, and the Economic and Social Council.

The *Organization of American States* (OAS) is an institution created in 1948 when the OAS Charter that entered into force in December 1951 was signed in Bogotá, Colombia. Its objective is to ensure that its member states have an order of peace and justice, promote their solidarity, strengthen their collaboration, and defend their sovereignty, their territorial integrity, and their independence, as stipulated in Article 1 of their Charter. To achieve its purposes, the OAS relies on democracy, human rights, security, and development as its main pillars. Currently, the OAS brings together the 35 independent states of the Americas and constitutes the main political, legal, and social governmental forum in the Hemisphere. In addition, it has granted the status of Permanent Observer to 69 States, as well as the European Union (EU).

The *European Court of Human Rights* (ECHR) established in 1959 and based in Strasbourg, France, is the highest European jurisdiction to guarantee the human rights and fundamental freedoms of citizens. The ECHR is made up of one judge for each member country of the Council of Europe. It currently has 47 judges elected by the Parliamentary Assembly of the Council of Europe from a short list of three proposed by each member country. The judges have a non-renewable term of nine years. For Amnesty International, this court is one of the most developed human rights protection mechanisms in the world inside and outside Europe.

The *African Commission on Human and Peoples Rights* (CADHP) is an institution established in 1986 to promote the values of the African Charter on Human and Peoples' Rights throughout the African continent. The Commission is composed of 11 members elected by the Assembly of the African Union from among several experts selected by the States. CADHP headquarters has its Secretariat in Banjul, The Gambia. For almost two decades after the creation of the Organization of African Unity (OAU) in 1963, the focus of the organization remained almost entirely on the process of decolonization of the continent and the elimination of apartheid, which was a system of legislation underpinning segregationist policies against black citizens of South Africa. After the support of the United Nations, the apartheid system was ended in 1994.

The *Organization for the African Union* (AU) is an institution made up of 54 African states with the exception of Morocco. It was created in 2001 in Addis Ababa, Ethiopia, in South Africa, although it started operating in 2002, replacing the Organization for African Unity (OAU).

The *International Criminal Court* (ICC) is an independent and permanent court to deal with crimes of international significance such as genocide, crimes against humanity and war crimes. The ICC observes the highest standards of impartiality and due process, and its competence and functioning are governed by the Rome Statute, which was the instrument adopted in the city of Rome, Italy, in 1998, during the Diplomatic Conference of Plenipotentiaries of the United Nations on the establishment of the International Criminal Court. The ICC is the first permanent court established to help end impunity for the perpetrators of the most serious crimes of significance to the international community. The ICC is a court of last resort based in The Hague, the Netherlands and is not part of the United Nations system. The expenses of the Court are mainly financed by the member states, although it also receives voluntary contributions from governments, international organizations, individuals, corporations, and other entities.

The ICC currently has 118 member countries, of which 32 are from Africa, 17 from Asia, 18 from Eastern Europe, 26 from Latin America and the Caribbean, and 25 from Western Europe.

The *International Federation for Human Rights* (FIDH) is one of the organizations founded in 1922 that brings together 178 organizations in more than 112 countries. Its objective is the protection of victims of human rights violations, the prevention of such violations and the prosecution of those responsible. FIDH has a general mandate to defend all the rights enshrined in the 1948 Universal Declaration of Human Rights, including civil, political, economic, social, and cultural rights.

There is even an institution called *Transparency International* (TI), which is a non-governmental organization, founded in the 1990s with headquarters in Berlin, Germany, in charge of developing measures with the aim of ending corruption.

We hope that these other institutions created to maintain peace and the good development of their regions do not deviate their objectives as the UN has done. At the same time, we also hope and wish for the UN to return to the path of freedom. Meanwhile, the people must continue defending their power and for this, political problems, and scandals, which do so much damage to democracy, as we have seen previously, must be avoided. To achieve this goal, the people must choose better officials with proven honesty and capable of developing mechanisms to detect any abnormality in time.

5.3 COLLAPSE OF THE ECONOMIC SYSTEM

Since the beginning of agriculture as the driving force of the economy, human beings have always been in search of the best method to manage their resources effectively and efficiently. Over the years, various methods have been tried to finally take the one that best suits society.

However, the selected economic system will depend on private property. If this is in the hands of citizens as in democracy, the economic system would be capitalism. But if private property is in the hands of the government as in socialism, the economic system would be state planning. There is also a mixed economic system between capitalism and state planning.

Currently, capitalism is an economic system that is based on private ownership of the means of production, as well as on the principle of free market, whose objective is the accumulation of capital. Therefore, capitalism is based on the ownership of the means of production and resources, from whose trade profits are extracted.

Capitalism presents free market as its basic principle. The market, according to the traditional capitalist model, is regulated by means of the law of supply and demand, aimed at satisfying consumption needs. In this sense, competitiveness among producers is a key aspect of this economic system.

This economic model uses capital and labor as its fundamental factors, which increase competition in the supply and demand of goods and services. Capitalism also uses the free market with a minimum participation of the State, it recognizes the company right as an individual right, so that any person or group that possesses the necessary economic resources can open a company and employ others. Furthermore, in capitalism people generate better income with which they can have a better quality of life.

Capitalism has been spreading in many parts of the world. At the end of the 20th century, one of the phenomena of capitalism could be observed, such as globalization, which is a process of expansion of economic integration driven by the low costs of products, as well as those of means of transport and the communication between the countries of the world.

However, the definition of traditional capitalism, as can be seen in democracy, may be affected by the country in which it is developed, especially by the type of political system or government that country has, especially socialist or communist systems of government. This usually ends up modifying the factors of capitalism such as the production, commercialization, distribution and price of the goods and services produced. For socialism is a sociopolitical doctrine based on the ownership and collective administration of the means of production, so the economic system would be based on state planning.

The state planning economy or socialist economy is one in which the state owns the means of production, that is, where there is no private property. In socialism there is generally a planned economy, although there are exceptions now. In 1978 China passed a reform to transform its planning socialist economy into a market one. We saw another case of a similar change in 1991, after the collapse of communism in the Soviet Union, its economy also became a market like that of China.

As for the mixed economic system, it is defined as one that combines the performance of the private sector with the participation of the public sector as regulator. This type of mixed economy is a mix of capitalism and central planning. Although most economic decisions are made by the private party according to the law of supply and demand, based on the needs of consumers and the market. However, the State normally creates and secures a framework of laws so that the market can function without problems, it could also intervene to avoid monopolies that affect free competition, as well as it could be investing in basic activities for the development of the country when said activities are not very profitable for the private sector such as supplying the population with public services.

The State could distribute part of its budget among people with services such as health care, basic education, affordable housing, food vouchers and aid in periods of unemployment or retirement. With this type of participation, the State would create social welfare so that people live with dignity in a more equitable society. Currently most countries have a mixed economy.

Capitalism is the economic system currently used by democratic countries to bring better socio-economic benefits to their people. However, this economic system is being affected by the influence of political fanatics of centrally planned communist economic models. These politicians, with the support of the media, have been in constant bombardment to try to impose their socialist and communist ideologies.

Many countries in the world, influenced by the communist model of the Soviet Union, adopted this economic model until they saw its collapse with the disintegration of the Soviet bloc in 1990 and returned to their market economies. After this, the world believed that communism would disappear, but it would not be so simple. Communist ideologies would pass to some so-called left-wing politicians who are entrenched in the traditional political parties of their respective countries, from where they try to influence the people on these ideas with the help of the media.

One of the ideas used by left-wing politicians to manipulate society is social assistance policy, with which some of the democratic governments would agree to win votes. This communist interference could weaken market economies and governments could gradually get closer to socialism. Other ideas used by left-wing politicians to achieve their goals also include high taxes and high state interventionism.

The problem that has been seen with social assistance is the huge corruption that this has generated, since a large percentage of people have abused it, to the point that they have even stopped working to live on social assistance. And the more people are receiving these benefits, the greater the public expenses will be, the less people work, the less the country's income will be, since governments do not generate any wealth, so they would have to increase personal taxes to meet the payment of social assistance expenses and if they are not yet enough, could also increase the tax on companies that generate jobs for the people and income for the governments, with the risk that these companies will go to other parts with better attractions to operate.

When the State cannot afford its expenses, they will resort to indebtedness and run the risk of impoverishment, which represents a condition of vulnerability very critical to the social and economic future of the country. However, reasonable help for social assistance for a person who cannot work would be justifiable as long as the help is genuine.

In the United States, more than 50% of public revenue is spent on social assistance including medical coverage. Some 80% of this income comes from personal tax and 11% comes from corporate taxes. However, there are many other countries with higher expenses.

The other idea of left-wing politicians is aggressive economic interventionism. In fact, when those politicians have tried to promote and implement ideas like the social assistance that we have just talked about, they are trying to make the State interfere in the country's economy. But this is not healthy. Under normal conditions, the State should not interfere in the economy, except during exceptional situations such as natural disasters or extraordinary crisis such as the current coronavirus crisis.

Active government interference in the economy could end in a host of new policies or laws that could negatively affect some companies and industries. However, the State must approve and apply the laws so that the entire economic system works properly. The state has earned a reputation as the worst administrator in the world. There must be a reason for it. As a sample, let us look at the following Chinese example.

China, with its centrally planned communist economic model, fell into a great state of poverty. Given this situation, the Chinese Communist Party, which exercises all of the power in the People's Republic of China, was forced, through the government leader in 1978; to undertake a process of reforms to liberate the economy, allow the emergence of the private sector and decentralize power. After these changes, the commercial relationship between the People's Republic of China and the western world began, giving way to the entry of foreign investments from capitalist countries and the Chinese communist economic model was transformed into a market economy.

Under the market economy model, China began to grow at record levels and steadily for three decades. According to the World Bank, it is estimated that more than 850 million Chinese people got out of poverty thanks to the reforms. Today, China is a modern country, with local and international companies manufacturing all kinds of products. Quite a technological giant thanks to capitalism, although the communist party is in all aspects of Chinese life.

In China when it comes to freedom, the story is different. Press freedom does not exist, and the media sector is under state control. According to the organization Human Rights Watch, the Chinese government maintains strict control over the internet, the mass media, and even persecutes religious communities and human rights defenders.

Now, in addition to all the normal events of the economy regarding its collapse, we have to add today the effects of the recent crisis caused by the coronavirus, which could be producing an economic collapse of great proportions, depending on the duration of the pandemic and of course, the measures taken to tackle the crisis.

To get out of this economic crisis, it is first necessary to definitively stop the spread of the virus and then apply the relevant economic measures. Public spending on health and social assistance will increase dramatically. On a personal level, unemployment will increase further, reducing people's purchasing power. And to add fuel to the fire, under this uncertain climate, capital markets will take time to reach positive levels.

The economy of some countries will recover as their income increases, which will of course depend on the values of their economic indicators. For this recovery, the governments of the countries must work together with financial institutions to economically help the reactivation of companies, including small and medium industries.

The economic recession of the coronavirus could cause the world economy a loss of between one and two trillion dollars. In addition to a slowdown in global annual growth below 2.5% according to the latest report of the United Nations Conference on Trade and Development (UNCTAD).

5.4 SOCIAL PROBLEMS

Social problems are situations that impede the development and progress of people in their society, as they cannot satisfy their basic needs. The social problems facing people around the world are many, however, we will only expose the most important: poverty, hunger, health, unemployment, discrimination, unsafety, drug addiction and corruption. In addition to listing social problems, we must also know their causes to prevent them and seek solutions.

Poverty is one of the great current problems of the world. By the UN standard, people living on $ 2.5 a day or less are considered poor. If they live on $ 1.25 a day or less, they are considered in extreme poverty. According to World Bank estimates, 12.7% of the world population lives on less than $ 1.9 a day. Many countries where poverty predominates are called third world countries. The parameters to measure poverty at the international level are established by organizations such as the World Bank, the International Monetary Fund, or the United Nations Development Program (UNDP). However, there are also within each country institutions responsible for evaluating poverty levels to develop programs aimed at fighting it. Poverty, in general, is more pronounced in countries that are underdeveloped. It also grows even more in countries in conflict than in peaceful and stable countries. Poverty itself also carries other problems such as hunger, health problems, and even lack of clean water.

Hunger in 2016 affected 815 million people worldwide, representing 11% of the world population, according to figures from the United Nations International Fund for Food and Agriculture. Hunger affects 520 million people in Asia, 243 million in Africa and 43 million in Latin America and the Caribbean. In fact, Africa has a large, undernourished population.

Health is also a serious problem in many countries of the world where there are more than 800 million people without access to any health care system, making them totally susceptible to contracting some diseases for which many of them die.

Furthermore, there are millions of people in the world who do not drink clean water and in some cases do not even have water of any kind. According to statistics almost 1 billion people do not have clean water.

Unemployment is another social problem since people do not generate any income to satisfy their needs, which can become a cause of poverty. In turn, unemployment can be caused by the country's economic problems. Currently, the countries with the highest unemployment rate are Greece and Spain with 27%; while the countries with the lowest unemployment rate are Rwanda and Qatar with 0.5%. According to World Bank data from 2013.

To alleviate poverty, the State must ensure that its country achieves sustainable economic growth capable of creating jobs with reasonable wages so that people can meet their fundamental needs for food, health, and hygiene.

Employment discrimination can be another social problem when people are not allowed to work due to their race, sex, gender, religion, nationality, etc. Labor discrimination can also affect the worker, after having been employed with different treatments or benefits compared to his colleagues for reasons that are not directly related to his job performance.

Unsafety is another social problem, as people have to face the dangers of living in violent cities. Unsafety, in addition to affecting the tranquility and security of society, also affects the interests of the countries, distancing investments, especially foreign ones, tourism and others.

Drug addiction is another great scourge, because the addiction or dependence of people to drugs generates, in addition to physical and psychological deterioration, it also generates a great social problem since the drug addict cannot satisfy his basic needs to live normally in society.

Corruption is a problem that damages everything healthy it touches and can even worsen any other existing social problem. Corruption uses simple practices of the people such as influence peddling, bribery, extortion, and fraud to obtain some benefit before a public official. These corrupt practices are very common for people to win a bid or to make a change related to it. These practices are also common in the opposite direction, that is, from the side of the official, who abuses his power to take advantage of the citizens. Corruption generates a chain of problems, making it extremely necessary to create more institutions such as "Transparency International" to attack this problem.

5.5 HOW TO AVOID THE COLLAPSE OF CIVILIZATION

So far, we have taken a journey since civilization emerged, going through all that it has created to bring us to the current world, where we found a host of problems as a clear dangerous trend that could lead humanity to the collapse of our civilization. Unless we do something to stop it.

We have seen in the exhibition on the origin and evolution of civilization, all that immense development and prosperity that the civilizations that brought us to where we are today reached. However, all its splendor has disappeared. We only have to take a look at two of them. For example, Mesopotamia; which was the cradle of civilization that lasted about 3 thousand years, where writing was invented, with which history began to be written and science emerged; and where the wheel was invented. For the glorious Mesopotamia ended in what is now Iraq. A country in deep chaos. Another example is Greece, which was the cradle of western civilization where democracy and great philosophical thought were born with exceptional figures forgers of freedom, science, and prosperity. However, Greece in today's world has fallen to very low levels of poverty.

To avoid the collapse of our current civilization, first of all, all the difficulties that threaten it must be addressed, such as the pandemic that currently plagues us, political decline, economic chaos, and social problems.

As for the coronavirus pandemic, the spread of this virus must first be stopped as soon as possible with quarantine, as is currently being done. Now, to avoid this type of crisis in the future, countries must prepare to handle biological and chemical crises mainly, in order to give a quick response to the problem. In addition, countries must promote leadership worldwide, not only to strengthen the global economy, but also to monitor more closely the health of financial institutions in order to avoid the collapse of some of them, which could be used by some unscrupulous governments to alter the world economy for their own benefit. This leadership must also be capable of holding the negligence or little cooperation of those countries in handling threats against humanity and world peace. We have seen how the entire world has been completely naked and vulnerable to the coronavirus. To achieve the desired leadership, you can think of a new organization, but very different from the existing ones, because these have failed today in the face of the problems of humanity, have even disrespected human rights, in a clear breach of objectives what they were created for.

As for political decline, the people must elect truthful and honest representatives and not allow themselves to be manipulated by left-wing politicians and the media. To avoid manipulation of the media, people should ignore them when they go against us. Furthermore, we the people should avoid voting for politicians involved in scandals.

In the face of any threat to the ethical and moral values of society, the people must raise their voices, and this can only be done in a democracy, where we have power. And to retain their power, then the people have to be on the side of democracy. People should become more involved in their democracy through greater direct participation to learn more about the management of their officials and to be involved in decision-making on matters of society. In this way the citizen can assume a more leading role in politics, both at the community, regional and national levels, through the use of some consultation mechanisms, such as the referendum or the plebiscite for the approval or repeal of laws or even for the revocation of the mandate of a ruler. So, if at any time this citizen who has become involved is elected to govern, know how to do it without making the mistakes that are leading our democracy to decline.

To avoid economic collapse, the people must defend the free market economy in a capitalist system, which is the economic system with the best socio-economic benefits for the people. Furthermore, capitalism is perfectly compatible with democracy.

To reduce the risk of collapse, the State of any country can also choose to provide greater social welfare for its people. In this sense, it must create the necessary legislation to make possible the development of economic activities oriented to this well-being with the participation of private companies, especially in the creation of jobs with remuneration that allows people to enjoy a better life. The State, together with private investment, can contribute to the country achieving a prosperous economy with good indicators of its gross domestic product (GDP), per capita income, distribution of wealth in social services, unemployment rate, poverty level, life expectation, protection against delinquency and organized crime, Social Security programs, etc. The better a country's economy is, the greater the chance that citizens will enjoy a better quality of life.

As for social problems, as they are public issues, the State has the responsibility and the obligation to advocate for the solution of social problems, by developing social policies necessary to solve or at least remedy social problems so that people have better quality of life. In this sense, the State must ensure that its country achieves sustainable economic growth capable of creating jobs with reasonable wages so that people can satisfy their fundamental needs.

However, society can also help in solving social problems through non-governmental organizations designed for this purpose. Although there are no countries without social problems, but the one with the least number of them could be considered a country of great social development.

One of the ways to help reduce poverty is through job creation. Now, to remedy the unemployment problem, the state must either review existing laws or develop and implement new laws that are fair and attractive to the private sector to make investments that create more jobs. So that the country has an economy that grows at the rate of the number of people seeking employment and thus achieve a stable labor market. Unemployment is one of the social problems with the greatest negative effects on the people and even worse if unemployment or employment is subject to discrimination.

Employment discrimination can also become a problem for companies with their respective impact on society. Discriminated workers may experience high levels of stress, making them prone to disorders such as nervous breakdown, personal dissatisfaction, or depression. All this can very negatively affect the company in terms of its productivity or its work climate. Although there are laws in many countries to prevent labor discrimination, if despite this some form of discrimination still occurs, companies must address them by applying measures to end the problem.

On the problem of drug addiction, its solution begins by preventing it and this responsibility falls on the parents. But to help their children, perhaps the parents will have to help themselves first. Also, parents need to watch what their children are doing and know whom they are with. However, when the problem of drug addiction already exists, there are social programs to help those affected to get out of the problem. However, the State must be updating these programs and ensure that the institutions that administer them fulfill such an important function.

Another of the social problems is unsafety and to solve it the State must create, plan, and invest in institutions of public security, justice, and prison systems, or reinforce existing ones. However, it is also recommended that citizens themselves assume a culture of preventive safety with actions necessary for their self-protection according to their possibilities, without having to face criminals directly.

In addition to advocating for the solution of people's social problems, the State could promote social welfare for its people, if the State can really afford it and without falling into populism. Social Welfare is the set of factors necessary for the members of a society to satisfy their fundamental needs to have optimal levels of quality of life. Social welfare normally includes all those things that have a positive impact on the quality of life of people such as a job with a salary sufficient to meet the needs of food, health, clothing, housing, etc.

Of course, social welfare will depend on the country where one lives. If there is a high purchasing power in that country, it would make people's salary enough to buy more goods or services to meet their needs. For example, in the United States today, a family of four needs to have an income of $ 4,700 per month to meet their basic needs, including expenses for housing with utilities and communications, plus a vehicle with maintenance and insurance costs, plus food expenses with medical insurance. However, the approximate minimum wage is $ 1,800 per person per month.

Now, for all the alternatives aimed at solving social problems and improving people's well-being to be effective, the immense problem of corruption must be attacked. The practices of corruption to obtain benefits against the people have come to undermine the foundations of all the social structures of humanity worldwide. This enormous scourge must be attacked from the highest levels of the State to the lowest strata of the people.

In the face of corruption, first of all, the integrity and independence of the judiciary must be strengthened so that the crime of the corrupt does not go unpunished. Like other measures, there must be transparency in public procurement to prevent public contracts from being assigned to the corrupt; monitor the financing of electoral campaigns, since much of that money is illegal and comes from criminal groups to obtain benefits from the corrupt rulers who are so elected; and debug the entire electoral process and review the immunity of the rulers.

The other part of the fight against corruption must come from the people. As we have already said, the people must first choose honest politicians to stop corruption and become more involved in matters related to their society, such as investigating the management of public money. The fight against corruption must be frontal to prevent it from further undermining the foundations of democracy and the rule of law, which in the long run could lead to a total collapse. However, we the people could have the media help us attack the effects of corruption. We hope that the media will help us in this noble and genuine mission to prevent the collapse of our civilization.

Another solution to avoid the collapse of our current civilization is to attend education so that people develop their mental and physical capacities to solve their problems. As well as for people to cultivate ethical and moral values such as respect and honesty. Education should not be put at the service of politicians to ideologize people. Rather, it must be put at the service of the people in order to be useful to their society. In other words, people must always be part of the Solution.

ABOUT AUTHOR

Ivanni Delgado is a graduate engineer at the University of Tulsa, Oklahoma, with a master's degree in business from NSU University in Tahlequah, Oklahoma. He is a member of the Texas Authors Association. And he is also the author of the books: "How We Get Here" and "Life Under a New Perspective". The first was written to answer one of the most important questions about the existence of the human being and with it opens an enlightened look at the past that can change the future. And the second was written for the purpose of helping people in the difficult task of living. In this new book "Where This Civilization Is Going," Ivanni tells how our civilization originated and the events that have brought it to where it is now. He thinks that if we do not do the right thing now, life will change drastically, so people need to know the history of our civilization to avoid its collapse.

NOTES

Chapter 1: CIVILIZATION: ORIGIN AND EVOLUTION

1. Delgado, I. How We Got Here, Houston: Carmen & Son, 2018
   http://www.carmen-usa.com/comollegamosaqui

2. Human Evolution, Smithsonian National Museum of Natural History, 2015

3. Encyclopedia Britannica
   https://www.britannica.com/place/Jarmo

Chapter 2: FIRST CIVILIZATIONS

4. Origen of Civilization
   https://www.uv.es/ivorra/Historia/Historia_Antigua/civilizacion.htm

5. Historia Universal
   https://mihistoriauniversal.com/edad-antigua/imperio-acadio/

Chapter 3:   WRITING AND SCIENCE

6. Encyclopedia Banrepcultural
    https://enciclopedia.banrepcultural.org/index.php/
    Origen_de_la_pol%C3%ADtica_en_el_mundo

Chapter 4:   WEALTH AND POWER

7. Filosofía & Co
    https://www.filco.es/riqueza-naciones-adam-smith/

8. Economipedia
    https://economipedia.com/definiciones/origen-de-
    la-economia.html

Chapter 5:   CURRENT WORLD:
A DANGEROUS TREND

9. Fox News
    http://foxnews.com

10. El Tiempo
    https://www.eltiempo.com/mundo/mas-
    regiones/analisis-sobre-la-situacion-geopolitica-
    mundial-reciente-263102

11. Visión Crítica.
    https://visioncritica.com/2017/05/21/10-signos-
    sociedad-decadencia/

12. ACNUR
    https://eacnur.org/blog/principales-problemas-del-
    mundo-actual-tc_alt45664n_o_pstn_o_pst/